COMPOSITES AND IRRADIATION TECHNIQUES

ENV BOOKS SERIES

COMPOSITES AND IRRADIATION TECHNIQUES

By

Dr. Hebatalrahman A.

Dr. Eng. Consultant

Materials Sciences & Material Applications,

Cairo, Egypt

Foreword by

Dr. Pawan Kumar 'Bharti'

Society for Environment, Health Awareness of

Nutrition & Toxicology (SEHAT)

B-225/5D, Top Floor, Subhash Gali, Road No. 7, Block B

Ashok Nagar, Shahdara, Delhi - 110 093

(India)

DPH

DISCOVERY PUBLISHING HOUSE PVT. LTD.

INDIA

Published by:
Namit Wasan
DISCOVERY PUBLISHING HOUSE PVT. LTD.
4383/4B, Ansari Road, Darya Ganj
New Delhi-110 002 (India)
Phone : +91-11-23279245; 23253475; 43596065
E-mail : discoverybooksindia@gmail.com
discoverypublishinghouse@gmail.com
namitwasan9@gmail.com
web : www.discoverypublishinggroup.com

***First Edition:* 2020**

ISBN: 978-93-88854-42-9

Composites and Irradiation Techniques

Printed at:
Infinity Imaging Systems
Delhi

Dr. Pawan Kumar 'Bharti'
(MSc, NET, PhD, FASEA, FANSF)
Vice President (Executive), *SEHAT-India, Delhi, India*
Editor-in-Chief, *ENVBOOKS series, India*
Member, *30th Indian Antarctic Expedition, MoES, Govt. of India*

Foreword

A composite is a combination of two materials with different physical and chemical properties. When they are combined they create a material which is specialised to do a certain job, for instance to become stronger, lighter or resistant to electricity. The reason for their use is because they improve the properties of their base materials and are applicable in many situations. Composite materials are inhomogeneous and anisotropic materials and usually made up by combining two or more materials which often ones with different properties. The most unique property of composites is the high strength to weight ratio. Another advantage of composite materials is that it provides flexibility in design in which the composites can be molded into complex shapes.

Composites are made up of matrix and fibre reinforcement. Currently, the dominating fibre used as the reinforcement are the fiberglass, graphite fibres or carbon and organic fibres such as aramid fibres, which are known as synthetic fibres. The choice of fibres depends on the cost, performance as well as the applications. However, with the raise of concern on environmental issues, the reinforcement has gain interest in replacing the synthetic fibre to natural fibre. In producing the composites, the improvement of the strength of the end product of the composites is essential. Various methods can be done to improve the strength of the materials such as using chemical treatment, addition of fibres especially for natural fibres, hybrid-ising the reinforcement and using radiation technique such as gamma radiation or electron beam machine (EBM).

In order to write a forward to the book of Prof. Hebatalrahman, focused on various issues/activities/ related to composites and irradiation techniques. I would like to appreciate the sincere efforts of the author, an proactive researcher/ activist along with his team to formulate a strategy to highlight the various relevant issues and bring them into notice via different medium including social platforms; conceptualization and publication of this compendium, which contains latest information on the various aspects of advance composites, smart materials, radiation technology, value addition of composites and many relevant information in the form of a handy book.

I hope this book will serve as a useful reference material and milestone to the new and current researcher and also help the scientist working in identifying and discovering the gaps in this research area. I consider this book a value addition to the scientific knowledge on composites and research world.

(Pawan Kumar 'Bharti')

PREFACE

Composite materials have been using for thousands of years, e.g. they have manufactured bricks with the help of mud which is thousand-year-old technology. Now days, we all depend on composite materials at some aspects of our lives. Composite material defined as a mixture of two or more than two materials (reinforcement, fillers and binder) different in composition. Composite materials also called composition materials or shortened to composites. Composite materials are materials made from two or more than two materials with considerably differ in physical and chemical properties, that when combined, make a material with appearances different from the individual components.

Composites comprise strong load carrying material is known as reinforcement and weaker materials is known as matrix. Reinforcement provides stiffness and strength which helps to support structural load. Composite materials do not lose their respective identities but still relate their properties to the product causing from their mixture. The benefits of composite materials have their great stiffness and strength. There are in many cases, the reinforcement is stronger, tougher, harder and stiffer than the matrix. It finds application in automotive, aerospace, electronic equipment, sport goods, furniture, medical equipment & packaging Industry. Composite materials used as an industrial material for their outstanding resistance to chemicals and most forms of corrosion. This property of composite material conventionally important is hardly the only useful property. There are many important and useful properties are, low mass, low weight unequalled manufacturing and processing possibilities, complex material body are easily produced, appropriate to very small products and very large product, tooling cost is very low, satisfactory surface finish can be an integral feature.

Composites have four to six times tensile strength as compare to steel or aluminium (depending on the reinforcements). Composites have less noise and lower vibration transmission than metals at the time of operations. Composite materials have torsional stiffness and impact properties. Composites have high fatigue strength, impact, environmental resistance and reduce maintenance, higher fatigue endurance limit (up to 60% of ultimate tensile strength. Composites exhibit fire retardancy and good corrosion resistance. Composites have improved surfaces properties and readily incorporable integral decorative melamine is other characteristics of composites, low electrical conductivity and thermal expansion. Composite parts can eliminate joints and providing simplification and assembly design compared to non composite metallic parts. Composite materials have high cost of material, long development time, manufacturing difficulties, low ductility, temperature limits, solvent or moister attack, hidden damages and damage susceptibility. Matrix used in composite materials is subject to environmental degradation and analysis is difficult, hot curing is necessary in many cases requiring special tooling, hot or cold curing takes time.

Applications of composites are in aerospace, automotive, medical field, electrical, chemical industries, sports and many more.

The present book updates the subject content on advances in composites, characterization, quality improvement, experiments on composites, impact of radiation technology on composites. Thanks are due to publisher and contributors from various institutions and universities. The book will be helpful for the researchers, academia working in the field of composites and recent developments in composites, advance composites, characterization, quality improvement, experiments on composites, different categories of composites, impact of radiation technology on composites.

Editors
(envbooks@gmail.com)

CONTENTS

1

Characteristics of Micro and Nano Composite from Marble and Granite Wastes

ABSTRACT

In this work, New composite material was developed from marble and granite waste, the unit for recycling of marble and granite wastes was designed, the prototype was tested in manufacturing of thermoplastic based composite from marble and granite wastes respectively, the main characteristics of both composite materials were measured, the structure of the new composite materials were determined by SEM, the composition were determined by EDX analysis, the particle size and elemental analysis were evaluated by the same technique, the volume resistivity and abrasive wear was evaluated. Thermogravimetric Analysis (TGA) was measured to determined the operation temperature of the new composite materials. Thermal conductivity of new composite material were calculated from the role of mixture. The main applications of the new composite materials were mentioned according to the characteristics measured.

Keywords : *Nano composite, granite, marble, waste recycling, characteristics.*

Introduction

Recycling waste as useful material is a very important environmental management tool for achieving sustainable development [1]. On the other hand, recycling waste without properly based scientific research and development can result in environmental problems greater than the waste itself[2],[3]. The successful research and development of a new building material or component using waste as raw material, is a very complex and multi disciplinary task having technical, environmental, financial, marketing, legal and social aspects. Now the cost of construction materials is increasing incrementally[4],[5]. For example, the cost of cement during 1995 was Rs.1.25/kg and in 2008 the price increased ~ three times. In case of bricks the price was 0.66 per brick in 1995 and the present rate is Rs.2.5 per brick[6],[7]. Similarly, over a period of 10 years from the year 1995 the price of 147 sand has increased four times[8]. Also due to high transportation costs of these raw materials, demand, environmental restrictions, it is essential to find functional substitutes for conventional building materials in the construction industry[9],[10]. Growth of population, increasing urbanization, rising standards of living due to technological innovations have contributed to an increase both in the quantity and variety of solid wastes generated by industrial, mining, domestic and agricultural activities[11],[12]. About 6 million tons of wastes from marble industries are being released from marble cutting, polishing, processing and grinding. The granite and marble dust is usually possesses a major environmental concern[13]. In dry season, the granite and marble powder or dust dangles in the air, flies and deposits on vegetation and crop. All these significantly affect the environment and local ecosystems. The granite and marble dust disposed in the river-bed and around the production facilities causes reduction in porosity and permeability of the topsoil and results in water logging. Further, fine particles results in poor fertility of the soil due to increase in alkalinity[14],[15]. Use of industrial wastes and by products as an aggregate or raw material is of great practical significance developing building material components as substitutes for materials and providing an alternative or supplementary materials to the housing industry in a cost effective manner and the conservation of natural resources[15].

Experimental Work

Materials

The matrix is polymethyl metha acrylate (PMMA. It is thermoplastic prepared from monomer (methyl methacrylate) by additional polymerization process; polymer was in the granule form with 5mm diameter.

Filler (Marble Wastes) Marble refuses consists wet refuse (sahla) (wet wastes):

It is a type of the wet refuse where its percentage of water reaches about 70%. It is sticky and it is produced from the processes of leveling and polishing. Commercially it is known as (Al Sahala) or Al Sahla. The sticky refuse is heavy in weight and big in size. This is due to the existence of water in it. but, they are very soft granules.

Chemically, they are crystalline rocks composed predominantly of calcite, dolomite or serpentine minerals. The other minor constituents vary from origin to origin. Average chemical composition of marbles, Table 1.1 shows the chemical composition of marble.

Table 1.1: The Chemical Composition of Marble

Compound	Symbol	Percent
Lime	(CaO)	28-32%
Silica	(SiO_2)	3-30%
Magnesium oxide	MgO	20 to 25%,
Iron oxides	$FeO + Fe_2O_3$	1-3%,
losses	Loss On Ignition (LOI)	20-45%

Impurities in Marble the major mineral impurities in marble are Quartz -Tremolite Actinolite -Chert -Garnet -Biotite -Muscovite -Microline -Talc -Fosterite, while the major chemical impurities in marble are SiO_2 -Fe_2O_3 -$2Fe_2O_3$ -$3H_2O$-Limonite -Manganese -Al_2O_3 -FeS_2(pyrite).

Filler (Granite Wastes) Granite Refuses Consists Wet Refuse (Sahla) (Wet Wastes)

Granite is an igneous rock with at least 20% quartz and up to 65% alkali feldspar by volume. Granite is nearly always massive (lacking any internal structures), hard and tough, and therefore it has gained widespread use throughout human history, and more recently as a construction stone. The average *density* of granite is between 2.65[2]and 2.75 g/cm^3, its compressive strength usually lies above 200 MPa, and its *viscosity* near *STP* is 3–6 • 10^{19} Pa·s.[3]

Melting temperature of dry granite at ambient pressure is or 1215–1260°C (2219–2300°F);[4] it is strongly reduced in the presence of water, down to 650°C at a few kBar pressure.[5]

Chemical Properties of granite

Table 1.2: A Worldwide Average of the Chemical Composition of Granite, by Weight Percent, Based on Standard Analyses

Compound	Symbol	Percent
Silica	SiO_2	72.04%
Alumina	Al_2O_3	14.42%
Potassium oxide	K_2O	4.12%
Sodium oxide	Na_2O	3.69%
Lime	CaO	1.82%
Iron oxide	FeO	1.68%
Iron oxide	Fe_2O_3	1.22%
Magnesium oxide	MgO	0.71%
Titanium oxide	TiO_2	0.30%
	P_2O_5	0.12%
Manganese oxide	MnO	0.05%

Preparation of Material

Grinding

A blinder with variable speeds is used to change the pieces of thermo-plastics into powder form, The blinder speed is about 15,500 rpm, work at 200 volt - 50 Hz, and the grinding time is about 90 sec. Switch off for cooling is lasted about 180 sec to prevent the agglomeration of the particles and achieve reasonable degree of quality in grinding. The retained granules after sieving will be returned to blinder.

Mixing

Treatment of Marble and granite Wastes

The wet refuse preparation consists of three consecutive steps:-.

A. **Preparation of wet refuse by drying phase**, the mixture is automatically pushed to the drying room The heaters are adjusted at 120°C for period from three to four hours, for guaranteeing the drying process. Wet refuse (Sahal) is got out of the dryer in the form of fragile masses which are transferred by a conveyor to the automatic turning over room as it is turned over and made in the form of powder suitable for sifting and mixing.

B. **Mixing and Sieving:** The outcome of the two phases is collected in the automatic sieve. Automatic mixing for thermoplastic in the powder form with at different aspects ratio was done. The amount of material required was calculated. The mixture moves to the final drying and mixing phase. This phase is fitted with heaters at 120°C for a period from 3 to 4 hours. This is for guaranteeing the final drying of the two mixtures.

C. **Manufacturing process:** Plastic powders and treated marble wastes were mixed together in the solid state. The mixture is heated at the required temperature, according to its components. The heating rate depends on the type of the joining material, compression and cooling were done for heated mixture. Nano composite material is fabricated, figure 1.1 shows the recycling of marble and granite wastes unit, the new composite material is distinguished with the light weight and the ability to endure scratch and damping capacity comparing with the natural marble. It is also liable for the easy formation and is distinctive with different colors and shapes

Fig. 1.1: The recycling of marble and granite wastes unit

Scanning Electron Microscope (SEM)

The specimens were examined by scanning electron microscope (SEM) operating at a nominal accelerating voltage of 30kv. Specimen preparation is very simply accomplished by cutting a thin slice of the specimen containing the surface of interest, chemical and electro etching were done at standard conditions, the samples were inserting into the specimen chamber for direct examination of the laser irradiation effects on the structure.

Energy dispersive X-ray " EDX"

The quantitative method of elemental analysis of the samples has been examined at the Chemical labs of the ministry of Telecommunication in Egypt by SEM JSM-T200 at 25KV acceleration voltage, 20mm working distance, and magnification 200x, (1peak omitted 0.02 KeV). Each value is at least an average of 2 readings

Electrical Measurements

Volume Resistivity

IEC 60093:1980, Method of test for volume resistivity and surface resistivity of solid electrical insulating materials.

American society for testing and materials-ASTM D257-07 standard test methods for DC resistance or conductance of insulating materials. Figure 1.2 shows the circuits for volume resistivity measurements

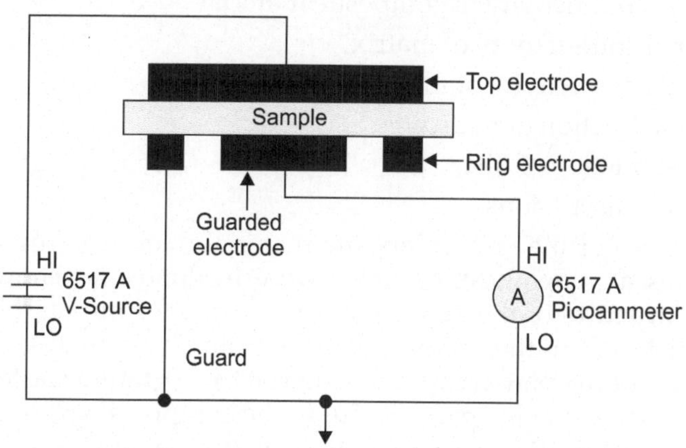

Fig. 1.2: The circuits for volume resistivity measurements

$\rho = RA/L$

ρ electrical resistivity

R electrical resistance of uniform material W (ohm)

A cross sectional area m^2

L specimen length m

Mechanical Measurements

Abrasive Wear

The Egyptian standard no 269/1 -2005 and The Egyptian standard no 269/2 -2005 for heavy duty services, test conditions are sliding distance 352 cycle, applied pressure 224 gm/cm^2 and the abrasive material is sand quartz. Egyptian standard is compatible with international standard of Abrasion Test according to ISO 9352 or ASTM D 4060. According to the Egyptian standard the limit for normal duty must achieve not more than 6 mm loss in thickness and average loss in thickness is not more than 5.2mm, for heavy duty services the limit is not more than 3.6 mm loss in thickness and average loss in thickness is not more than 3mm.

Thermogravimetric Analysis (TGA)

Thermogravimetry thermal analysis (TGA) testing - ASTM E1131, ISO 11358, **Thermogravimetric Analysis (TGA)** measures the change in mass of a material as a function of time and temperature. Ideally, it is utilized to assess volatile content, degradation characteristics, thermal stability, aging and lifetime breakdown, and sintering behavior/reaction kinetics.

Thermal properties

The thermal conductivity of the new composite materials are calculated by role of mixtures,

$$V_m K_m + V_f K_f = K_{Composite}$$

K_c thermal conductivity of composite material

K_m thermal conductivity of matrix

K_f thermal conductivity of filler

V_m volume fraction of matrix

V_f volume fraction of filler

Results and discussions

The structure of the new composite material materials from marble and granite wastes at magnification 5000x were evaluated as shown in figure 1.3(a) is the structure of the new composite material from marble waste, the average particle size in the sample is ranges from 50mm to 300mm. While (b) is the structure of the new composite material from granite waste at the same magnification , the average particle size in the sample is ranges from 150mm to 500mm. the distribution of particles in both samples are semi homogeneous in the micro and nano size.

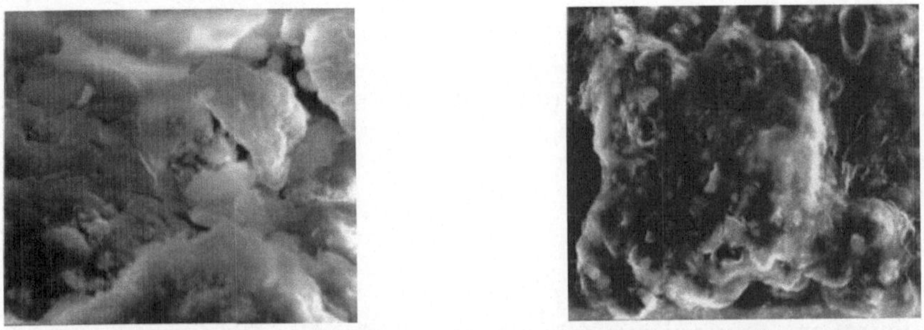

(a) SEM for composite from marble waste (b) SEM for composite from marble waste

Fig. 1.3: SEM of composite materials from marble and granite wastes at 5000x

Spectroscopic Analysis

The chemical composition where evaluated by spectroscopic analysis techniques. Elemental analysis for composite material from marble waste was shown in table 1.3 , and table 1.4 shows the elemental analysis of the composite material from granite waste. the distribution of the elements in the two composites were seem to be different , in composite from marbles waste there was some sulfur content about 0.24% while the composite from granite waste was free of sulfur content. The major element in composite from marbles waste is Calcium while silicon is the main element in composite from granite waste. the two composite material have great difference in structure and composition which explain that they have great difference in manufacturing parameters and electrical and mechanical properties.

Table 1.3: Elemental Analysis of the Composite Material from Marble Waste

Marble							
Element	S	Al	Si	Na	K	Fe	Ca
Concentration %	0.24	0.54	2.51	0.79	0.26	1.94	10

Table 1.4: Elemental Analysis of the Composite Material from Granite Waste

Granite						
Element	Al	Si	Na	K	Fe	Ca
Concentration %	7.12	31.58	3.53	3.93	1.68	1.18

Figure 1.4 shows the EDX analysis distribution of all elements in the composite from marbles wastes, while figure 1.5 shows the EDX distribution of all elements in the composite from granite wastes

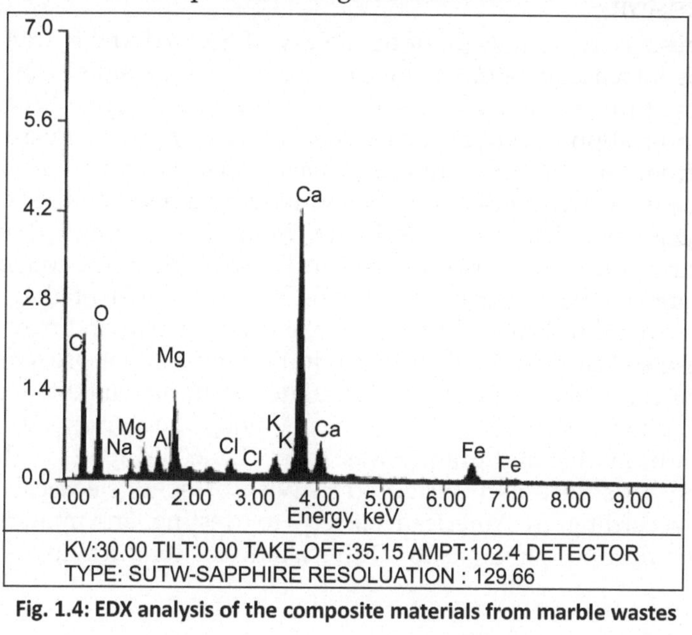

Fig. 1.4: EDX analysis of the composite materials from marble wastes

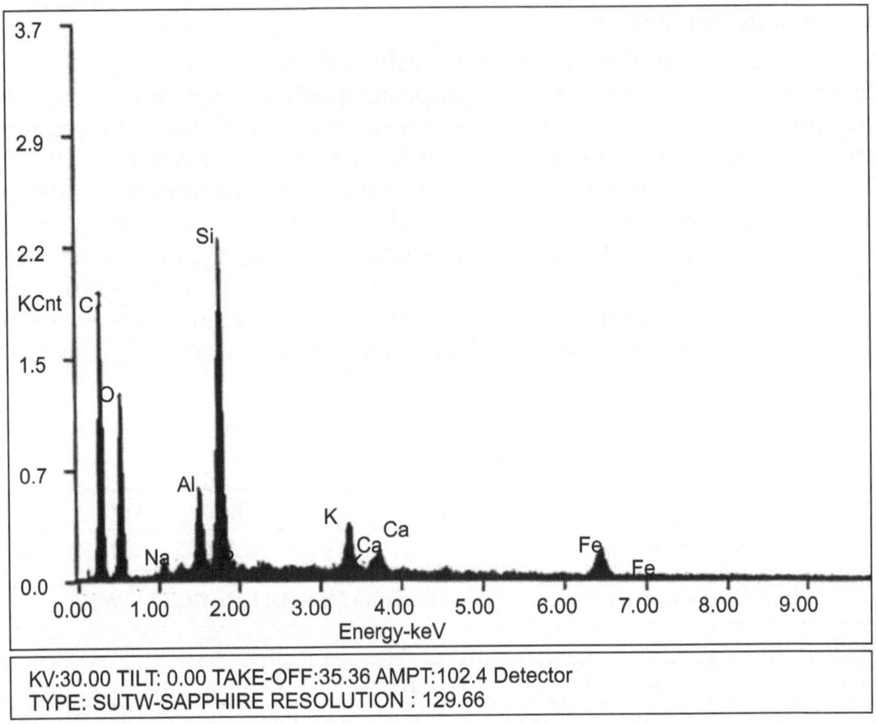

Fig. 1.5: EDX analysis of the composite materials from granite wastes

Electrical Resistance

Volume Resistivity

Electrical resistivity is measure of the ability of the material to flow electrical current, the increase in value of volume resistivity is considered as indication that the structure is free of defects, the electrical resistivity is directly related to the concentration of charge carriers and to their mobility, micro and nano particles from marble and granite wastes work as impurities inside the structure cause a sharp reduction in conductivity, the structure is considered as heterogeneous dielectric material in randomly distributed composite, this structures have sharp rise in electrical resistivity ρ due to scattering of electrons and charge disturbances to the potential field of the lattice, the superior electrical resistance in the material due to micro and nano additives which cause structure and substructure imperfections that prevent vibration of ions, the composite materials are insulated material suitable for different electrical applications. Table 1.5 shows Volume resistivity of composite material from marble and granite wastes by IEC 60093:1980, Method of test for volume resistivity and surface resistivity of solid electrical insulating materials according to American society for testing and materials-ASTM D257-07 standard test methods for DC resistance or conductance of insulating materials.

Table 1.5: Volume Resistivity of Composite Material from Marble and Granite Wastes

	Volume resistivity	Sample dimension	
		Thickness(cm)	Diameter (cm)
Marble 1	> 0.66 *10^{14}	1	5.3
Marble 2	>1.16*10^{14}	1.9	9.7
Granite	>1*10^{14}	2.20	9.7

Mechanical measurements

Abrasive Wear

Abrasive wear data were obtained from pin-on-drum tests where the wear path is essentially linear, all tests were carried out in dry ambient air laboratory conditions. According to the Egyptian standard, the sliding distance is 352 cycle under pressure 632 gm/cm^2. Abrasive wear rates with different kinds of the reinforcement relative to the abrasive medium, quartz sands abrasive which is substantially harder than either the matrix (PMMA) or the reinforcement (marble and granite) was used. abrasive wear in ductile composites reinforced with a hard second phase is presented based on the salient mechanisms of sliding wear, namely plowing, cracking at the matrix/reinforcement interface or in the reinforcement, and particle removal. In the test beginning during the first cycles under load any portion of reinforcement that is removed as wear debris can contribute to the wear resistance of the material; and work as self lubricant . The strong bond energy between the matrix and reinforcement plays a significant role in improving the wear resistance at the interface for both composite material from marble waste and granite waste respectively, composite material from marble wastes have superior wear resistance relative to composite from granite although granite reinforcements are harder secondary phase relative to marble, Self lubrication action is the main reason for these phenomena, during sliding the marble particles are fragmented in the beginning more easily and work as self lubricant media which prevent more fragmentation. Table 1.6 shows abrasive wear of composite material from marble and granite wastes from the above table both composite materials from marble (0.34mm loss in thickness) and granite wastes (0.49mm loss in thickness) are suitable for heavy duty and normal duty applications. According to the Egyptian standard the limit for normal duty 6 mm loss in thickness and average loss in thickness is 5.2mm and for heavy duty services 3.6 mm loss in thickness and average loss in thickness is 3mm.

Table 1.6: Abrasive Wear of Composite Material from Marble and Granite Wastes

Sample	Sample dimensions		Weight Before (gm)	Weight After (gm)	Density (gm/cm^3)	Thickness Loss (mm)	Average (hickness loss (mm)
	Diameter (cm)	Thickness (cm)					
Marble	5.34	1.16	34	33	1.31	0.34	0.34
Granite	3.18	1.07	11	10.5	1.30	0.49	0.49

Thermogravimetric Analysis (TGA)

The TGA curve (below) is labeled in terms of the identity of the components. The sample was heated from room temperature to 900°C at a rate of 5°C/min in air. as shown in the figure 1.6 and 1.7, TGA measures the amount of weight change of a material, either as a function of increasing temperature, or isothermally as a function of time, thermal analysis was used for studying reactions in the solid state, weight change sensitivity less than 0.01 mg. Samples was analyzed in the form of small pieces so the interior sample temperature remains close to the measured gas temperature. In practice thermal analysis gives indication about the dimension stability, Determines temperature and weight change of decomposition reactions, which often allows quantitative composition analysis. the un-change in weight of the composite materials until 100°C to 120°C used to determine water content in a material and reactions with air, oxygen, or other reactive gases

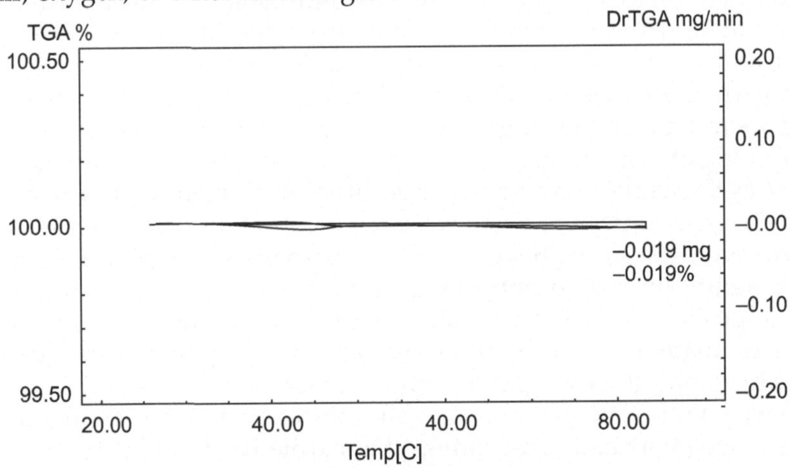

Fig. 1.6: (TGA) Analysis of composite material from marble waste

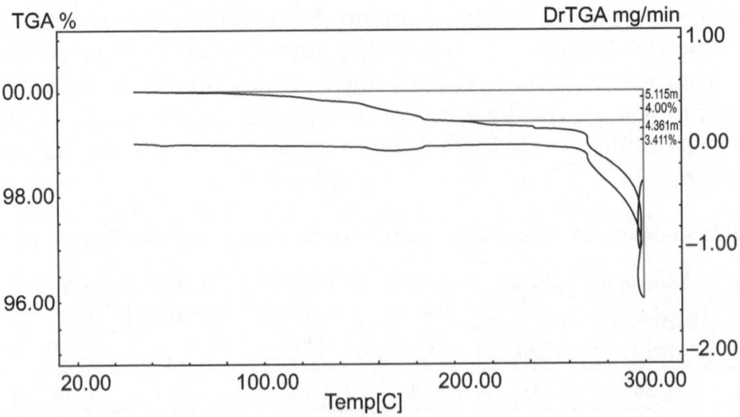

Fig. 1.7: (TGA) Analysis of composite material from granite waste

Thermal Properties

The thermal conductivity of the new composite materials are calculated by role of mixtures, table 1.7 shows the thermal conductivity of both matrix and additives at room temperature.

Table 1.7: Thermal Conductivity of Matrix and Additives

Material	Thermal conductivity [$W{\cdot}m^{-1}{\cdot}K^{-1}$]	Temperature [K]	Notes
Acrylic Glass (Plexiglas V045i)	0.17[2]-0.19[2]-0.2[3]	296[2]	
Granite	1.73[48] - 3.98[48]		(72% SiO_2 + 14% Al_2O_3 + 4% K_2O etc.)
Marble	2.07[48]-2.08[6]-2.94[6][48]	298[6]	Mostly $CaCO_3$

$$0.17 \times 0.75 + 2.07 \times 0.25 = 0.1275 + 0.5175 = 0.645\ (\mathbf{W{\cdot}m^{-1}{\cdot}K^{-1}})$$

$$0.2 \times 0.75 + 2.94 \times 0.25 = 0.15 + 0.735 = 0.885\ (\mathbf{W{\cdot}m^{-1}{\cdot}K^{-1}})$$

Thermal conductivity of composite from marble waste 0.645 to 0.885 ($\mathbf{W{\cdot}m^{-1}{\cdot}K^{-1}}$) at room temperature

$$0.17 \times 0.75 + 1.73 \times 0.25 = 0.1275 + 0.4325 = 0.56\ (\mathbf{W{\cdot}m^{-1}{\cdot}K^{-1}})$$

$$0.2 \times 0.75 + 3.98 \times 0.25 = 0.15 + 0.995 = 1.145\ (\mathbf{W{\cdot}m^{-1}{\cdot}K^{-1}})$$

Thermal conductivity of composite from granite waste 0.56 to 1.145 ($\mathbf{W{\cdot}m^{-1}{\cdot}K^{-1}}$) at room temperature. The new composite materials are considered as thermal insulated material

Conclusions

1. The new composite material consists of micro and nano particles from marble and granite waste impeded in thermoplastic matrix.
2. The new randomly distributed composite material are special type of heterogeneous dielectric materials.
3. The superior electrical resistance in the material due to micro and nano additives which cause structure and substructure imperfections that prevent vibration of ions, the composite materials are insulated material suitable for different electrical applications.
4. Composite material from marble wastes have superior wear resistance relative to composite from granite although granite reinforcements are harder secondary phase relative to marble, Self lubrication action is the main reason for these phenomena, during sliding the marble particles are fragmented in the beginning more easily and work as self lubricant media which prevent more fragmentation.
5. The new composite are suitable for heavy duty and normal duty wear applications. According to the Egyptian standard

6. The new composite materials are considered as thermal insulated material with dimension stability until 100°C to 120°C.
7. The unique structure of the new composite materials are resulting from the new manufacturing technique and the manufacturing unit design.
8. The new composites are economic and suitable for electrical and thermal insulation techniques beside heavy duty tribology applications

REFERENCES

1. Acchar, W., Vieira, F. A. & Hotza, D., 2006. Effect of marble and granite sludge in clay materials, Materials Science and Engineering, A 419, 306-309.
2. John, V. M. & Zordan, S. E., 2001. Research and development methodology for recycling residues as building materials - a proposal. Waste management, 21, 213-219.
3. Menezes, R. R., Ferreira, H. S., Neves, G. A., Lira, H de L. & Ferreira, H. C., 2005. Use of granite sawing wastes in the production of ceramic bricks and tiles. Journal of the European Ceramic Society, 25, 1149-1158.
4. Monteiro, S.N., Alexandre, J., Margem, J.I., Sanchez, R. & Vieira, C.M.F., 2008. Incorporation of sludge waste from water treatment plant into red ceramic. Construction and Building Materials, 22, 1281-1287.
5. Murad, E. & Wagner, U., 1989. Pure and impure clays and their firing products, Hyperfine Interactions, 45, 161-177.
6. Pappu, A., Saxena, M. & Asolekar, S. R., 2007. Solid wastes generation in India and their recycling potential in building materials. Building and Environment, 42, 2311-2320.
7. Russel, J.D., 1987. A Hand Book of Determinative Methods in Clay Mineralogy (edi.) M.J. Wilson and Blackie, London.
8. Segadaes, A.M., Carvalho, M.A. & Acchar, W., 2005. Using marble and granite rejects to enhance the processing of rejects to enhance the processing of clay products. Applied Clay Science, 30, 42-52.
9. F. G. Bell, Engineering properties of soils and rocks, Blackwell Science Publishers, 2000.
10. J.C. Jaeger, N.G.W. Cook, Fundamentals of rock mechanics, Chapman and Hall Publishers, 1979.
11. Ghosh, S. N., 1978. Infra-red spectra of some selected minerals, rocks and products. Journal of Material Science, 13, 1877-1886. John, V. M. & Zordan, S. E., 2001.
12. Manoharan, C., Veeramuthu, K., Venkatachalapathy, R., Radhakrishnan, T. & Ilango, R., 2008. Spectroscopic and ancient geomagnetic field intensity studies on archaeological pottery samples, India. Lithuanian Journal of Physics, 48 (2): 195-202.
13. Monteiro, S.N., Alexandre, J., Margem, J.I., Sanchez, R. & Vieira, C.M.F., 2008. Incorporation of sludge waste from water treatment plant into red ceramic. Construction and Building Materials, 22, 1281-1287.
14. Saxena, M. & Asolekar, S. R., 2007. Solid wastes generation in India and their recycling potential in building materials. Building and Environment, 42, 2311-2320.
15. Menezes, R. R., Ferreira, H. S., Neves, G. A., Lira, H de L. & Ferreira, H. C., 2005. Use of granite sawing wastes in the production of ceramic bricks and tiles. Journal of the European Ceramic Society, 25, 1149-1158 .

2

Nano Indentation Effects on Ti6A14VELI during Excimer Laser Irradiation

ABSTRACT

*In this work, the effects of laser as method of surface treatment in nanoscale on the properties of alloys were evaluated. In order to study the effect of UV laser irradiation on **Ti6Al4VELI**, it was irradiated by 308nm Excimer laser at different number of pulses in the range from 2000 pulses to50000pulses. The nano-indentation measurements were performed on the surface of both untreated **Ti6Al4VELI** and on laser irradiated samples in order to determine their hardness, stiffness and elastic properties such as reduced modulus, the effect of irradiation process on the microstructure of **Ti6Al4VELI** was evaluated by qualitative analysis. This work discuss the effect of laser processing parameters on the microstructure and compare the results obtained by various researchers. Therefore, an overview of the difficulties involved in the laser processing of titanium is provided with a discussion of future prospects. The research emphasis that laser irradiation is a promising technique for surface hardening of materials in nano scale rather than conventional methods*

Keywords:** Laser, irradiation, nano-indentation, microstructure, **Ti6Al4VELI.

Introduction

The benefits of titanium to the world are endless. This metal has completely changed opportunities in medical, chemical processing, energy, drilling, aerospace, marine, weaponry, and consumer industries for ever[1],[2]. Titanium is available in several different grades. Pure titanium is not as strong as the different titanium alloys[3].

The alloy offers the best all-round performance for a variety of weight reduction applications in aerospace, automotive and marine equipment. The high strength, low weight ratio and outstanding corrosion resistance inherent to titanium and its alloys has led to a wide and diversified range of successful applications which demand high levels of reliable performance in surgery and medicine as well as in aerospace, automotive, chemical plant, power generation, oil and gas extraction, sports, and other major industries. In the majority of these and other engineering applications, titanium replaces heavier, less serviceable or less cost-effective materials. Designs made using the properties provided by titanium often result in reliable, economic and more durable systems and components[4],[5]. These titanium components often substantially exceed performance and service life expectations at a lower overall cost[6],[7].

Ti6Al4V is the most widely used titanium alloy. It features good machinability and excellent mechanical properties[8],[9]. Ti6Al4V also has numerous applications in the medical industry. The biocompatibility of Ti6Al4V is excellent, especially when direct contact with tissue or bone is required[10],[11]. Neither grade of Ti 6Al-4V has corrosion properties quite as good as CP titanium, but both are corrosion resistant in seawater, oxidizing acids, aqueous chlorides, wet chlorine gas, and sodium hypochlorite[12],[13].

Ti 6Al-4V and Ti 6Al-4V ELI are the most widely used titanium alloys and account for more than half of all the titanium sponge used worldwide[14],[15]. Aerospace applications account for 80% of that usage. The remainder is found in defense, marine, medical, chemical, and other industries[16],[17].

Ti6Al4V ELI (Grade 23) is very similar to Ti6Al4V (Grade 5), except that Ti6Al4V ELI contains reduced levels of oxygen, nitrogen, carbon and iron[18],[19]. ELI is short for "Extra Low *Interstitials*", and these lower interstitials provide improved ductility[20],[21].

Altering the interstitial levels tends to enhance certain properties; Ti 6Al-4V ELI (Extra Low Interstitials) is a popular alloy where medium strength and good toughness are required[22]. The strength and ductility are similar, but the fracture toughness of the ELI grade is about 25% higher than the standard grade. The ELI grade is usually specified for seawater applications (MIL-T-9047) and for medical use (ASTM F136). A medical grade of Ti 6Al-4V (ASTM F1472) also exists[23],[24].

ELI is the extra low interstitial version of Ti-6AL- 4V that offers better ductility and fracture toughness in air and salt water with a low modulus[25]. Grade 23 titanium, commonly known as ELI has some of the most coveted properties of all the grades of titanium[26]. Grade 23 ELI Titanium will continue to be one of the highest standard alloys. It is a top choice for any application where good corrosion resistance, strength, toughness and light weight are required. The many benefits of the alloyed titanium grade 23 are the biomedical application opportunities as well as aerospace. This amazing grade can be used in implants, surgical devices, orthodontic applications, bone fixation, space vehicles structures, missile components, aircraft ducting, hydraulics, tubing. You will find grade 23 in several product forms including titanium bars, billets, plates, sheets, wire, seamless tubing, and foils[27]. Make sure to consult a well known and well stocked titanium processing center for your next project with titanium[28].

Property Ratings and Comparisons: Titanium grade 23 Ti-6AL-4V ELI has an excellent combination of properties beneficial to medical, industrial and applications where high speed and great force are factors[29]. It has good corrosion resistance, excellent strength and toughness as well as high ductility and formability ratings. These properties make ELI the perfect choice whenever those factors are present; for example, it's ideal for coils, wires, cables, medical devices or implants, aerospace applications and pressure vessels.it is worth noting advances in the development of laser coatings on Ti-TiN. Since the 1990s, it has been known that it is possible to obtain a hard coating of TiN on titanium by laser alloying with nitrogen gas. However, this is an unstable process, and it is difficult to obtain thick and dense layers without defects. Recently, this technique was used with a Nd:YAG pulse laser and various combinations of Ar/N2 and new Ti-Nb-Zr biomedical alloys. Greater adhesion and hardness were achieved, although a fine network of microscopic cracks also formed due to the formation of TiN dendrites. However, major difficulties have been encountered in these processes, and these include changes in the components, cracking, and poor adhesion between the coating and substrate, surface faults are one of the major causes of failure in these joints.[30],[31]

Experimental Work

The alloy used throughout this work was supplied by Sandvik Co, France in the form of bars of **Ti6Al4VELI**. Table 2.1 shows the chemical composition of the alloy used in the current **work.**

Table 2.1: The Chemical Composition of Ti6Al4VELI (Grade 23)

Type Analysis			
Carbon (Maximum)	0.08%	Titanium	Balance
Aluminium	5.50 to 6.50%	Vanadium	3.50 to 4.50%
Nitrogen (Maximum)	0.05%	Iron (Maximum)	0.25%
Oxygen (Maximum)	0.130%	Hydrogen (Maximum)	0.013%
Other, Total (Maximum)	0.40%		

*Other, Each (Maximum) = 0.1%

**For AMS 4930 rev. D, Hydrogen = 0.0125% and Yttrium = 0.005%.

Laser Surface Irradiation

The surface irradiation of the alloys was studied. Samples used in this investigation were in the standard size for every test according to ASTM. All the experiments were performed at room temperature in air at atmospheric pressure; it was shown elsewhere [10] that the presence of air has no measurable influence on the process of irradiation by UV laser [11]. The irradiation is done on one side of the sample and covers all the surface area of the sample. The main goal of this work is optimize condition for laser irradiation of the samples by Excimer laser at 308nm Table (2) shows data for used rare gas halide XeCl Excimer laser[32].

Table 2.2: Data for Excimer Laser (Rare Gas Halide)

Gas type	λ (nm)	r (A)	ω (cm–1)	σ (cm^2)	τ (ns)
XeCl	308	2.9	194	50	11

λ = transition wavelength

r (A) = equilibrium inter-nuclear separation

ω = fundamental vibration frequency of the excited state

σ = stimulated emission cross section

τ = irradiative life time (pulse duration)

The number of pulses and the effect of energy per pulse on the hardness were recorded to indicate the energy required (fluence) to improve the mechanical properties. In the shape of a rectangle with width (w = 4mm) and length (l = 10 mm) was used in the laser process, the power density ranges from (0.75 W/Cm^2 to 0.1 W/Cm^2) without any focusing. The laser irradiation condition is listed in Table 2.3.

Table 2.3: The Laser Irradiation Conditions of the Samples

Type	Wavelength nm	No. of pulses	Energy per pulse mJ	Repetition rate (Hz)
Eximer	UV 308.6	0, 2000, 5000, 10250, 15000, 5000	6	200

time = 6nano second & total energy = energy per puke "number of pulses

Excimer laser irradiation is performed directly in the air and without any intermediate media[27].

Indentation Data Analysis

Surface and near-surface mechanical properties of thin films and coatings can be critical to their final performance. The rapidly expanding field of depth-sensing nano-indentation provides a quantitative method for mapping the mechanical properties, such as hardness and elastic modulus, of the surface/near-surface region. Quantification is possible through the use of diamond indenters with well defined tip geometry, combined with established models for determining the mechanical properties from the measured data. Nano-indentation has been employed extensively to characterize the mechanical properties of a wide range of hard coatings and surface-modified layers. The principle behind nano-indentation is similar to micro hardness testing, which employs greater applied load so that the residual indent can be measured optically.

The depth vs. load raw unloading data was fitted to a power-law function, as originally proposed by Oliver and Pharr, to determine the hardness and modulus of the film, after correction for the effects of instrument compliance

Contact compliance C = total compliance (C_t) – machine compliance (C_m)

Where contact compliance = 1/contact stiffness. The power-law function has the form

$$P = a(h-h_f)^m \tag{1}$$

where P is the load, (h - h_f) is the elastic displacement, a and m are material constants. The indenter contact (or plastic) depth, h_c is determined from the expression:

$$h_c = h_{max} - v(CP_{max}) \tag{2}$$

where C is the contact compliance equal to the tangent at maximum load (P_{max}). The value of v is a function of the indenter geometry and depends on the pressure distribution that is established after the plastic deformation. For flat punch indenter v is 1, whereas for a Berkovich indenter, as used in this study, v is taken as 0.75 since most indenters have a rounded tip. The plastic depths correspond to these indenter geometries. The diamond area function A(h_c) was determined separately from indentations into fused quartz.

The hardness (H) is determined from the peak load (P_{max}) and the projected area of contact, A:

$$H = P_{max}/A \tag{3}$$

To obtain the elastic modulus, the unloading portion of the depth-load curve is analyzed according to a relation, which depends on the contact area:

$$C = v^{0.5}/(2E_r A^{0.5}) \tag{4}$$

where C is the contact compliance and E_r is the reduced modulus defined by

$$1/E_r = (1-v_s^2)/E_s + (1-v_i^2)/E_i \tag{5}$$

where v_s the Poisson's ratio for the sample, v_i, the Poisson's ratio for the indenter (0.07), E_s the Young's modulus for the sample and E_i, the Young's modulus for the indenter (1141 GPa).

In all the data reported in this paper, the loading data have been fitted to a power law function in the instrument software to determine this depth offset, as has been done previously.

$$P = a(h - h_0)^n \tag{6}$$

where P is the load, h_0, the real depth zero, a, a material parameter and n, the index of the deformation (indentation exponent)[11].

Qualitative analysis

Metallographic Examinations

The specimens were prepared for examination first by grinding on different grades of silicon carbide "SiC" papers coarse grinding followed by fine grinding at 180, 240, 320, 400, 600, and 800 finally polishing was conducted with Alumina powder (3 μm) size. The details of the microstructure were revealed after etching by standard etching solution of the alloy selected. All specimens had to be etched and polished several times to obtain best results and to produce a uniform level of sample examination. The surfaces of the samples before and after laser irradiation were examined using an Olympus optical microscope Model BHM at selected magnification[20].

Alloy	Etchant	Conditions	Remarks
T6A14VELI	Dist water	100 ml	Swep
	Hydrofluric acid (40%)	1.3 ml	Sample
	Nitric acid (1.40)	2-6 ml	3-10s (Toxic)

Results and Discussions

In order to determine the sub-surface changes resulting from excimer laser irradiation at different number of pulses, nano-indentation measurements were done at the same test conditions mentioned before. Figure 2.1 and figure 2.2 show the variation of hardness with load and depth respectively as a function of number of pulses. At 5000 pulses, the maximum value of hardness was 11.8 GPa at unloaded conditions. at 10250 pulses the hardness at the unloaded conditions 8.8GPa , the untreated sample record 1.4 GPa at the same conditions, at other pulses 15000, 50000, 2000 the improvement in the hardness at un loaded conditions were in the range from 3.5 to 5 GPa, when the load increase the hardness decrease almost at all number of pulses. sudden decrease in hardness are recorded at load increase to 4.3 mN. at 5000 pulses and 10250 pulses while gradual decrease were recorded at other conditions. the disturbance in the behavior due to hardening during manufacturing and error range of the measurements tools, this work confirmed that it is possible to produce layers in Ti6Al4V with a good metallurgical characteristics different in microstructure with the microstructure of substrate and without cracks or pores. Moreover, the layer becomes harder and more resistant to erosion.[18]

At figure 2.2 similar behavior was recorded with depth, the hardness always decreased with depth at all number of pulses, The hardness increased gradually with number of pulses and reach maximum value 12GPa at 5000 pulses. The rate of hardness decrease from 5000 to 15000 pulses was very narrow. The hardness value almost remained constant from 15000 to 50000 pulses, the maximum value at the sub surface was 7GPa at 5000 pulses also. It was found that the laser hardened layer is strong function of laser irradiation conditions and number of pulses. The previous research prove that various types of laser treatment can be used to enhance mechanical properties of Ti 6Al 4V ELI improve its poor resistance to wear by hardness increase. Our results agree well with published results(10),(12). Typical hardness in the annealed condition for the same alloy is Rockwell C 30-34, and about Rockwell C 35-39 in the solution and aged condition[30].

Scientists study microhardness as a function of the distance from the surface is gradually decrease with the distance from the surface. On the other hand the microhardness fluctuates with the distance (the distance parallel to the surface). These results suggest that thermal strain or heterogeneity has been accumulated perpendicular to the moving direction of the laser beam. When solution –annealing has done, a decrease in microhardness and smoothing of microhardness profile along the surface are attributed to the annealing effect. Current results have the same trend in nano-scale and the same hardness profile was appeared[25]. The microhardness along the depth of the hardened zones, and the microstructures observed are greatly the same with the results of some former researchers[8],[9].

In current technique cracks were reduced, and the roughness and hardness of the layer created were controlled through strict control of the power applied and the laser characteristics. The result in both cases was a significant improvement in mechanical properties beside reduction in defects. Figure 2.3 shows the variation of modulus with depth as a function of number of pulses. the maximum value of modulus was 330 GPa recorded at 10250 pulses while at 5000 pulses the modulus value was 270 GPa. the untreated sample record 100 GPa, at other conditions there was slight improve in the modulus in the range from 150 to 220 GPa. Figure 2.4 shows the variation of modulus with load as a function of number of pulses. At 10250 pulses, the maximum value at the surface was 320 GPa and almost unchanged until 4mN. At 5000 pulses, the modulus value almost at 270 GPa. The modulus of the untreated sample at unloaded conditions are 100 GPa. In general the modulus decreases gradually to reach the value of base metal with load increase, the modulus improvement at other pulses in the range from 150 GPa to 200 GPa. The great amount of energy absorbed at 50 000 pulses lead to an oxidized, contaminated surface layer that is often stressed and plastically deformed, non-uniform and rather poorly defined. Such "native" surfaces are clearly not appropriate for different applications and some surface treatment must be performed. Previous published data emphasis that, the various surface modification technologies pertaining to titanium and titanium alloys including mechanical treatment, thermal spraying, sol–gel, chemical and electrochemical treatment, and ion implantation from the perspective of biomedical engineering. all previous techniques have shown that the wear resistance, corrosion resistance, and biological properties of titanium and titanium alloys can be improved selectively using the appropriate surface treatment techniques while the desirable bulk attributes of the materials are retained[18],[20].

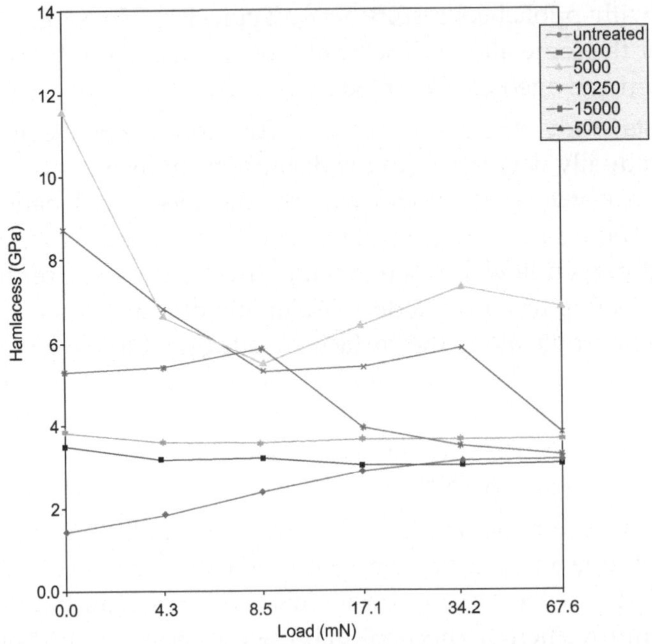

Fig. 2.1: The variation of Hardness with Load for Titanium irradiated by excimer Laser 308 nm, 6 mJ, 200 Hz at Different Number of Pulses

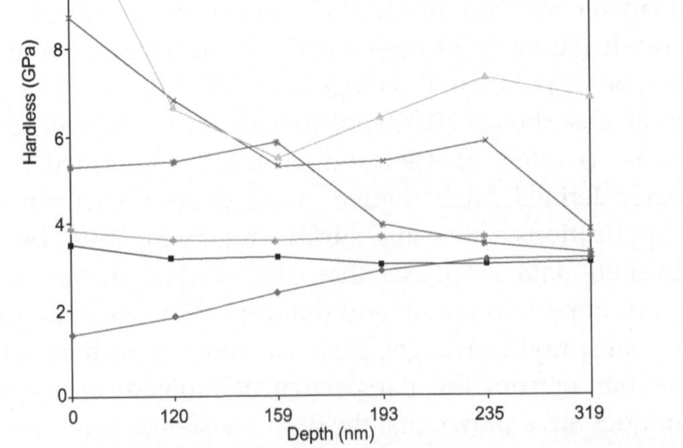

Fig. 2.2: The variation of Hardness with Depth for Titanium irradiated by excimer Laser 308 nm, 6mJ, 200 Hz at Diffrent Number of Pulses

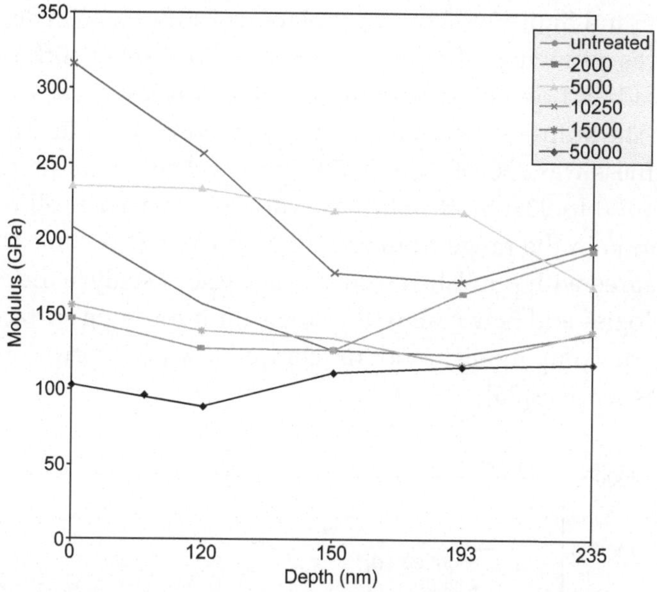

Fig. 2.3: The variation of Modulus with Depth for Titanium irradiated by excimer Laser 308 nm, 6mJ, 200 Hz at Different Number of Pulses

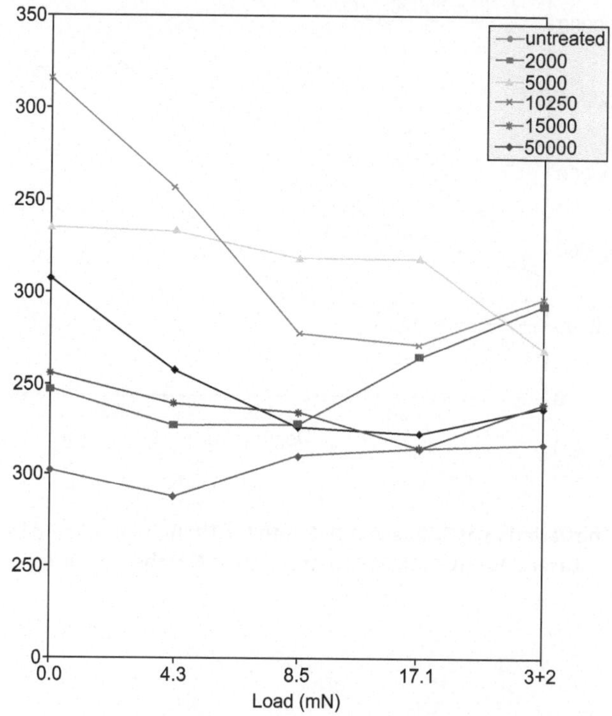

Fig. 2.4: The variation of Modulus with Load for titanium irradiated by excimer Laser 308 nm, 6mJ, 200 Hz at Different Number of Pulses

Figure 2.5 and figure 2.6 show the variation of stiffness with depth and load respectively as a function of number of pulses. The rate of stiffness increased with both load and depth. Minimum values of stiffness were 100000 N/m at the surface. The stiffness increased with both load and depth. The maximum value of stiffness was 750000 N/m at 5000pulses. The rate of increases almost the same from 0 to 236nm, the stiffness values increased at all conditions of laser irradiation in the range from 650000 N/m to 750000 N/m. The results of these work agree with published results, the authors analyze the effect of new laser technologies and new materials as tools for improving surface properties specifically, biocompatibility and resistance to wear, corrosion, and high temperatures services[26].

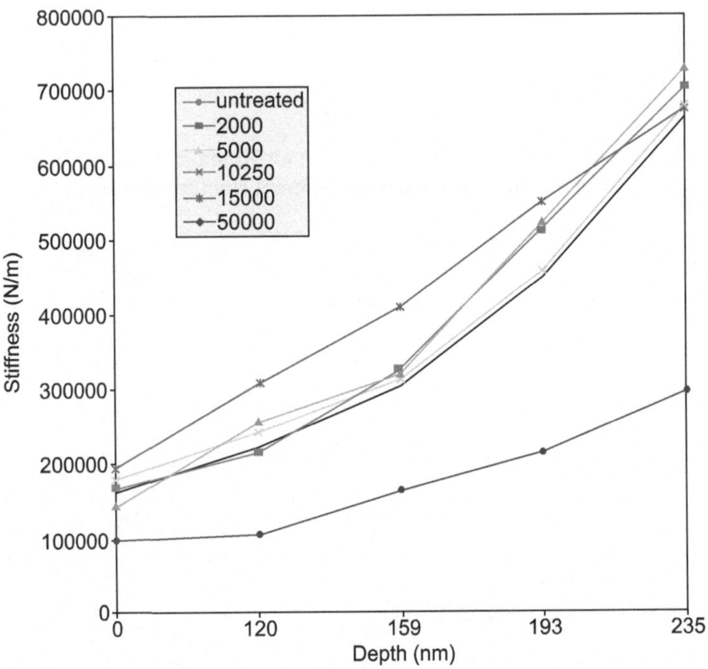

Fig. 2.5: The variation of Stiffness with Depth for Titanium irradiated by excimer Laser 308 nm, 6mJ, 200 Hz at Different Number of Pulses

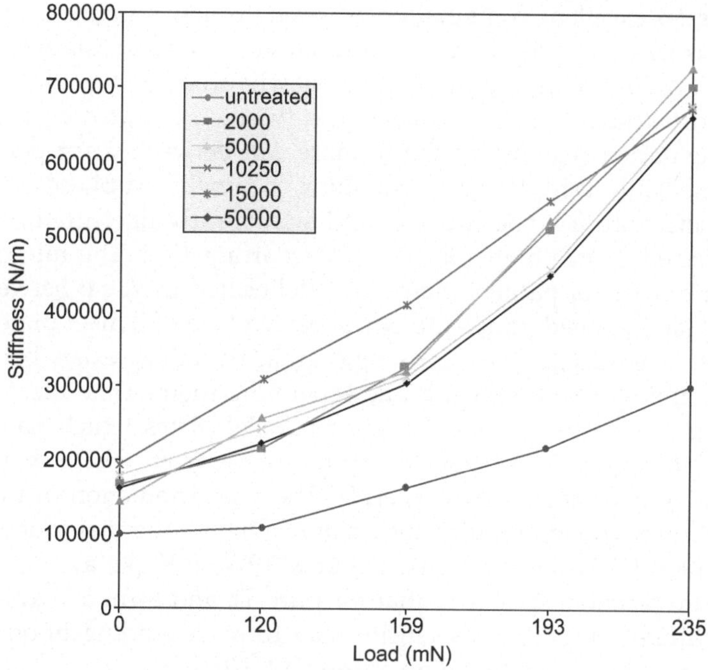

Fig. 2.6: The variation of Stiffness with Load for Titanium irradiated by excimer Laser 308 nm, 6mJ, 200 Hz at Different Number of Pulses

Titanium alloy used in this study as shown in figure 2.7-a is an alpha-beta type, the structure is globular particles of b in a matrix of a. It is a two phase $\alpha + \beta$ titanium alloy, The formation of inter-metallic compounds in situ is another approach for improving the surface properties of Titanium. Two alloying elements are especially important Aluminum as the alpha stabilizer and Vanadium as the beta stabilizer[19].

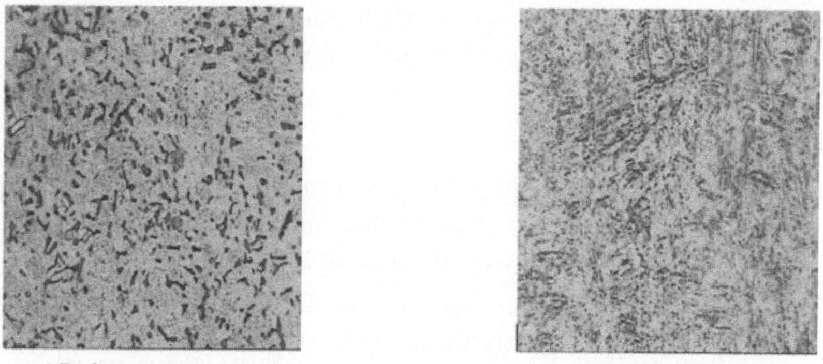

Before treatment After treatment

Fig. 2.7: Microstructure of Ti6Al4VELI at 750X before and after laser irradiation by Excimer laser 308nm, 200Hz, 5000 pulses, 6 mJ.

It has an excellent combination of strength and toughness along with excellent corrosion resistance, the formation of Widmanstatten structure in Ti6Al4V alloy achieved by cooling slowly from above the β transus, final microstructure consists of plates of α (white) separated by the β phase (dark). The darker regions are the β phase, left between the α plates which have formed[28]. Ti6Al4V ELI containing a lamellar α-phase with larger β-grains, and with a higher density and significantly finer grain, When the alloy subjected to treatments in air by laser irradiation. The microstructure change, it consists of parallel plates of α delineated by the β between them. Where α plates formed parallel to one specific plane of β meet plates formed on another plane[20],[21]. A high-angle grain boundary exists between the α crystals and etches to reveal a line separating them. This microstructural morphology, consisting of these sets of parallel plates which have formed with a crystallographic relationship to the phase from which they formed, is called a Widmanstatten structure[21]. The laser irradiation of the alloy is similar action to cooling rapidly, the relatively higher thermal conductivity of titanium alloy Ti6Al4VELI which is about 0.219W/cmK, β may decompose by a martensite reaction, similar to that for pure Ti, and form a Widmanstatten pattern. Different types of martensite may form depending upon the alloy chemistry and the quenching temperature[29],[30].

Since in a given β grain there are six sets of nonparallel growth planes, then a structure of *a* plates is formed consisting of six nonparallel sets. The Widmanstatten microstructure developed So laser treated Ti-6Al-4V has an excellent combination of strength and toughness along with excellent performance there is no change in shape and appearance, it has found extended application of laser irradiation techniques mentioned in this work because of useful mechanical properties produced by surface treatments. Wear resistance, corrosion resistance, paint adhesion, and decorative effects have been improved[14],[15].

Typical uses include aerospace applications, pressure vessels, aircraft turbine and compressor blades and disks. Surgical implants, and building elements[22].

Conclusions

1. Using ultra violet Excimer laser 308nm at different number of pulses which is high power cold beam does not have any thermal effect this prevent alloy reaction with the atmosphere
2. Laser photon energy is absorbed on the surface of the Ti6AL4V ELI alloys and causes change in the microstructure leads to change in the mechanical properties
3. The Hardness, reduced modulus and stiffness are changed with the amount of laser energy absorbed and with number of pulses

4. The maximum value of hardness was 11.8 GPa at unloaded conditions. at 10250 pulses the hardness at the unloaded conditions 8.8GPa , the untreated sample record 1.4 GPa at the same conditions.
5. The variation of modulus with depth as a function of number of pulses. the maximum value of modulus was 330 GPa recorded at 10250 pulses while at 5000 pulses the modulus value was 270 GPa. the untreated sample record 100 GPa.
6. The hardness increased gradually with number of pulses and reach maximum value 12GPa at 5000 pulses. The rate of hardness decrease from 5000 to 15000 pulses was very narrow.
7. The modulus decreases gradually to reach the value of base metal with load increase, the modulus improvement at other pulses in the range from 150 GPa to 200 GPa.
8. The variation of stiffness occurs with depth and load respectively as a function of number of pulses. The rate of stiffness increased with both load and depth. The maximum value of stiffness was 750000 N/m at 5000pulses. The rate of increases almost the same from 0 to 236nm, the stiffness values increased at all conditions of laser irradiation in the range from 650000 N/m to 750000 N/m
9. The Widmanstatten microstructure is developed so laser irradiation of Ti6AL4V ELI in the room temperature is similar to quenching process of the same alloy due to high thermal conductivity of titanium .
10. Laser treated Ti-6Al-4V has an excellent combination of strength and toughness along with excellent corrosion resistance. Typical uses include aerospace applications, pressure vessels, aircraft turbine and compressor blades and disks. Surgical implants, and building elements.

REFERENCES

1. Moiseyev, Valentin N. (2006). Titanium Alloys: Russian Aircraft and Aerospace Applications. Taylor and Francis, LLC. p. 196. ISBN 978-0-8493-3273-9.
2. Andrew E. Kramer (5 July 2013). "Titanium Fills Vital Role for Boeing and Russia". The New York Times. Retrieved 6 July 2013.
3. Wang, Hongtao, Z. Zak Fang, and Pei Sun. A critical review of mechanical properties of powder metallurgy titanium. International journal of powder metallurgy 46, no. 5 (2010): 45-57.
4. Yan, M., S. D. Luo, G. B. Schaffer, and M. Qian. TEM and XRD characterisation of commercially pure α-Ti made by powder metallurgy and casting. Materials Letters 72 (2012): 64-67.
5. Yan, M., S. D. Luo, G. B. Schaffer, and M. Qian. Impurity (Fe, Cl, and P)-Induced Grain Boundary and Secondary Phases in Commercially Pure Titanium (CP-Ti). Metallurgical and Materials Transactions A 44, no. 8 (2013): 3961-3969.
6. Yan, M., Qian, M., Kong, C., & Dargusch, M. S. (2014). Impacts of trace carbon on the microstructure of as-sintered biomedical Ti–15Mo alloy and reassessment of the maximum carbon limit. Acta biomaterialia, 10(2), 1014-1023.

7. Y. Yang, D. Zhang, W. Yan, and Y. Zheng,(2010), "Microstructure and wear properties of TiCN/Ti coatings on titanium alloy by laser cladding," Opt.Lasers Eng. **48**, 119–124.
8. S. Sathish, M. Geetha, N. D. Pandey, C. Richard, and R. Asokamani,(2010) "Studies on the corrosion and wear behavior of the laser nitrided biomedical titanium and its alloys," Mater. Sci. Eng., C **30**, p376–382.
9. Y. Zhang, Z. Wei, L. Shi, and M. Xi, (2008),"Characterization of laser powder deposited Ti–TiC composites and functional gradient materials," J. Mater.Process. Technol. **206**, p438–444.
10. J. J. Candel, V. Amigó, J. A. Ramos, and D. Busquets,(2010), "Sliding wear resistance of TiCp reinforced titanium composite coating produced by laser cladding," Surf. Coat. Technol. **204**, p 3161–3166.
11. M. Zheng, D. Fan, X. Li, J. Zhang, and Q. Liu,(2010), "Microstructure and in vitro bioactivity of laser-cladded bioceramic coating on titanium alloy in a simulated body fluid," J. Alloys Compd. **489**, p211–214.
12. R. Comesaña, F. Quintero, F. Lusquiños, and M. J. Pascual,(2010), "Laser cladding of bioactive glass coatings," Acta Biomater. **6**, p953–961.
13. http://www.essentialchemicalindustry.org/metals/titanium.html
14. https://www.elsevier.com/books/additive-manufacturing-of-titanium-alloys/
15. http://www.titanium.org.
16. Velasco-Ortega, E (Sep 2010). "In vitro evaluation of cytotoxicity and genotoxicity of a commercial titanium alloy for dental implantology". Mutat Res. **702**: 17–23.
17. The Essential Chemical Industry online. York, UK: CIEC Promoting Science at the University of York. 15 January 2015 "Titanium"
18. https://en.wikipedia.org/wiki/Titanium
19. http://www.nature.com/nmat/journal/v3/n2/abs/nmat1058.html
20. http://cartech.ides.com/datasheet.aspx?i=101
21. http://continentalsteel.com/titanium/titanium- grades/grade-23/
22. http://titaniumprocessingcenter.com/guide-to- titanium-grades.htm
23. http://asm.matweb.com/search/SpecificMaterial.asp?bassnum=MTP641
24. Murr, L. E.; Quinones, S. A.; Gaytan, S. M.; Lopez, M. I.; Rodela, A.; Martinez, E. Y.; Hernandez, D. H.; Martinez, E.; Medina, F. (2009-01-01). "Microstructure and mechanical behavior of Ti–6Al–4V produced by rapid-layer manufacturing, for biomedical applications". Journal of the Mechanical Behavior of Biomedical Materials. **2** (1): 20–32
25. Vydehi Arun Joshi. (2006), Titanium Alloys: An Atlas of Structures and Fracture Features. CRC Press.
26. https://www.jim.or.jp/journal/e/pdf3/46/09/2020.pdf
27. http://www.arcam.com/wp-content/uploads/Arcam-Ti6Al4V-Titanium-Alloy.pdf
28. https://en.wikipedia.org/wiki/Ti-6Al-4V
29. http://onlinelibrary.wiley.com/doi/10.1002/mawe.201600515/full
30. https://www.atimetals.com/Documents/ati_6-4_tds_en_v1.pdf
31. W. C. Oliver, G. M. Pharr, J. Mater. Res. 7 (1992) p. 1564.
32. Hebatalrahman patent number 24014,Egyptian patent office,2008.

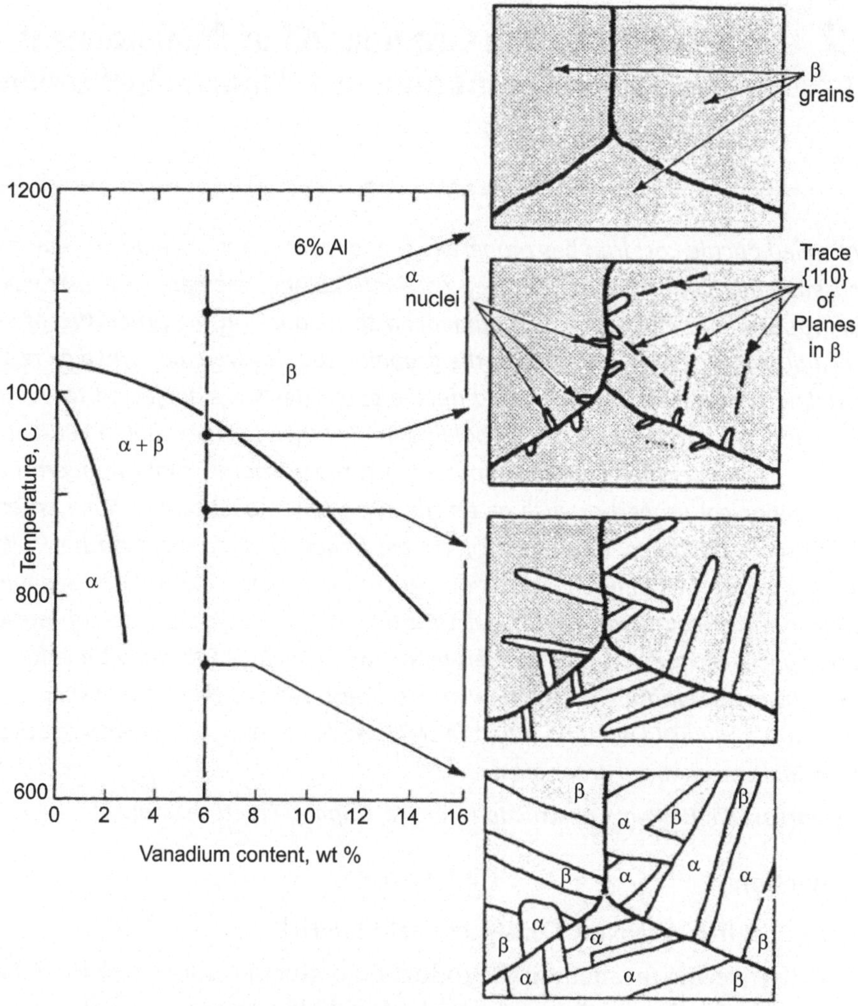

Achieved by cooling slowly above the β transus. Final microstructure consists of plates of α (white) separated by the β phase (dark).

3 Rolled Ductile Cast Iron DCI as Reinforcement Element in Construction and Building Applications

ABSTRACT

Hot rolled ductile cast iron has properties similar to steels with relatively low cost and easy fabrication. It can be used as reinforcement element in construction applications. The effect of double annealing techniques on the properties of hot rolled ductile cast iron was studies. the graphite nodules were deformed as result of rolling progresses. The hot rolled ductile cast irons were subjected to double annealing by heating to 900°C and holding for 3hr then furnace cool to 700°C and holding at this temperature for 3hous then furnace cool to room temperature. The mechanical properties such as tensile strength, impact and yielding criteria of DCI were discussed. The effect of double annealing treatment on hot rolled DCI was studied at different reduction percentages from 26% to 52%. Scanning electron microscope was carried out to examine the fracture surface of tension and impact specimens. Stress analysis model was developed to study the effect of microstructure variation on the flow stress. The results of these study show that the cost of rolled DCI was less than the steel used in reinforcement with relatively reasonable mechanical properties.

Keywords: *DCI, Rolling, Construction, Tensile, Impact, Fracture Analysis.*

Introduction

Ductile Cast-Iron as a New Constructional Material

Before discovering the method of production of ductile cast-iron with globular graphite or simply ductile cast dated May 1948, designers used only two types of cast-iron: gray cast-iron with zero plasticity and malleable cast-iron with graphite of flaky shape, which was made by means of long and power-consuming high-temperature annealing of so called white cast-iron. Till the beginning of fifties the only constructional material for medium and big cast details, which should have high plastic and ductile characteristics, there was a cast steel[1]. Ductile cast-iron, having high technological, operational and economic qualities, replaced during the last four decades great part of castings of steel, malleable and gray cast-iron and welded constructions.

In narrow minded understanding cast-iron is something fragile and unstable. This opinion may fairly refer to the products of gray cast-iron. Due to unique properties of ductile cast-iron products the growth of production of this material in the world is impressive[2],[3]. At year 2000 total production of ductile cast-iron was more than 20 million tones per year. The importance of ductile cast iron can be appreciated from production statistics, which that they represent 21% (by weight) of all ferrous castings produced in the world. Up to the first half of the last century, only malleable irons were able to partially offer a combination of grey iron cast-ability and steel mechanical properties (first of all, toughness). These cast irons were obtained as a result of extended annealing treatment of white iron, with a matrix microstructure that was characterized by different ferrite and pearlite volume fractions, as a function of the cooling cycle[4],[5]. The main problems of this procedure were the high costs and the difficulty to cast sound white iron components. In 1943, in the International Nickel Company Research Laboratory, a magnesium addition allowed to obtain a cast iron containing not flakes but nearly perfect graphite spheres.

In 1948, at the American Foundry man Society Convention, it was announced that a small amount of cerium allowed to obtain the same result[6].

After more than fifty years, ductile iron should be considered as a family of materials offering a wide range of properties depending on the chemical composition and heat treatment and the consequent microstructure modifications[7],[8].

Matrix microstructure importance is emphasized by the use of matrix names to commonly designate the different types of ductile irons

(a) Ferritic DCI: this DCI is characterized by a good ductility and impact resistance; ultimate tensile and yield strength are equivalent to a low carbon steel.

(b) Pearlitic DCI: a pearlitic DCI is characterized by high strength, good wear resistance and reduced ductility and impact resistance.

(c) Ferritic-pearlitic DCIs: these are the most common DCI; properties are intermediate between ferritic and pearlitic grades and good machinability is obtained with low production costs.

(d) Austenitic DCI: this DCI shows a high corrosion and oxidation resistance, with good strength and dimensional stability at high temperature.

(e) Martensitic DCI: these DCI are obtained controlling both the chemical composition (to prevent pearlite formation) and the heat treatment (quench and temper): very high strength and wear resistance are obtained, but with lower values of ductility and toughness.

(f) Bainitic DCI: this DCI is obtained controlling chemical composition and/ or heat treatment: the result is a hard and wear resistant material.

(g) Austempered DCI (also ADI): ADI are obtained after an austempering heat treatment, with very high tensile strength values (twice than a pearlitic DCI), high elongation and toughness.

Compared with steel, ductile cast iron has generally inferior ductility, weld-ability, toughness and fatigue resistance however, it has superior cast-ability (high Ca and Si), machine-ability, wear, corrosion resistance and damping capacity[9],[10].

Ductile cast-iron is also widely used in construction. During the last 15 years almost all leading firms, that work in this field, began in producing new grades of this material, which allowed increasing loads and decreasing the price the production of casting of ductile cast-iron needs the use of special technologies, equipment, high-quality materials, trained staff and special means of control[11].

Experimental Work

Material

The ductile cast iron used in this work is obtained from El-Nasr Casting Company. The slab cut from centrifugal casting pipe with 1000 mm diameter and 10 mm thickness, which consider as the main commercial product in the Company. The chemical composition of the ductile cast iron is shown in table 3.1.

Table 3.1: The Chemical Composition of the Ductile Cast Iron

Contents	C	Si	Mg	S	Mn	Fe
Percentage %	3.68	2.1	0.0042	0.017	0.35	Balance

Treatment before Rolling

- Slices were double annealed (L.H.T) to 900°C and hold for 2hr prior to furnace cooling to 700°C, then held at this temperature for 3hr before the furnace cooling to the room temperature.
- Some of the slices were feritizing annealed (F.H.T) at 920°C for 30min then furnace cooled for 30min Full feritizing Annealing used to remove carbides and stabilized Pearlite, heat to 900°C, holding long enough to dissolve carbides, then cooling at a rate of 85°C/h to 705°C, and still air cooling to room temperature. It improves low temperature fracture resistance but reduces fatigue strength.

Preheat before Rolling

- The L.H.T specimen is soaked at 950°C for one hour before rolling, while the F.H.T specimen is soaked at 900°C for one hour before rolling.

Rolling Process

Rolling was carried out on the slices in the circumference direction of the pipe by using a laboratory two - high reversing mill with 320mm diameter rolls and

450mm length. The slices were heated to a temperature range between 900°C and 950°C there soaked for one hour at this temperature. The rolls speed was 25m/min. Reduction in cross sectional area was carried out on 2 to 4 passes. Some of the rolled strips were air cooled A.C, while the others were furnace cooled, F.C at 700°C. Figure 3.1 shows schematic diagram for the steps of manufacturing, rolling and treatment

Heat Treatment

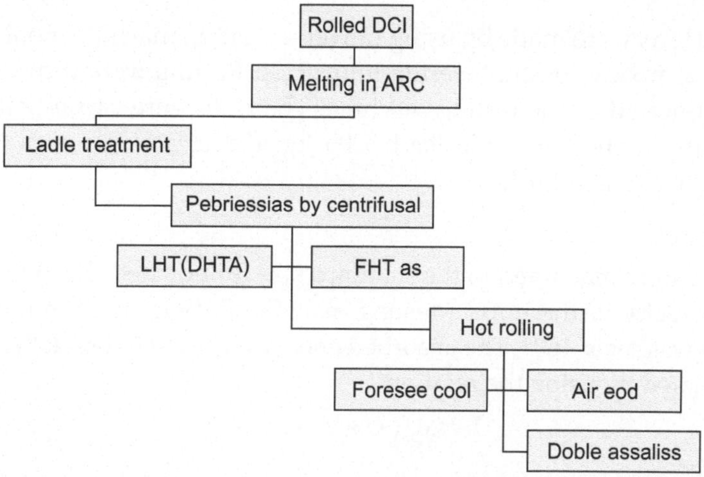

Fig. 3.1: Schematic diagram for the steps of manufacturing, rolling and treatment

All specimens were double-heat-treatment annealed (DHTA) by heating in the muffle furnace to 900°C : 910°C and holding for 3 hr. then furnace cool to 700°C and holding at this temperature for 3 hours and then furnace cool to room temperature. Figure 3.2 shows the cycle of double annealing heat treatment (DHTA).

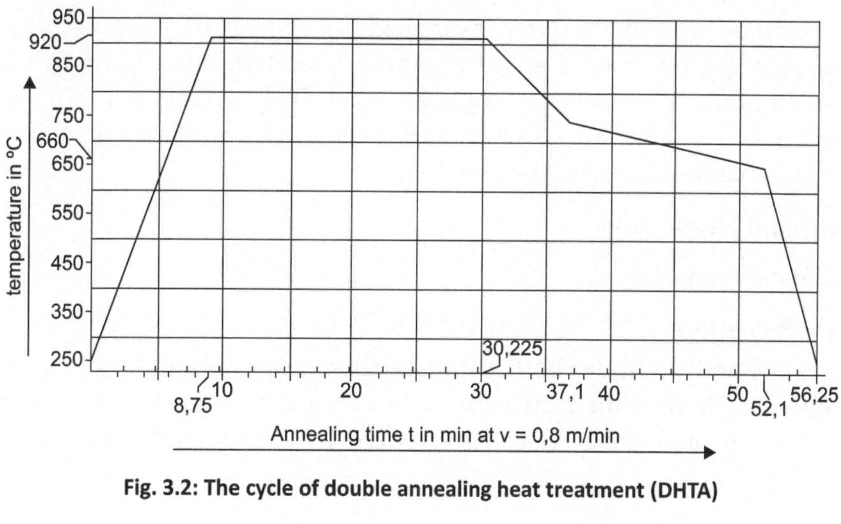

Fig. 3.2: The cycle of double annealing heat treatment (DHTA)

Metallographic Examination

All specimen wear prepared by grinding on different grades of silicon carbide "Sic" emergency paper, coarse grinding and fine grinding were done to produce a uniform level of graphite matrix, finally polishing with alumina were done. The details of the microstructure were revealed after etching in 3% nital solution (3% nitric acid solution in ethanol).

Tensile Testing

All tensile tests were made by using universal testing machine model 2M1090. in Maadi company for engineering industries. Results were recorded on x-y plotter connected to the testing machine. The tests were carried out at room temperature at the full scale load 5000 kg and strain rate was 6mm/min. according to B.S standard.

Impact Testing

Specimens were machined to the standard size for notched charpy impact test as. The capacity of the impact testing machine is 15 kg-m. The initial lifting angle (θ1) was set at 160°· The absorbed energy required to break the specimen was calculated by using the relation

$$I = GL\ (\cos\theta - \cos\phi) \tag{1}$$

Where

I = capacity of the machine 15kg-m

G = wt of pendulum

L = the length of the pendulum arm

ϕ = the impact angle

Fracture Analysis

The fractured specimens were examined by means of scanning election microscope (SEM) operating at a nominal accelerating voltage of 30kv. Specimen preparation is very simply accomplished by cutting a thin slice of the specimen containing the fracture surface of interest and inserting it into the specimen chamber for direct examination.

Results and Discussions

Mechanical Properties

Tensile Properties

Figures 3.3 and 3.4 show both Ultimate tensile strength and yield strength respectively. Both of them increase with increase in reduction percentages. As the result of ductility decrease gradually by increasing the amount of reduction.

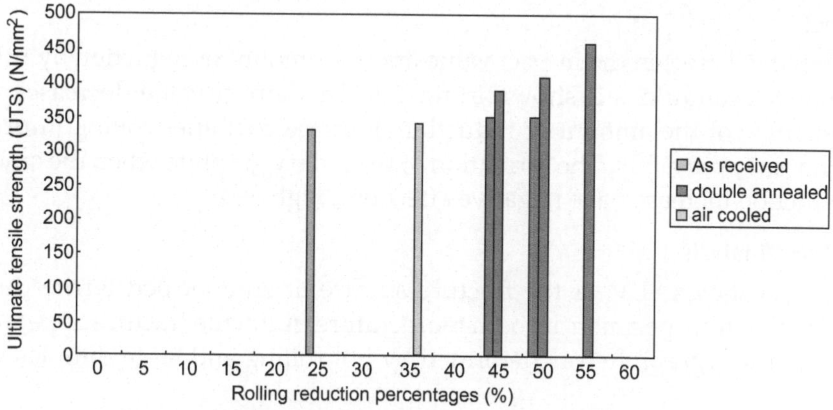

Fig. 3.3: The effect of reduction percentages on ultimate tensile strength (UTS) at different rolling conditions

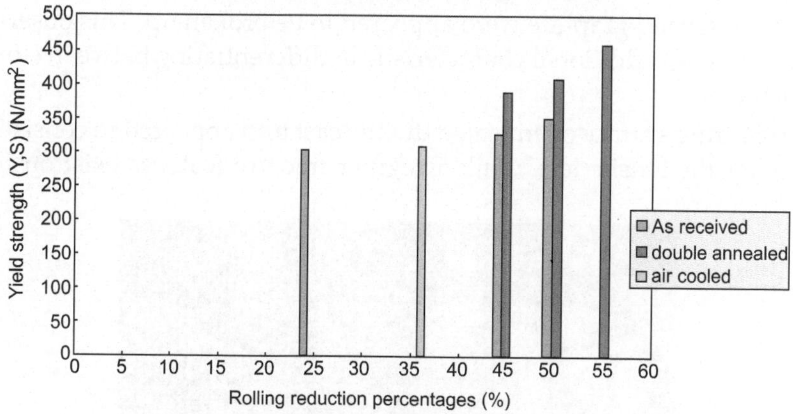

Fig. 3.4: The effect of reduction percentages on yield strength (YS) at different rolling conditions

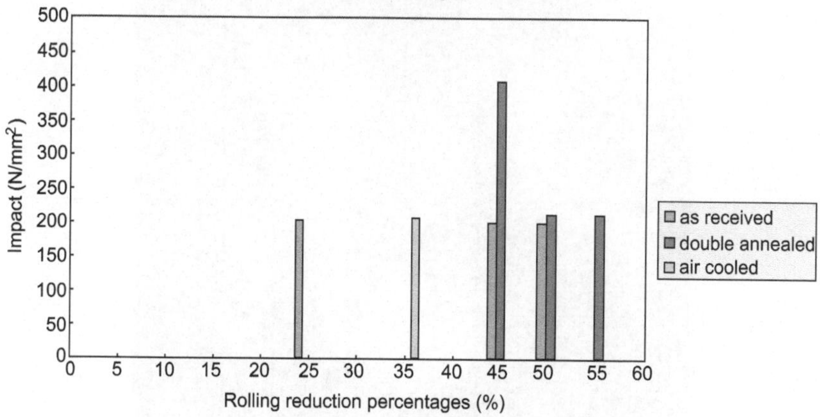

Fig. 3.5: The efect of reduction percentages on toughness at different rolling conditions

Impact

The relation between the impact value and the amount of reduction by rolling at different conditions is shown in fig. 3.8. The impact value decreases with the increase of the amount of reduction. Furnace cool after rolling improves toughness appreciably. The formation of secondary graphite when the amount of reduction increase have negative effect on toughness.

Fracture Analysis

Figure 3.6 shows SEM of the fracture surface of an annealed ferrite ductile iron tension test specimen at room temperature. A ductile fracture appearance was recorded, graphite was deformed by hot rolling and large dimples were appeared.

Figure 3.7 shows impact fracture at room temperature indicates a minimal amount of deformation with no stretching was occured in graphite nodules. In addition, several graphite were appeared to be broken up. This observation could serve as an additional characteristic in differentiating between slow and fast fracture.

The fracture surface of annealed ductile cast iron appeared to consist of big dimples for the tensile test, while irregular fracture features exist on impact test.

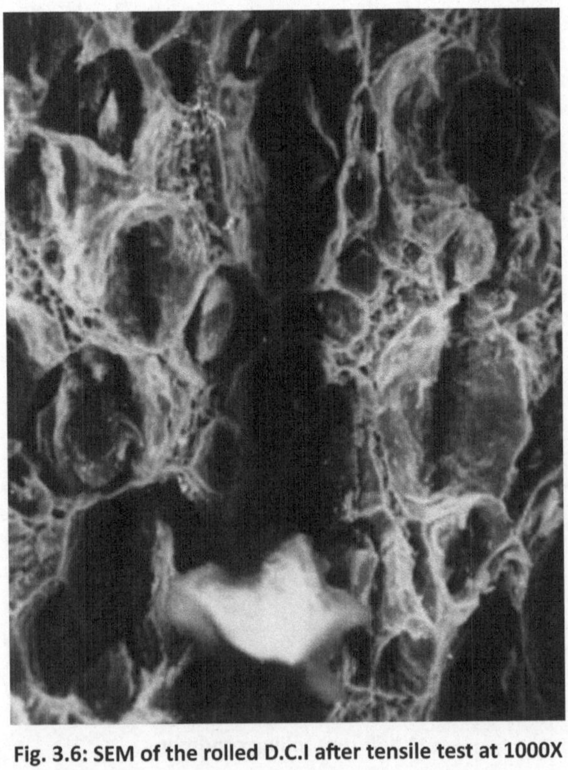

Fig. 3.6: SEM of the rolled D.C.I after tensile test at 1000X

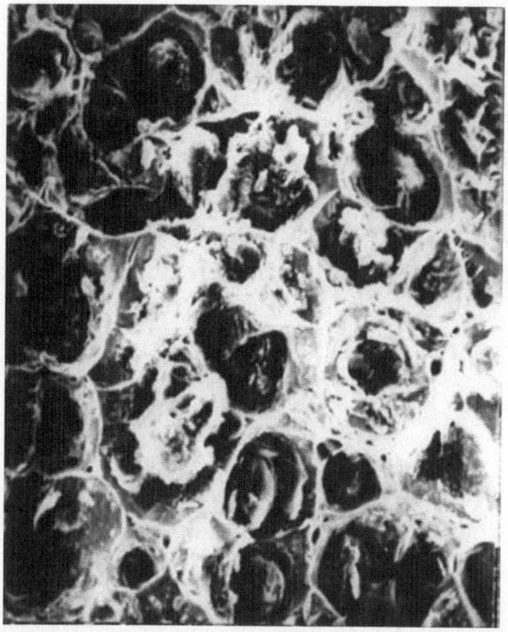

Fig. 3.7: SEM of the rolled D.C.I after Impact test at 1000X

The ferrite grain size became finer with the graphite nodules diameter decrease. When the microstructure was very fine, the inter-granular fracture can be eliminated due to elongation increase with decreasing ferrite grain size.

Above (40%) reduction graphite start to break and the shape ratio of graphite decreases with increase in the reduction percentage because the formation of secondary graphite. The ferrite grain size decrease is dropped due to enhance nucleation due to decrease in M.F.P and increases stress concentration[11].

Stress Analysis

The determination of the stress analysis for the specimen chosen for Fracture analysis (fractography) the following relationships may be used, Fig. 3.8 shows model of stress analysis:-

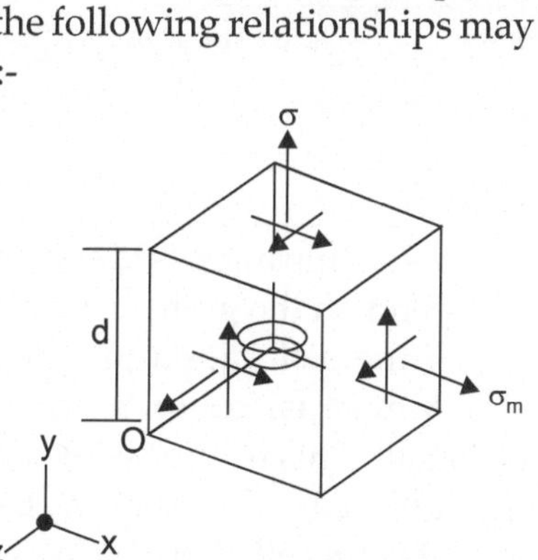

Fig. 3.8: Model for hydrostatic tensile stress analysis

$$a = \frac{d}{2n} - r_2 \quad (2)$$

a is half of M.F.P (mean free path)

d lattice constant

n Shape factor r_o/r (S.F) (shape factor)

r_2 average graphite radius in the transverse direction

σ_m the maximum hydrostatic tensile stress and can be calculated from :

$$\sigma_m = \left(\frac{x}{2} + \frac{1}{3}\right)\sigma_{re} \quad (3)$$

6_{re} Tensile stress

$$X = \frac{a}{r_2} \quad (4)$$

The flow stress as a function of graphite volume fraction and ferrite grain size as follow:-

$$\sigma_u = (1 - K_1 V_g)(s_o + K_2 d_f^{-1/2}) \quad (5)$$

σ_o, K_1, K_2 is constant determined by experimental work and the equation becomes:-

$$\sigma = (1 - 2.2 V_g)(394 + 26.7 d_f^{-1/2}) \quad (6)$$

V_g graphite volume fraction

d_f ferrite grain size μm

s_u flow stress Results are recorded in table 3.2

Inter granular fracture will occur when the ratio of the hydrostatic stress (equivalent stress) is larger than one

$$(\sigma_m / \sigma_u > 1). \quad (7)$$

Table 3.2: The stresses as function of ferrite grain size

Ferrite grains size d_1 mm		Hydrostatic stress σ_m (N/mm²)	Equivalent flow stress σ_i (N/mm²)
Impact specimen	85.77	389.83	311.76
Tensile specimen	84.01	500.75	302.78

$\sigma_m/\sigma_u = 1.1 : 1.2$ in this case within a stressed specimen. The stress necessary for crack nucleation will depend on the grain size because the size of the grain will determine the length of the dislocation pile up and the intensity of the stress concentration[12],[13]. A material could be made infinitely strong if the grains are made infinitely small. This is impossible though, because the lower limit of grain size is a single unit cell of the material. Even then, if the grains of a material are the size of a single unit cell, then the material is in fact amorphous, not crystalline, since there is no long range order, and dislocations can not be defined in an amorphous material. The effect of grain boundaries on resistance to deformation described by equation is shown in fig. 3.9.

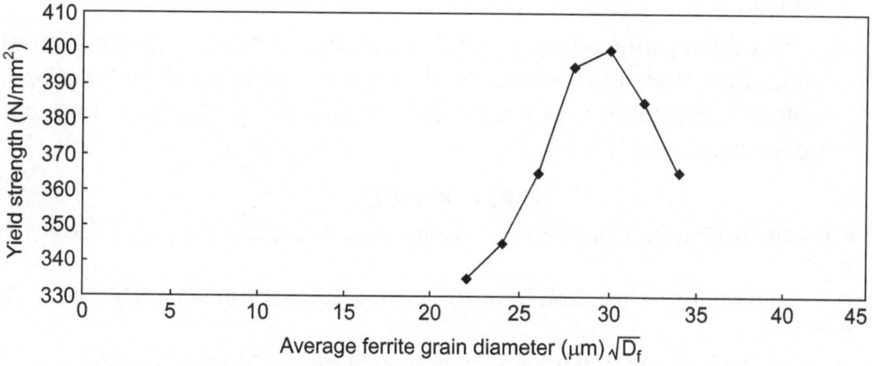

Fig. 3.9: Hall_Petch relationships

Fine microstructure can eliminate intergranular fracture the effect of ferrite grain size and triaxial stress field around graphite nodules on intergranular embrittlement. It is based on the observation that grain boundaries impede dislocation movement and that the number of dislocations within a grain have an effect on how easily dislocations can traverse grain boundaries and travel from grain to grain. So, by changing grain size one can influence dislocation movement and yield strength.The hot rolling of ductile cast Iron leads to plastic deformation , heat treatment after plastic deformation and changing the rate of solidification are ways to alter grain size.[4]

Conclusions

Based on the results obtained in this work the following conclusions are presented :-

1. Hot rolling play a great role in the improving the mechanical properties of DCI such as tensile and yield in the rolling direction(Longitudinal direction), it also changes the microstructure of matrix and graphite nodules.The tensile properties also improved by raising the amount of rolling reduction.
2. Toughness decreases gradually by increasing the amount of reduction by rolling but furnace cooling after rolling improve toughness.
3. The fracture surface of annealed ductile cast iron were appeared to consist of big dimples for the tensile test, while irregular fracture features exist on impact test. Hot rolled DCI was similar to steel in fracture behavior so it is recommended in different construction applications
4. The effect of grain boundaries on resistance to deformation described by the equation is manifest indirectly through the effect of strain hardening with a more rapid increase of dislocation density.

5. The barrier effect of cell boundaries is evident in hot rolled ductile cast Iron with large deformations, which leads to deviation of $\sigma_f = f(d^{-2})$ from linear.
6. With decreasing relative length of grain boundaries (large grains) or enrichment of grain boundaries in impurities and precipitates of second phase the number of potential dislocation sources near grain boundaries decreases.

REFERENCES

1. C.F. Walton, Gray and Ductile Iron Castings Handbook, Iron Founder's Society, 1971, p 193
2. C.F. Walton and T.J. Opar, Iron Castings Handbook, Iron Casting Society, 1981, p 235 & p 297- 321
3. "Chrome-Moly White Cast Irons," Publication M – 630, AMAX, Inc., 1986
4. Davis, J.R., Cast Irons, ASM International, Materials Park, OH, 1996
5. G. Lambert, Ed., Typical Microstructures of Cast Metals, 2nd ed., The Institute of British Foundrymen, 1996, p 47
6. H.T. Angus, Physical and Engineering Properties of Cast Iron, BCIRA, 1960, p 21
7. http://www.msm.cam.ac.uk/doitpoms/miclib/index.php
8. http://www.matweb.com/search/GetSubcat.asp
9. http://www.wynndanzur.com/glossary.htm
10. T. El-Bitar and E. El-Banna, Characteristics of Hot Rolled Ductile Cast Iron Strips, 4th Intern. Conf. on PEDD, Ein Shams Univ., Cairo, 1993, pp. 404-414.
11. R. Grosby et al., Experiments in Hot Rolling and Forging of Ductile Cast Iron (US Dept. of Interior, Bureau of Mines, Washington, DC, 1980).
12. R.G. Ward, An Introduction to the Physical Chemistry of Iron and Steel Making, Arnold, London (1962).
13. ASTM Standard test Method for Measurements of fatigue crack growth rates (E647-93), Annual Book of ASTM Standards (1993), 0301, American Society for Testing and Materials.

4 The Microstructure Variation of Ti6Al4VELI during Excimer Laser 308nm Irradiation

ABSTRACT

In these work, the effects of laser irradiation on microstructure and performance of Ti6Al4VELI alloy have been studied by qualitative and quantitative analysis techniques, volume fraction of secondary phase, shape factors, number of particles of secondary phase, mean free path and grain size number were studied at different laser irradiation conditions. The effect of the amount of absorbed energy were represented by the variation in the number of pulses from 2000 pulses to 50000 pulses. Excimer laser irradiation is performed directly in the air and without any intermediate media. The volume fraction of the secondary phase β and α phase changed in the microstructure of Ti6Al4VELI alloy gradually with increase in laser dosages. Physical metallurgy considerations is the tool to understand the microstructure of any alloy system at specified laser irradiation conditions, the phase relationships and constitution of the system being studied.

Keywords: *Surface Treatment, Titanium Alloys, Microstructure, Laser Applications, Ultraviolet Sources.*

Introduction

Titanium is an allotropic element: that is, it exists in more than one crystallographic form. At room temperature, titanium has a hexagonal close-packed (hcp) crystal structure, which is referred to as "alpha" phase. This structure transforms to a body-centered cubic (bcc) crystal structure. Called "beta" phase, at 883°C (1621°F). It is common to separate the alloys into three categories[(1),(2)]. Referring to the common phases present. The alloy categories are alpha, beta and alpha + beta :

*α. Or alpha

Alloys are non-heat treatable and are generally very weldable. They have low to medium strength; good notch toughness, reasonably good ductility and possess excellent mechanical properties at cryogenic temperatures[(3)]. The more highly alloyed alpha and near-alpha alloys offer optimum high temperature creep strength and oxidation resistance as well[(4),(5)].

*β. Or beta

Beta or near-beta alloys are readily heat treatable, generally weldable, and capable of high strengths and good creep resistance to intermediate temperatures. Excellent formability can be expected of the beta alloys in the solution treated condition. Beta-type alloys have good combinations of properties in sheet, heavy sections, fasteners and spring applications(6).

*α - β. Or alpha plus beta

Alloys are heat treatable and most are weldable. Their strength levels are medium to high. Their hot-forming qualities are good, but the high temperature creep strength is not as good as in most alpha alloys(7),(8).

These categories describe the origin of the microstructure in terms of the basic crystal structure favored by an alloy composition. Crystal structure and grain structure (microstructure) are not synonymous terms. The important fact to keep in mind is that basic crystal structure changes from α to β and back again play the major role in defining titanium properties(9),(10).

Alloying elements generally can be classified as α and β stabilizers(11). This transformation temperature from α + β or from α to all β is known as the β transus temperature. The β transus is defined as the lowest equilibrium temperature at which the material is 100%β. The β transus is critical in deformation processing and heat treatment. Below the beta β transus temperature, Titanium is a mixture of α + β if the material contains some β stabilizers; otherwise it is all α if it contains limited or no β stabilizers(12):(14). The β transus is important. Because processing and heat treatment often is carried out with reference to some incremental temperature above or below the β transus. Alloying elements that favor the α crystal structure and stabilize it by raising the β transus temperature include Aluminium, gallium, Germanium, Carbon, Oxygen, and Nitrogen(15).

2. Experimental Work

A. Materials

The alloys used throughout this work was supplied by Sandvik Co, France in the form of bars of Ti6Al4VELI. Table 4.1 shows the chemical composition of the alloy used in the current work.

Table 4.1: The chemical composition of Ti6Al4VELI (grade 23)

Material	C%	N%	10%	Fe%	Al%	V%	0%
Ti6Al4VELI	0.08	0.05	0.015	0.25	5.75	3.5	0.13
Rod	max	max	max	max	6.75	4.5	max

ϕ (omm)

B. Laser Surface Irradiation

The surface irradiation of the alloys was studied. Samples used in this investigation were in the standard size for every test according to ASTM. All the experiments were performed at room temperature in air at atmospheric pressure; it was shown elsewhere[(10)] that the presence of air has no measurable influence on the process of irradiation by UV laser[(11)]. The irradiation is done on one side of the sample and covers all the surface area of the sample. The main goal of this work is optimize condition for laser irradiation of the samples by Excimer laser at 308nm Table 4.2 shows data for used rare gas halide Excimer laser.

Table 4.2: Data for Excimer Laser (Rare Gas Halide)

Gas type	λ (nm)	r (A)	ω (cm^{-1})	σ (cm^2)	τ (ns)
XeCl	308	2.9	194	50	11

λ = transition wavelength

r(A) = equilibrium inter-nuclear separation

ω = fundamental vibration frequency of the excited state

σ = stimulated emission cross section

τ = radiative life time (pulse duration)

The number of pulses and the effect of energy per pulse on the hardness were recorded to indicate the energy required (fluence) to improve the mechanical properties. Source in the shape of a rectangle with width (w = 4mm) and length (l = 10mm) was used in the laser process the power density ranges from (0.75 W/Cm^2 to 0.1 W/Cm^2) without any focusing. Excimer laser irradiation is performed directly in the air and without any intermediate media. The laser irradiation condition is listed in Table 4.3.

Table 4.3: The Laser Irradiation Conditions of the Samples

Type	Wavelength nm	No. of pulses	Energy per pulse mJ	Repetition rate (Hz)
Excimer	UV 308.6	0, 2000, 5000, 10250, 15000, 50000	6	200

time = 6nano second & total energy = energy per puke * number of pulses

C. Qualitative Analysis

Metallographic Examinations

The specimens were prepared for examination first by grinding on different grades of silicon carbide "SiC" papers coarse grinding followed by fine grinding at 180, 240, 320, 400, 600, and 800 finally polishing was conducted with Alumina powder (3μm) size. The details of the microstructure were revealed after etching by standard etching solution of the alloy selected. Table 4.4 the etching solution composition and characteristics of Ti6Al4VELI. All specimens had to be etched and polished several times to obtain best results and to produce a uniform level of sample examination. The surfaces of the samples before and after laser irradiation were examined using an Olympus optical microscope Model BHM at selected magnification.

Table 4.4: The Etching Solution Composition and Characteristics of Ti6Al4VELI

Alloy	Etchant	Conditions	Remarks
T6A14VELI	Dist water	100 ml	Swap
	Hydrofluric acid (40%	1.3 ml	sample
	Nitric acid (1.40)	2.6 ml	3-10s (toxic)

D. Quantitative Analysis

Quantitative Metallography Measurements

A quantitative analysis of the microstructures was produced carried out over four (4) fields across the surface to indicate:

1. The volume fraction V_f of each phase (count analysis was applied).
2. Average grain size by linear intercept technique.
3. Average particles radius D_A using number of modules per unit area and can calculated as follows: (118)

$$D_A = (4\,V_f / N_g)^{1/2} \qquad (1)$$

Inter nodule spacing (MFP) by measuring P_L no of particles per unit length and sustain in the equation(118)

$$MFP = (1 - V_f) / P_L \qquad (2)$$

The shape factor by using equation(118):

$$S.F = 2/3(P_L)/ V_f\,N_g \qquad (3)$$

V_f volume fraction of secondary phase

N_g average grain size number

D_A Average particles radius

P_L no of particles per unit length

MFP Inter nodule spacing

S.F the shape factor

The terms were determined according to ASTM E112. Calculations were carried out in several areas in each specimen investigated at 100X projected on a screen measuring 500 mm^2. The measurement is an average of over five readings for each condition. The scattering value for each specimen was +1%. All calculations were measured around a circle to consider all directions 360°

Results and Discussions

(a) Qualitative analysis

Figure (1)-(a) shows the initial microstructure of the alloy before laser irradiation, the structure is alpha-beta (equiaxed) system contain one or more alpha stabilizers or alpha-soluble elements plus one or more beta stabilizers. The structure constituent is related to chemical composition and the effect of alloying elements on the microstructure. Alpha stabilizers such as Aluminium and oxygen, increase the temperature at which the α phase is stable. Beta stabilizers such as Vanadium result in stability of the β phase at lower temperatures.

When the surface of the alloy irradiated by Ultraviolet Excimer laser 308nm as shown in figure 4.1 from (b) to (e). The processes was done at room temperature in the normal atmosphere these rate allow the Martensitic transformation. The white plates are α. and the dark regions between them are β. This is a typical Widmanstatten structure.

Beta phase decomposes, usually by martensitic transformations in the alpha-beta alloys. Martensitic reactions are fast. Diffusionless (no composition change' transformations in crystal structure and microstructure, the morphology (shape location) of the phase changes with prior treatment. The *a* phase may remain relatively globular (equiaxed). But the transformed beta (martensites or alpha may be very acicular or elongated. The amount of equiaxed alpha and the coarseness or fineness of the transformed beta products will affect titanium's alloy. Metastable beta can show more variety in decomposition than does the supersaturated alpha or martensitic alpha structure. The omega phase can form, as can alpha phase and a low-solute-contend beta phase. Other intermetallic compounds also may form. and. under certain circumstances, ordering of the beta phase can occur. (Ordering removes the randomness in atom location which normally exists and puts atoms in specific locations.

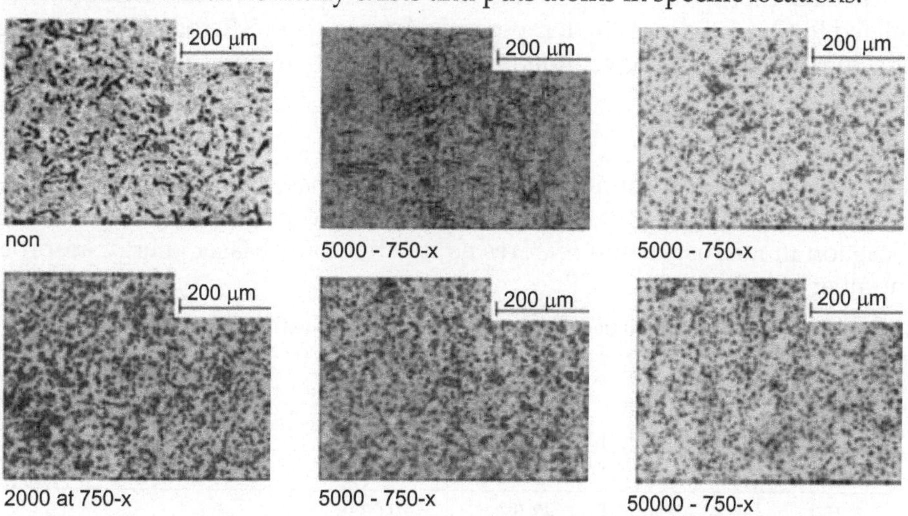

(a) untreated (b) 2000pulses (c) 5000pulses (d) 15000pulses (e) 50000pulses

Fig. 4.1: Qualitative analysis for the Effect of Excimer Laser irradiation at 308nm, 6mJ, 200Hz, 750x at Different Number of Pulses on the microstructure of TI6Al4VELI

Hardenability of a titanium alloy is a phrase that refers to its ability to permit full transformation of the alloy to martensitic phases or to retain beta to room temperature. Alpha prime (α') and alpha double prime (a") martensites are brought out by cooling and decompose, on subsequent aging, to alpha and beta phases.

The β transus is important. Because processing and heat treatment often is carried out with reference to some incremental temperature above or below the β transus . Alloying elements that favor the α crystal structure and stabilize it by raising the β transus temperature.

Transformation kinetics, transformation products, and specific response of a given alloy can be quite complex. A mechanism of laser irradiation at high power rating was explained according to the following procedures: a point on the surface within the path of the beam is rapidly heated as the beam passes. This area is subsequently cooled rapidly by heat conduction to the interior after the beam has passed. By selecting the correct power density and repetition rate of the process. The material will harden to the desired depth. According to The Law of conservation of energy the laser photons absorbed according to Einstein principles

$$E = h\nu = \Delta G\ (T) \tag{4}$$

Photon energy (laser energy) will transform to Energy for phase transition, the Gibbs Energy (which cause phase transition) is function of temperature

$$\Delta G\ (T) = A + BT\ \log T + CT \tag{5}$$

$$\Delta G\ (T) = H - T\Delta S \tag{6}$$

So ΔG Gibbs free Energy related to amount of absorbed energy which related to phase diagram by temperature (appendix I). Microstructure change is a function of phase constituent which depends mainly on ΔG Gibbs free Energy

(b) Quantitative analysis

The amount and distribution of the secondary phase β phase plays the most significant role during the laser irradiation process, table 4.5 shows the variation in microstructure features as function of the laser energy absorbed (number of pulses).

Table 4.5: The Variation in Microstructure Features with Number of Pulses

Number of Pulses	Number of particles per unit length	Volume fraction V_f	MFP (Mean Free Path)	S.F. (shape factor)	ASTM grain size number
0	14	38.6%	0.04385	2.41	10
2000	17	42.5%	0.0336	2.7	9.5
5000	20	30%	0.035	4.44	7.5
10250	16	34.3%	0.04107	3.14	10
15000	10	28.6%	0.07142	2.33	10
50000	14	38.6%	0.04388	2.4	10

Figure 4.2 shows the relation between the amount of absorbed energy and the volume fraction of the secondary phase according to the phase diagram of the Ti6Al4VELI. The maximum amount of secondary phase appears at 2000 pulses, While the amount of secondary phase in the material irradiated by Excimer laser 308nm as function of the number of pulses in the range from 5000 pulses to 50000 pulses were less than the non irradiated samples. The phenomena can be explained in terms of the phase diagram (appendix I) and kinetics of the reaction when the material absorb more energy at the same composition. Ti6Al4V is a structure which is HCP structure vanadium which found in 3.5:4.5% which β-BCC phase stabilizer at room temperature so the final micro structure is a combination between α and β structure this micro-structure produce 34% improvement in the micro-hardness. Not only the constituent of the alloys or the amount of alloying elements but the microstructure also have the most significant effect on the irradiation process.

Laser irradiation work as method of hardening and softening at the same time. The initial microstructure of the irradiated alloy (the room temperature microstructure) plays the significant role in that case. The chemical composition and the amount of alloying elements in the alloy plays a significant effect on the laser irradiation process.

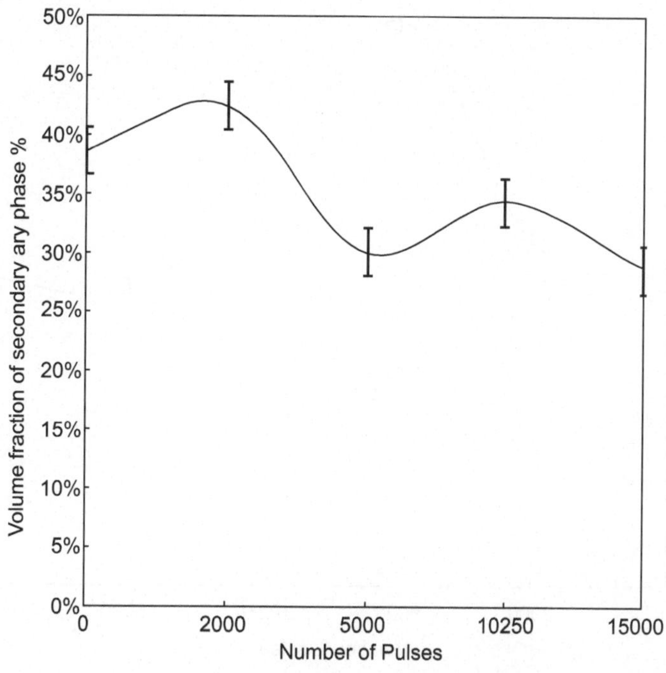

Fig. 4.2: The relation between number of pulses and volume fractionof secondary phase for Ti6Al4VELI irradiated by 308 nm, 6mJ, 200 Hz

Figure 4.3 shows one of the most important features during microstructure changes which is the shape factor of the secondary phase during laser irradiation, the maximum value was recorded at 5000 pulses, at this amount of energy the homogeneity in the secondary phase is less while at different number of pulses the homogeneity in the structure were less than the non irradiated samples, the variation in shape factor give impression about martensetic transformation due to laser irradiation and the formation of typical Widmanstatten structure.

The phase distribution in the microstructure can be expressed by the number of secondary phase particles per unit length and the mean free path (edge to edge spacing) as shown in the Figures 4.4 and 4.5 respectively, The maximum amount of the secondary phase was recorded at 5000 pulses while the minimum amount was recorded at 15000 pulses. The alpha- beta alloys is the strongest structure in Titanium alloys. The absorption of more amount of energy above the alpha- beta transformation temperature lead to grain coarsening and affect the grain size number as shown in table 4.5. According to the theory of dislocations, laser irradiation effects have explained. The strain hardening effect is due to an increase in dislocation density under the action of external force resulting from the transformation of energy of the laser photons. The external force resulting from laser photons lead to the interaction

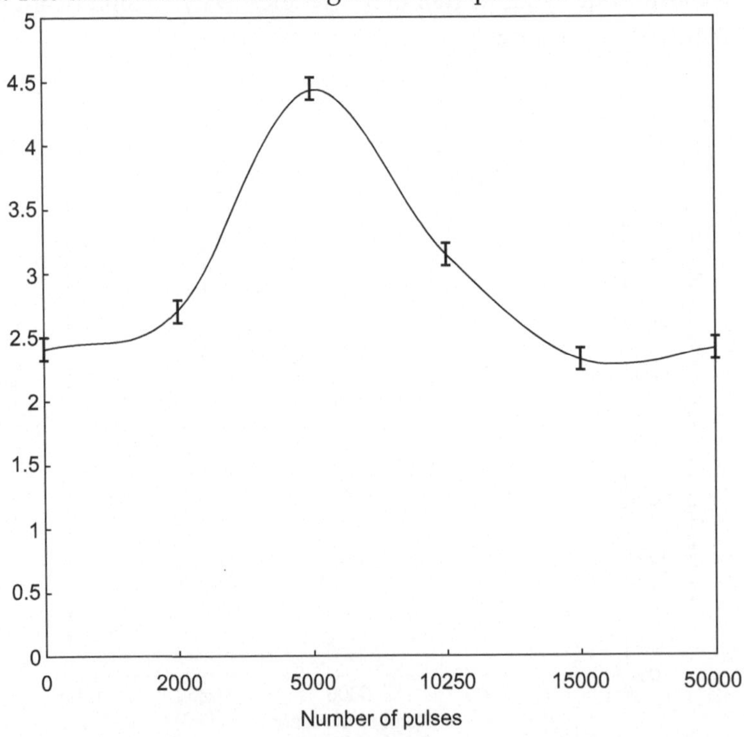

Fig. 4.3: The relation between number of pulses and Shape factor of secondary phase for Ti6A14VELI irradiated by 308 nm, 6m, 200 Hz

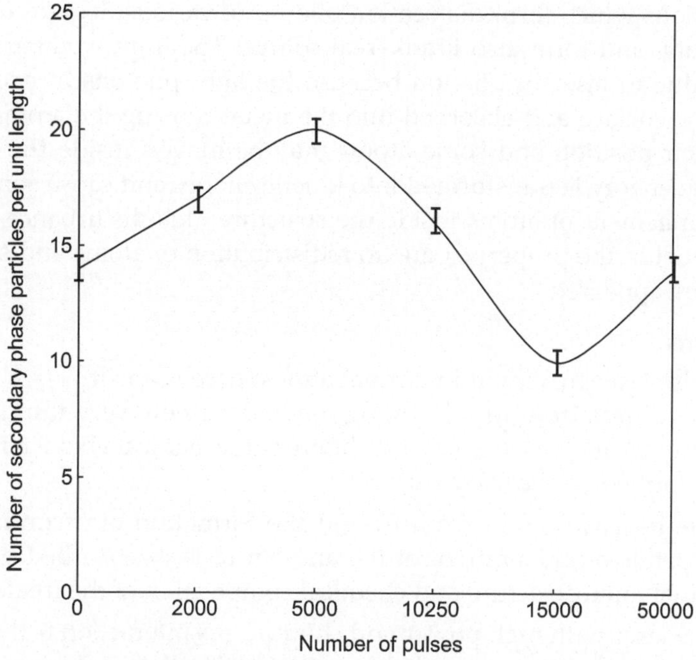

Fig. 4.4: The relation between number of pulses and Number of Particles per Unit Area of secondary phase for Ti6a14VELI irradiate by 308 nm, 6mJ, 200 Hz

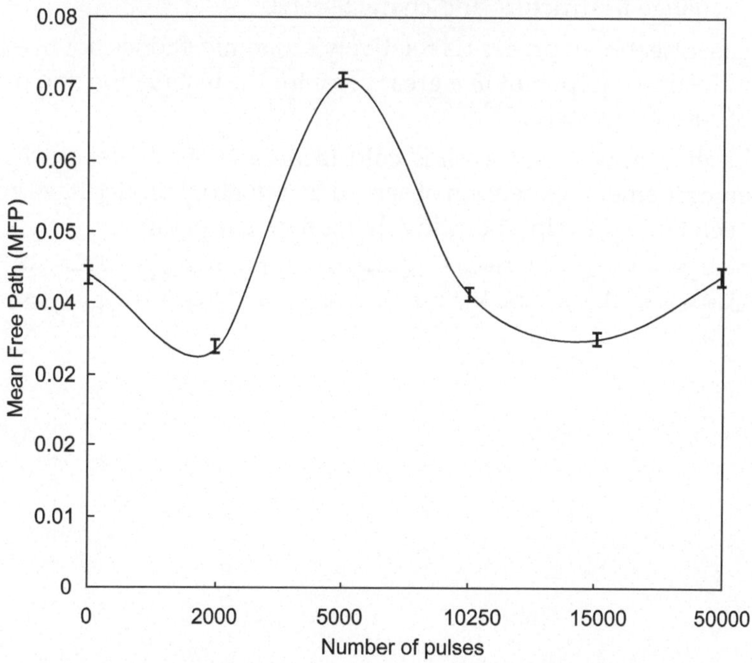

Fig. 4.5: The relation between number of pulses and Mean Free Path for Ti6Al4VELI irradiated by 308 nm, 6mJ, 200 Hz

of dislocations which form dislocation pile up of various degrees of stability and mobility, and form also Frank–real source. The improvement in micro-hardness due to laser irradiation because the light photons of energy is go through the surface and absorbed into the metal causing the atoms to move around their position and some atoms may be moved inside the structure. The photon energy is transformed into kinetic energy and cause some change in the arrangement of atoms inside the structure; this disturbance cause the improvement in the properties due to redistribution of atoms and some hard phases were appeared.

Conclusions

1. Pulse laser treatment in normal atmosphere is an attractive technique that differs from usual coating methods, a new very thin layer with different microstructure and different mechanical characteristics will be formed on the alloy surface.
2. The microstructure features and the formation of secondary phase depends on the amount of the amount of laser absorbed besides the initial microstructure and chemical composition of the treated alloy.
3. The laser with high power and short pulses interaction is the basis for an effective treatment suitable for Ti6Al4VELI. to induce the physical reaction in the atmospheric environment without external media leads to change in structure and characteristics.
4. Laser treatment process is relatively economic. It does not need a huge industrial equipment in a great place for the installation and operation of such equipment.
5. Laser irradiation process is cold technique, so it prevent hydrogen embrittlement of titanium observed in industrial service have generally been limited to situations involving high temperatures.

*الطريقة الجديدة لا تحتاج لاستخدام معاملات كيميائية مكلفة مثل عمليات التغطية السطحية و تفاعلات معقدة ينتج عنها غازات ضارة بالبيئة و مخلفات.

APPENDIX-1

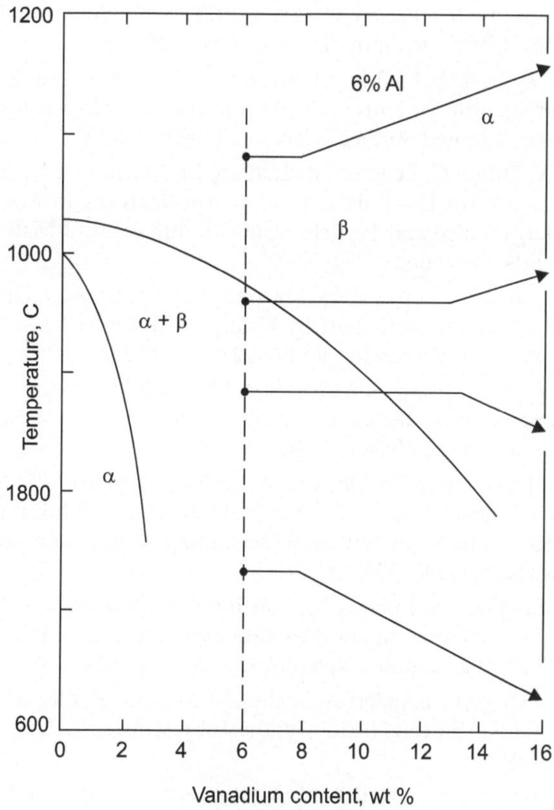

Phase diagram of TI6Al4VELI

REFERENCES

1. E. D'Anna, G. Leggieri, A. Luches, M. Martino, S. Luby, I. N. Mihailescu: Pulsed Laser Synthesis of Titanium Silicides and Nitrides, Laser Assisted Processing SPIE. 1022 (1988) 130-135
2. V. Craciun, I. N. Mihailescu, I. Ursu, F. Craciunoiu, A. Corici, G. Leggieri, A. Luches, V. Nassisi, M. Martino: Multi-layer Metallization Structures With Titanium Nitride and Titanium Silicate Prepared by Multipulse Laser Irradiation, Applied Physics Letters 52 (1988) 1225-1227
3. I. Ursu, V. Craciun, I. N. Mihailescu, L. C. Nistor, A. Popa, V. S. Teodorescu, A. Luches, V. Nassisi, M. Martino, F. Cracinoiu, A. Corici, A. Andrei, G. Semenescu, G. Onicioiu: Diffusion Barrier with TiN/TiSi2 Prepared By Multi-Pulse Excimer Laser Irradiation, New Laser Technologies and Applications, Olympia, Editrice Compositor Bologna (1988) 195-203
4. E. D'Anna, G. Leggieri, A. Luches, G. Majni, M. Martino, P. Mengucci, I. N. Mihailescu: Multipulse Laser Synthesis of Metal Silicates, High Power Lasers and Laser Machining Technology SPIE 1132 (1989) 120-127

5. I. Ursu, I. N. Mihailescu, V. Craciun, A. M. Prokhorov, V. I. Konov, V. G. Ralchenko, S. A. Uglov, A. Luches, M. Martino, G. Leggieri, A. V. Drigo: Laser Scanning Synthesis of Surface Compound by Irradiation of Metals and Semiconductors in Chemically-Active Gases, Ernst Abbe Conf. On Optics Eac Jena (1989) 257-269
6. V. Craciun, G. Leggieri, A. Luches, M. Martino, I. N. Mihailescu, I. Ursu: Synthesis of Metallic and Semiconductor Nitrides by Multipulse Laser Irradiation of Solid Samples In Ambient Gases, Applied Surface Science 43 (1989) 304-307
7. V. Craciun, A. V. Drigo, G. Leggieri, A. Luches, M. Martino, I. N. Mihailescu, I. Ursu: Nitride Synthesis With UV-Pulsed Lasers: Applications in Microelectronics and Metallurgy, Energy Pulse and Particle Beam Modification of Materials, K. Hohmuth And E. Richter Eds. , Dresden (1990) 57-65
8. E. Deanna, G. Leggieri, A. Luches, M. Martino, A. Perrone, A. V. Drigo, J. Zemek, I. N. Mihailescu: Nitride Layer Formation by Multipulse Excimer Laser Irradiation of Solid Samples, Laser Assisted Processing II SPIE 1279 (1990) 182-194
9. E. Deanna, G. Leggieri, A. Luches, M. Martino, Materials Processing with Pulsed Electron Beam, High Energy Density Technology in Materials Science, F. Garbassi and E. Occhiello Eds. , Kluwer Academic Publishers (1990) 89-103
10. V. Craciun, I. N. Mihailescu, Gh. Oncioiu, A. Luches, M. Martino, V. Nassisi, E. Radiotis, A. V. Drigo, S. Ganatsios: Direct Oxinitride Synthesis by Multipulse Excimer Laser Irradiation of Silicon Wafer in Nitrogen Containing Ambient Environment, Journal of Applied Physics 68(5) (1990) 2509-2511.
11. V. Craciun, G. Leggieri, A. Luches, M. Martino, I. N. Mihailescu, E. Radiotis, I. Ursu: One-Step Surface Implantation and Reaction by Laser Irradiation of Multi-Structures Deposited on Si and Ge Samples, Vacuum 41 (1990) 912-914
12. E. D'Anna, A. V. Drigo, G. Leggieri, A. Luches, M. Martino, P. Mengucci, I. N. Mihailescu, A. Perrone, J. Zemek: Silicon Nitride Synthesis by Multipulse Laser Irradiation, Vuoto XX(2) (1990) 430-434
13. E. D'Anna, G. Leggieri, A. Luches, M. Martino, A. V. Drigo, G. Majni, P. Mengucci, I. N. Mihailescu: Nitridation of Titanium by Multipulse Excimer Laser Irradiation Applied Surface Science 46 (1990) 365-370
14. E. D'Anna, G. Leggieri, A. Luches, M. Martino, A. Perrone, G. Majni, P. Mengucci, A. V. Drigo, I. N. Mihailescu: Surface Nitride Synthesis by Multipulse Excimer Laser Irradiation, Excimer Lasers and Applications III, SPIE 1503 (1991) 256-268
15. E. Deanna, G. Leggieri, A. Luches, M. Martino, P. Mengucci, I. N. Mihailescu: Synthesis of Pure Titanium Nitride Layers by Multipulse Excimer Laser Irradiation, Quantum Electronics and Plasma Physics G. C. Righini Ed. (1991) 175-181.
16. Hebatalrahman patent number 24014,Egyptian patent office, 2008.

5

The Effect of Hot Rolling on the Tribology of Ductile Cast Iron

ABSTRACT

Important applications of graphite bearing ferrous metals such as graphite steel and iron are wear - resistant ones. In these work, The ductile cast iron samples were hot rolled. The hot rolled ductile cast irons were subjected to double annealing by heating to 900°C and holding for 3hr then furnace cool to 700°C and holding at this temperature for 3hous then furnace cool to room temperature. The effect of cooling rate after rolling on the microstructure of rolled DCI and wear characteristics were determined. The hardness and the wear resistance of hot rolled ductile cast iron were significantly enhanced, the maximum rolling reduction percentages at fast cooling rate (air cool) and slow cooling rate (furnace cool) were evaluated.

Keywords: *Hot Rolled, DCI, Microstructure, Hardness, Wear, Double Annealing.*

Introduction

Wear can be defined as the progressive loss of material from the operation surface of a body occurs as a result of relative motion at the surfaces[1],[2]. As wear occurs in a wide variety of industries, it is also an item causing major annual expense through construction industry specially bridges[3],[4]. The factors which affect wear are numerous such as the type and method of loading, speed, temperature and material, the lubricant type and quantity is considered as the most important factor beside the chemical nature of the environment. The variety of conditions makes the study of wear is very complex subject[5],[6].

Gray cast irons are widely used in applications where lubrication is not feasible[7],[8]. Graphite detached from the cast iron the result will be the generation of series of mico-voids and that is act as emergency reservoir for oil[9]:[11]. The resistance to wear is also influenced by the form of the graphite[12],[13]. A nodular form in D.C.I is superior to wear resistance and can be considerably improved by work hardening[14].

Some characteristics are beneficial if high resistance wear is required in ductile cast iron (D.C.I) such as :

1. Amount of graphite should be high
2. Bainitic structure of ductile cast iron[15].
3. Upper limits of the phosphorous content must be at 0.25%.

4. White iron have a full pearlitic matrix is recommended for abrasive wear applications[16],[17].

Wear and Rolled Ductile Cast Iron

The main application of the rolled ductile iron as building elements are the metal structures for bridges and tunnels[18,19]. This category of building elements are subjected to different types of wears and frictions such as:

- Abrasive wear arises from the presence of gritty particles between the moving parts, the result is bad appearance scratched surface.
- Pitting arises in the parts from sub-surface fatigue cracks[20]:[22].
- Repeated sliding of the parts ultimately allows the start of very small cracks below the surface of the metal.
- Over load wear is resulted from high load and low speeds lead to rupture[23]:[26].
- Sapling is more destructive effect than pitting
- Corrosion wear take the from of pits of the surface[27].
- Rippling is caused by plastic yielding and characterized by a peculiar fish-scale pattern is the result of heavy sliding[28],[29].
- Burning the discoloration following oxidation and accompanied by loss of hardness is due to excessive friction resulting from either over load or over speed[30],[31].
- Scoring is indicated by tears in the direction of sliding due to welding and metal transfer.
- Interference wear has constructional rather than operational origins. It can result from poor design or bad manufacture[32].

Experimental

Material

The ductile cast iron used in this work is obtained from El-Nasr Casting Company. The slab cut from centrifugal casting pipe with 1000 mm diameter and 10 mm thickness, which consider as the main commercial product in the Company. The chemical composition of the ductile cast iron is shown in table 5.1.

Table 5.1: Chemical composition of D.C.I

Contents	C	Si	Mg	S	Mn	Fe
Percentages %	3.68	2.1	0.0042	0.017	0.35	Balance

Manufacturing and Treatment

Treatment before Rolling

1. Slices were double annealed (L.H.T) to 900°C and hold for 2hr prior to furnace cooling to 700°C, then held at this temperature for 3hr before the furnace cooling to the room temperature.
2. Some of the slices were feritizing annealed (F.H.T) at 920°C for 30min then furnace cooled for 30 min.
3. Annealing: Full feritizing Annealing used to remove carbides and stabilized Pearlite by heat to 900°C, holding long enough to dissolve carbides, then cooling at a rate of 85°C/h to 705°C, and still air cooling to room temperature. It improves low temperature fracture resistance but reduces fatigue strength.

Preheat before rolling

The L.H.T specimen is soaked at 950°C for one hour before rolling, while the F.H.T specimen is soaked at 900°C for one hour before rolling.

Rolling Process

Rolling was carried out on the slices in the circumference direction of the pipe by using a laboratory two - high reversing mill with 320mm diameter rolls and 450mm length. The slices were heated to a temperature range between 900°C and 950°C then soaked for one hour at this temperature. The rolls speed was 25m/min. Reduction in cross sectional area was carried out on 2 to 4 passes. Some of the rolled strips were air cooled A.C, while the others were furnace cooled F.C at 700°C. Table 5.2 shows rolling and preheat conditions of ductile Cast Iron

Heat Treatment

All specimens were double-heat-treatment annealed (DHTA) by heating in the muffle furnace to 900°C : 910°C and holding for 3hr then furnace cool to 700°C and holding at this temperature for 3 hours and then furnace cool to room temperature.

Table 5.2: Rolling and Preheat Conditions of Ductile Cast Iron

Specimen Number	Before rolling			After rolling		
	FHT	IHT	Soaking Temperature °C	Hot Rolling Reduction %	Cooling rate (After rolling)	Rate Sec-1
11	xx		900	36	A.C	7.82
31	xx		900	42	F.C.	8.68
32	xx		900	50	F.C	10.06
42	xx		900	26	F.C	6.13

43	xx		900	26	F.C	6.13
52		xx	950	46	F.C	9.23
53		xx	950	44	F.C	9.11
54		xx	950	50	F.C	10.06
62		xx	950	51	F.C	10.35
63		xx	950	48	F.C	9.75

Metallographic Examination

The specimens were prepared for examination first by grinding on different grades of silicon carbide "SiC" papers coarse grinding followed by fine grinding at 180, 240, 320, 400, 600, 800, 1000 and 1200 finally polishing was conducted with Alumina powder (3μm) size. The details of the microstructure were revealed after etching by standard etching solution of the alloy. All specimens had to be etched and polished several times to obtain best results and to produce a uniform level of sample examination. The surfaces of the samples before and after rolling and heat treatment were examined using an Olympus optical microscope Model BHM at selected magnification. The details of the microstructure were revealed after etching in 3% nital solution. The etching process was done by emerging the surface of the samples in nital solution. Specimen must be etched and polished several times to obtain best results and produce a uniform level of graphite matrix.

Mechanical Test

Hardness

The hardness of the specimens were measured by using Vickers testing machine at 15kg. Each hardness value is an average of 5 readings at least with scatter + 4%.

Friction and Were Testing

The test was carried out in normal atmosphere include weighing the test specimen before and after test for assessing the wear properties in such contacts, pin-on disc wear test machine are used in this work. The tested specimen was held in sliding contact with rotating hardned alloy steel (Mn-Cr) disc with hardness (HRC65). The test specimen is mounted on to holder which was designed for easy change of pin (tested samples). The normal load range (0.2 - 3 kg) is applied by dead weight at the end of level to cause the actual normal applied load on the test specimen to increase by a factor (liver ratio = 2.75). At the end of loading beam there was a counter weight for oppose the beam weight, so the applied forces on the specimen come from the applied dead weight only cause a sliding speed ranges from (0.12:1.31) m/sec applied for 10min. The friction force between the vertical stationary specimen and rotation hardened steel disc was measured by strain gauges fixed on a cantilever attached to the tribo-testing machine from the signal, strain gauges was fed through an electric circuit F10MK11. Digital strain bridge reading are calibrated to read frictional force value by applying known dead weight later on the arm. The effect of Brinell hardness number of different specimen on properties are recorded.

The coefficient of friction is determined by :

$$U = \frac{F}{N} \quad (1)$$

F is the friction force.

N is the normal load.

U is the coefficient of friction

The wear volume is calculated from the relation

$$V = \frac{w}{\rho} \quad (2)$$

W is the wear weight the difference in weight of specimen before and after test.

ρ is the density of D.C.I equals to 7.2gm/cm^3.

The sliding distance calculated from the relation

$$L = 2\pi rn \quad (3)$$

r is the mean radius of the rotating disc.

L is determined to be 78.5m (sliding distance)

n is the number of revolution

The following relation is used to calculated wear coefficient:

$$V = K\frac{LW}{3P} \quad (4)$$

V the volume removed by wear from the surface.

K The wear coefficient.

L Length of travel.

W The normal load.

P The Indentation hardness of the softer body.

Liver ratio = 2.75

Results and Discussions

Microstructure

The microstructure features at different conditions before rolling were evaluated, figure 5.1 shows metallographic representation of as-cast ductile cast iron specimens, the microstructure of the alloy was studied, the microstructure consists mainly of pearlite and graphite nodules in ferritic matrix. The ferrite was free from sub-boundary structure, the high cooling rates achieved by centrifugal pipe casting process was responsible for the existence of cementite with ferrite in some areas of the matrix. The pearlite volume fraction was recorded at 23.81%.

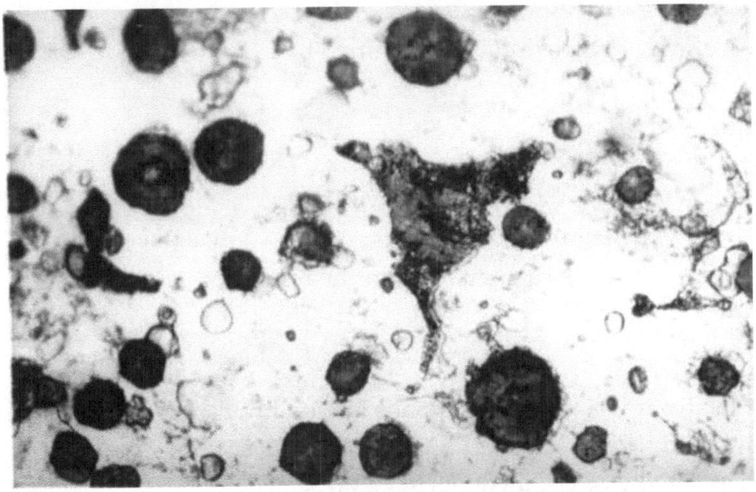

Fig. 5.1: As-cast ductile cast iron specimen

Full Feritizing Annealing as Received (F.H.T)

The foundry heat treaded (F.H.T) annealing process was done, the microstructure constituent of these sample was shown in Figure 5.2, which is carried out after casting. The structure consists of graphite, pearlite (5%) and ferrite but with sub boundaries. Full feritizing Annealing used to remove carbides and stabilize Pearlite.

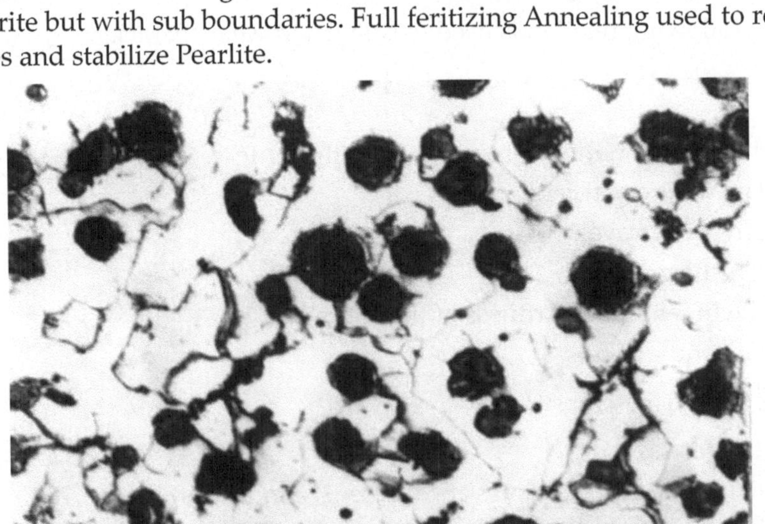

Fig. 5.2: Structure after foundry heat treaded (F.H.T) full feritizing annealing

Double Annealing LHT (DHTA)

The sample treated in the lab by (DHTA) was shown in figure 5.3, which represents a double annealing cycle lead to decomposition of all cementite and produce nodules impeded in full ferritic matrix which increases workability. It was necessary to preheating all samples in the range from 900°C to 950°C to produce adequate ductility for rolling and achieve fully austenite structure.

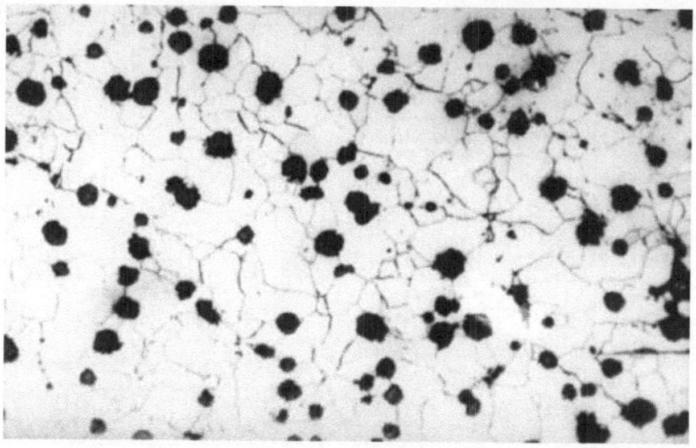

Fig. 5.3: Structure of ductile cast iron after double annealing cycle

Furnace Cool Specimen after Rolling

Fig. 5.4 shows microstructure of hot rolled and then furnace cool specimens, it was deformed by different amount of reduction, graphite is deformed in the rolling direction, further increase in the amount of reduction lead to progressive elongation of graphite accompanied with decrease in the average thickness of the ferrite envelope. Furnace cooling creates sub-boundaries in ferrite while the amount of pearlite decreases, further increase in the amount of reduction more than 40% leads to crumble graphite where secondary graphite is formed all over the matrix.

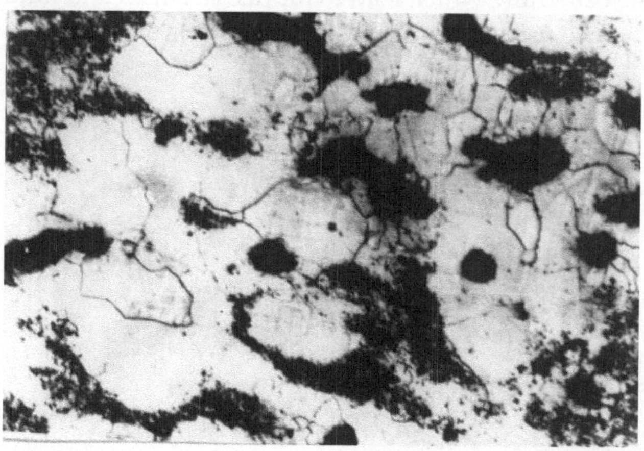

Fig. 5.4: DCI after rolling reduction furnace cool (before heat treatment)

Air Cool Specimen after Rolling

Figure 5.5 indicates microstructure of hot rolled specimen then air cooled, the nodules of graphite are enveloped in ferrite free from sub-boundaries and the remaining matrix is pearlite this emphasizes that air cooling rate is fast enough to ensure that carbon in solution of the austenite forms pearlite which causes raising of hardness, it can also be noted that graphite nodules are deformed by hot rolling into lens shaped disks ellipsoidal in plane which are flattened more as the amount of reduction increases.

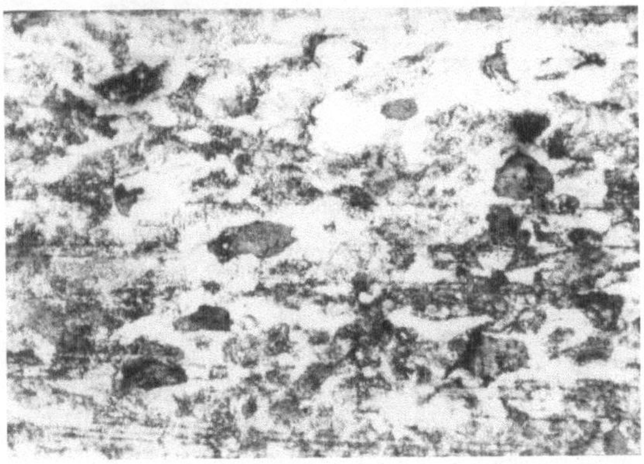

Fig. 5.5: DCI after rolling Air cool (before heat treatment)

Fig. 5.6 and figure 5.7 show the effect of heat treatment double annealing on hot rolled ductile cast iron, they represent the microstructure of heat treated specimens after rolling which divided into two main groups air cooled after rolling and furnace cool after rolling specimen respectively. Heat treatment produce full ferritic matrix the ferrite grain is elongated in the rolling direction, and also the graphite flattened as the amount of reduction increases. Heat treatment does not eliminate directionality (anisotropy remain) but only decompose the cementite which lead to reduce strength and improve ductility in order to enhance impact properties necessary for machining.

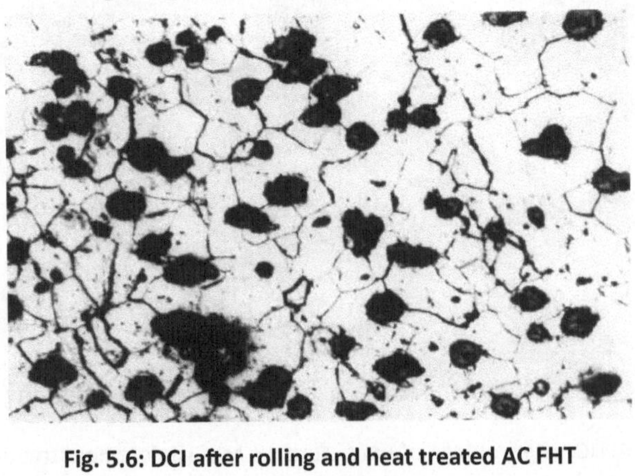

Fig. 5.6: DCI after rolling and heat treated AC FHT

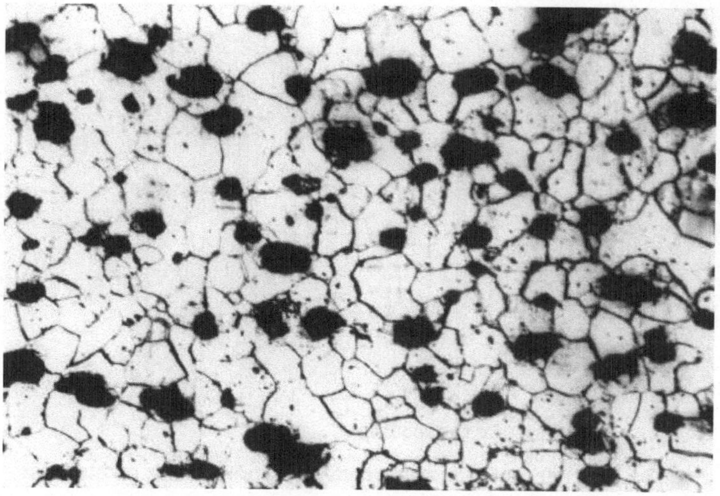

Fig. 5.7: DCI after rolling and heat treated FC FHT

Mechanical Properties

Hardness

The mechanical properties of the samples were recorded, table 5.3 shows the relation between Vicker hardness value and microstructure constitute before rolling at room temperature, each value was the mean of five (5) readings. Hardness value is strong function of the phases presented due to heat treatment process. The maximum value was recorded for as cast structure and the minimum one was recorded for the fully ferritic structure (L.H.T).

Table 5.3: The Relation between Micro-structure Constituent of D.C.I and Hardness before Rolling

Conditions	Vicker Hardness (VH)	Brinell Hardness (BHN)	Microstructure	Pearlite %
As Cast	211	201	graphite + ferrite + pearlite	23.8%
Laboratory heat treated (L.H.T.)	166.67	158	graphite + ferrite + pearlite	5.1%
Foundry heat treated (as received) F.H.T.	86	90.5	graphite + ferrite + pearlite	0%

The correlation between the Vickers hardness of the rolled specimen and the amount of total reduction by rolling is shown in figure 5.8. It is clear that hardness increases by increasing the amount of reduction by rolling which may be attributed by the accumulative strain hardening effect.

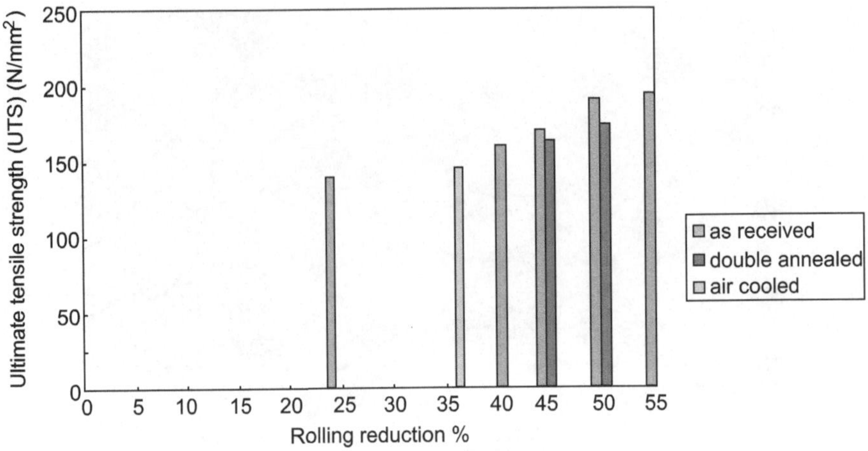

Fig. 5.8: The effect of reduction percentage during rolling on hardness

The manufacturing condition include the type of heat treatment cycle has significant effect up on hardness, table 5.4 shows The relation between manufacturing and rolling conditions of D.C.I on Hardness. The air cooled specimens have always higher hardness value than that of furnace cooled specimen ones. In case of air cooled specimens the rate of cooling was higher. The double annealing is lower the hardness value due to the formation of soft fully ferritic matrix as result of double annealing process.

Table 5.4: The Relation between Manufacturing and Rolling Conditions of D.C.I on Hardness

Specimen Number	Treatment Before rolling	Cooling rate (After rolling)	Hot Rolling Reduction %	V.H.	B.H.N
11	F.H.T (as received)	A.C	36	147	140
31	F.H.T (as received)	F.C	42	165	156
32	F.H.T (as received)	F.C	50	183	174
42	F.H.T (as received)	F.C	26	140	133
43	F.H.T (as received)	F.C	26	140	133
52	L.H.T	F.C	46	165	156
53	L.H.T.	F.C.	44	162.5	154
54	L.H.T	F.C	50	174	166
62	L.H.T	F.C	51	177	168
63	L.H.T	F.C	48	173.5	164.5

Friction and Wear

The different wear and friction characteristics are determined by pin on desk technique, digital strain bridge reading are calibrated to read frictional force value by applying known dead weights laterally on the arm, figure 5.9 shows the calibration curve of the digital strain bridge.

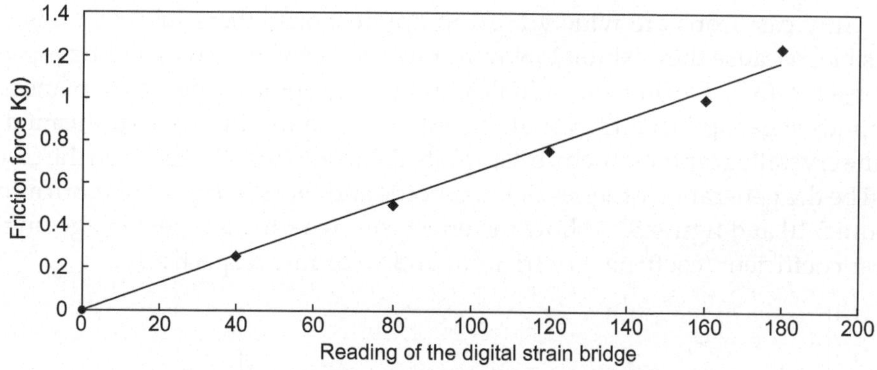

Fig. 5.9: The calibration curve to read friction force value

The particles of graphite were deposited from the matrix on the surface of hardned alloy steel disc work as dry lubricant. The wear tracks are formed on polished tested specimens. After subbing against rotating hardned alloy steel disc. The grooved appearance of the tracks indicates the breaking of the hardned layers and suggests many wear mechanisms involved. The surface damage is less pronounced with low surface hardness as may be noticed by comparing various types of damage to sliding surface have been observed such as removal of graphite particles from matrix of test specimens reduced deformation micro cutting and tearing in depth, so the loose of graphite particles is the source of dry lubrication, all results are recorded in table 5.5. The wear tested specimens at constant load and constant sliding speed is dependent on the hardness and microstructures of tested specimens, during sliding deformation of surface may occur.

Table 5.5: Wear Properties Data Calculated

Specimen Number	Hot Rolling Reduction %	Wear Weight	Wear Volume	Wear Rate	Wear coefficient
11	36	1.7783	0.2470	3.1465×10^{-4}	1.0777×10^{-5}
31	42	1.6143	0.2242	2.8561×10^{-4}	1.0036×10^{-5}
32	50	1.8641	0.2589	3.2981×10^{-4}	1.0264×10^{-5}
42	26	1.6321	0.2267	2.8879×10^{-4}	1.00195×10^{-5}
43	26	1.2418	0.1725	2.1475×10^{-4}	0.8798×10^{-5}
52	46	1.3126	0.1823	2.3223×10^{-4}	0.89869×10^{-5}
53	44	1.8923	0.2628	3.3478×10^{-4}	0.64032×10^{-5}
54	50	1.6141	0.2242	2.8561×10^{-4}	1.04807×10^{-5}
62	51	1.5943	0.2214	2.8204×10^{-4}	1.05380^{-5}
63	48	1.6068	0.2232	2.8433×10^{-4}	1.04972^{-5}

Gray cast irons are widely used in applications where lubrication is not feasible, because they exhibit low wear rates and can be used as sliding against themselves(35). During the initial sliding of graphite. The basal planes of graphite shear appear and provide a continuous source of a solid lubricant due to the crystallographic structure, Graphite detached from the cast iron the result will be the generation of series of mico-voids and there is act as self lubrication, figure 5.10 and figure 5.11 show the effect rolling reduction percentage on the wear coefficient (coefficient of friction) and wear rate respectively.

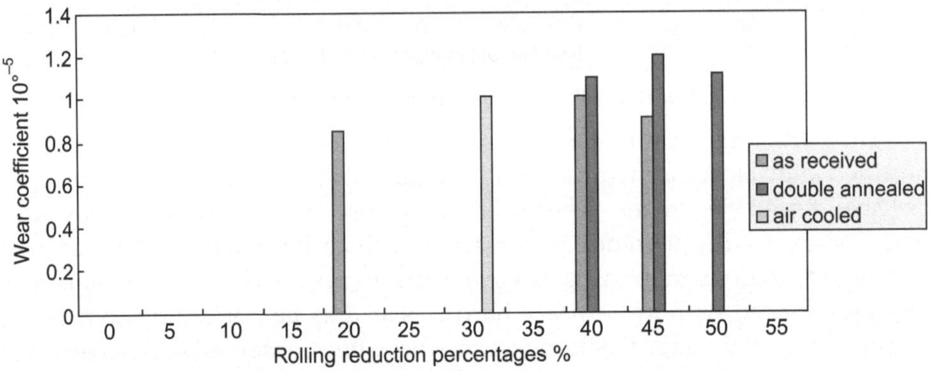

Fig. 5.10: The effect of reduction percentages on friction coefficient at different conditions

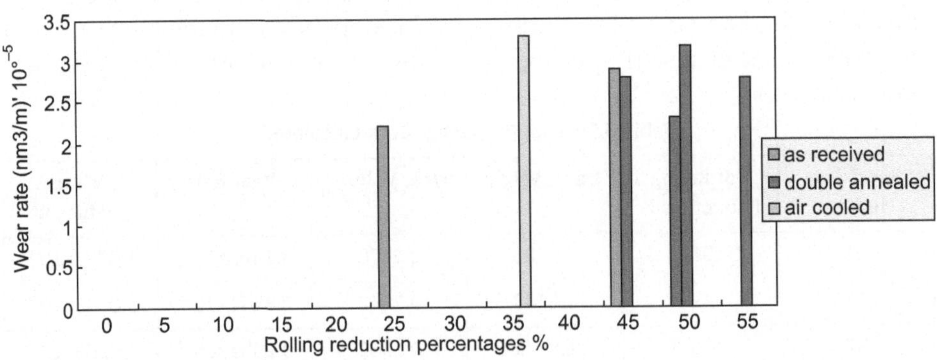

Fig. 5.11: The effect of reduction percentages on wear rate at different conditions

The fraction behavior of different conditions was function on hardness, figure 5.12 shows the relationship between the hardness and the friction coefficient of the annealed specimen of hot - rolled ductile cast iron which vary with the hardness of the tested specimens.

The wear resistance is also influenced by the graphite form. nodular form in D.C.I is superior to wear resistance also can be considerably improved by work hardening due to rolling

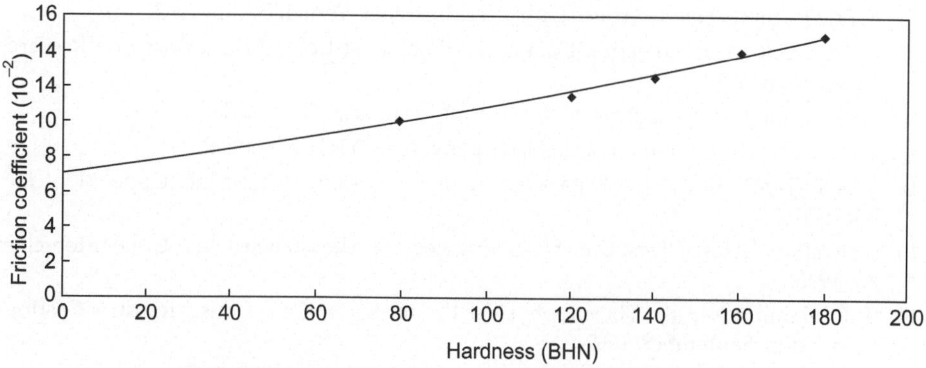

Fig. 5.12: The effect of hardness on the coefficient of friction

The wear coefficient K of hot rolled ductile cast iron is similar to that of tool steel, So it is recommended for building elements in moving parts.

Conclusions

1. Rolling of ductile cast iron can improve properties in the rolling direction such as hardness, wear and friction.
2. Hardness increases linearly with increase of the percentage of rolling reduction due to strain hardening.
3. The pearlite percentages have significant effect on hardness and wear
4. Ferrite grain size was dropped sharply with increasing rolling reduction percentages which may be attributed to enhance of nucleation process.
5. Friction coefficient decrease with increasing of reduction percent which may be attributed to stress concentration in vicinity of graphite nodules that work as self lubricant element.
6. Superior wear properties were relate to rolling of D.C.I because graphite work as a dry lubricant minimizing wear.
7. Rolled ductile cast iron consider as more economical relative to carbon steel so it may be recommended in construction and building applications

REFERENCES

1. S. I. Karsay, Ductile Iron II, Quebec Iron and Titanium Corporation, 1972.
2. Annual Book of ASTM Standards, Volume 01.02, Ferrous Castings, 1987.
3. Engineering Properties and Applications of the Ni-Resists and Ductile Ni-Resists, The International Company, New York, NY, 1978.
4. The Iron Castings Handbook, Iron Castings Society, Inc., 1981.
5. Metals Handbook, American Society for Metals, Vol. 1, 8th edition, 1961.
6. E. Soehnchen and O. Bernhofen, "The Thermal Expansion Coefficient of Cast Iron," Archive fur das Eisenhattenwesen, Vol. 8, 1935.
7. H. T. Angus, Cast Iron: Physical and Engineering Properties, 2nd ed., Butterworths Inc, 1967.

8. E. Piwowarsky, Hochwertiges Gusseisen, Springer-Verlag, Berlin, 1942.
9. G. N. J. Gilbert, Engineering Data on Nodular Cast Irons, British Cast Iron Research Association, 1968.
10. High Strength Irons, Climax Molybdenum Company, New York.
11. Ductile Iron, International Nickel Company, New York, NY, 1956.
12. "Ductile Iron" Alloy Digest Data Sheet, Engineering Alloys Digest, Inc., Upper Montclair, NJ, 1956.
13. "Ductalloy, " Alloy Digest Data Sheet, Engineering Alloys Digest, Inc., Upper Montclair, NJ, 1956.
14. B. E. Neimark, et al, "Thermophysical Properties of Cast Irons," Russian Castings Production, September, 1967.
15. A Design Engineer's Digest of Ductile Iron, 5th Edition, 1983, QIT-Fer et Titane Inc., Montreal, Quebec, Canada.
16. Ductile Iron, Metals Handbook, American Society for Metals, 9th edition, Vol 15, 1988.
17. W. Fairhurst and K. Rorhrig "High-silicon Nodular Irons." Foundry Trade journal, March 29, 1979, pp. 657-681.
18. http://www.ductile.org/didata/Section5/5intro.htm#Elastic Properties
19. C.F. Walton, Gray and Ductile Iron Castings Handbook, Iron Founder's Society, 1971, p 193
20. C.F. Walton and T.J. Opar, Iron Castings Handbook, Iron Casting Society, 1981, p 235 & p 297-321
21. "Chrome-Moly White Cast Irons," Publication M – 630, AMAX, Inc., 1986
22. Davis, J.R., Cast Irons, ASM International, Materials Park, OH, 1996
23. G. Lambert, Ed., Typical Microstructures of Cast Metals, 2nd ed., The Institute of British Foundrymen, 1996, p 47
24. H.T. Angus, Physical and Engineering Properties of Cast Iron, BCIRA, 1960, p 21
25. Shackleford, Introduction to Materials Science for Engineers, Chapter 4, (2nd ED.).
26. Van Vlack, Elements of Materials Science and Engineering, Chapter 7, (6th ED.) or Chapter 4 (5th ED.).
27. Smith, Principles of Materials Science and Engineering, Chapter4, (1st Ed.).
28. http://www.msm.cam.ac.uk/doitpoms/miclib/index.php
29. http://www.matweb.com/search/GetSubcat.asp
30. http://www.wynndanzur.com/glossary.htm
31. http://www.sciencepub.net/researcher/research0401/003_7556bresearch0401_15_23.pdf
32. http://www.sciencepub.net/researcher/research0312/009_7555breseach0312_46_56.pdf

6 Pollution Control in Building Material Industries

ABSTRACT

In this work, the wastes resulting from building and construction sectors are divided into two main version. First, wastes resulting from mining of building material during their manufacturing. Second, wastes resulting from construction process and activity. a survey about mining industries as feeding industry to building and construction sector has been done.

Another survey was done for different kinds of pollutants and their effects on the environment in the near future and on the long run. It differentiates between pollutants by their sources and effects. Feeding industries pollutants are mentioned according to the national and international statistical data and technical reports. The kind of wastes and their amounts were evaluated. The most common examples of industrial hazardous waste were included and the source of each were explained. The data were collected by author. The precautions and Laws for pollution control in Egypt are also discussed in this work. Finally the results are discussed. Materials recycling, materials replacement and green building procedures are the best methods for reduction and elimination of pollution resulting from construction sector wastes. Recommendations emphasizing on the pollution control and the importance of environmental protection according to national and international waste management programs.

Keywords: *Pollution, wastes, building materials, construction, feeding industries.*

Introduction

Extraction is the first phase of hardrock mining which consists of the initial removal of ore from the earth. It is the initial attempt at liberating and concentrating the valuable mineral from the extracted ore. After the beneficiation step, the remaining material is often physically and chemically similar to the material (ore or mineral) that entered the operation, except that particle size has been reduced. The extraction and beneficiation of minerals generates large quantities of waste. Mineral processing waste streams typically bear little or no resemblance to the materials that entered the operation, producing product and waste streams that are not earthen in character, these wastes cause pollution to air, water and land. Fig. 6.1 shows Waste emission to the environmental (land and water) resulting from different types of minerals

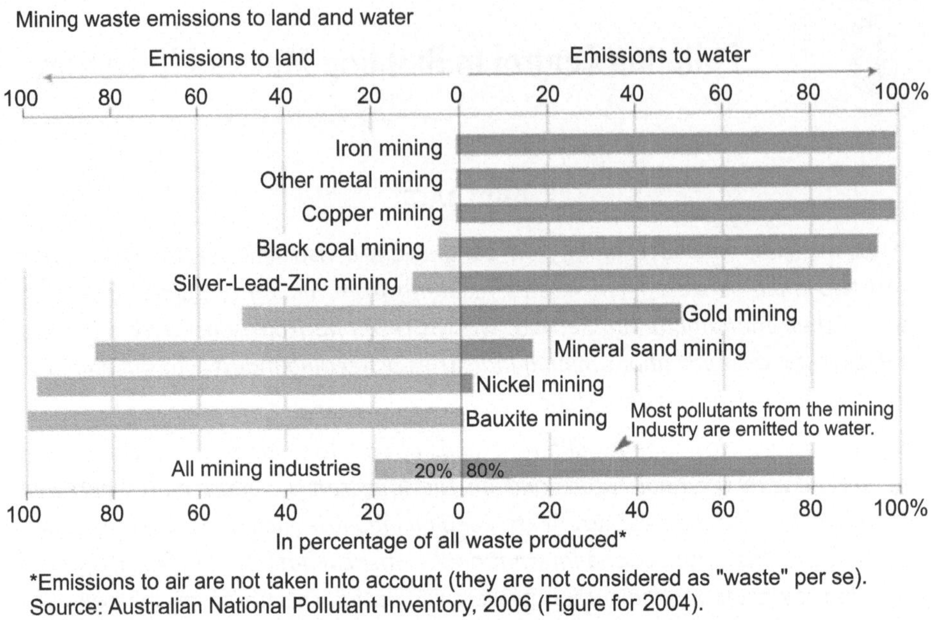

Fig. 6.1: Waste emission to the environmental (land &water)

Negative Impacts of Wastes

The amount of wastes resulting from construction process are increased rapidly every year. According to the last statistical analysis, it is about 1228 million ton per year distributed to all construction sectors. Fig. 6.2 shows The amount of wastes in each building sector.

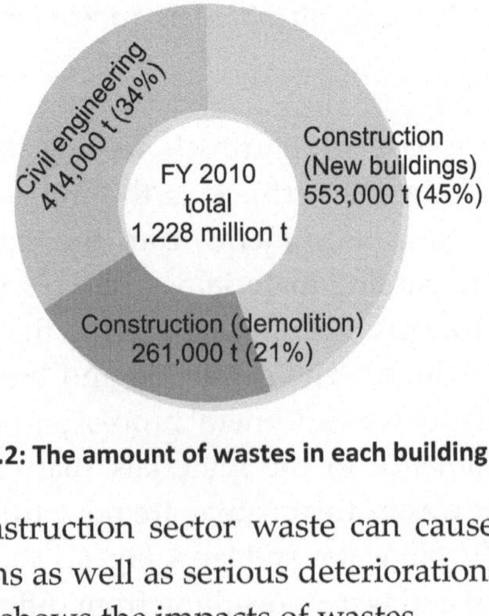

Fig. 6.2: The amount of wastes in each building sector

Building and construction sector waste can cause short and long term public health problems as well as serious deteriorations in the environmental quality[(18),(19)]. Fig. 6.3 shows the impacts of wastes

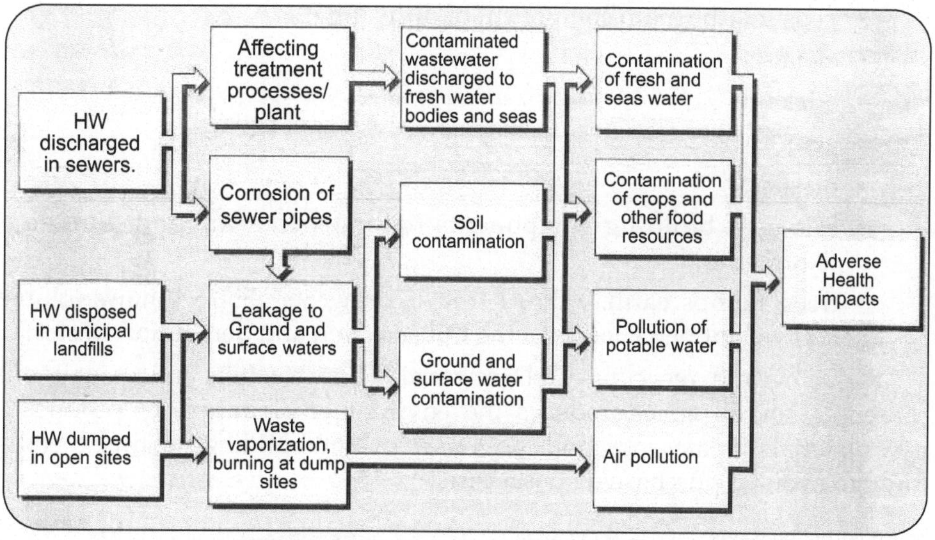

Fig. 6.3: Environmental impacts of hazardous wastes

Classification of Hazardous Wastes

Solid, liquid, or gaseous wastes are considered hazardous if they possess one or more hazardous characteristics which may be summarized as: -

1. Ignitability (capable of burning or causing fire); for example waste ethyl ether, methanol, acetone, toluene, benzene, peroxides.
2. Corrosivity (able to corrode steel or harm organisms because of extreme acidic or basic properties); for example waste sodium hydroxide and sulphuric acid.
3. Reactivity (reacts violently with air and/or water to liberate or produce toxic gases), such as waste cyanide solutions.
4. Toxicity (containing substances which are poisonous); for example waste chromium (VI), arsenic, cadmium, and other heavy metals.
5. Ecotoxicty (due to its bioaccumulation and persistence in the environment); for example PCB waste (poly chlorinated Biphenyls), DDT (p, p`-Dichlorodiphenyltrichloroethane)

Construction and Demolition Wastes Materials

Construction and demolition (C&D) materials consist of the debris generated during the construction, renovation, and demolition of buildings, roads, and bridges. C&D materials often contain bulky, heavy materials that include:

- concrete,
- wood (from buildings),
- asphalt (from roads and roofing shingles),

- gypsum (the main component of drywall),
- metals,
- bricks,
- glass,
- plastics,
- salvaged building components (doors, windows, and plumbing fixtures), and
- trees, stumps, earth, and rock from clearing sites. Fig. 6.4 shows volume and weight percentages of the Construction and demolition wastes.

Reducing and recycling C&D materials (Construction and demolition) conserves landfill space, reduces the environmental impact of producing new materials, creates jobs, and can reduce overall building project expenses through avoided purchase/disposal costs

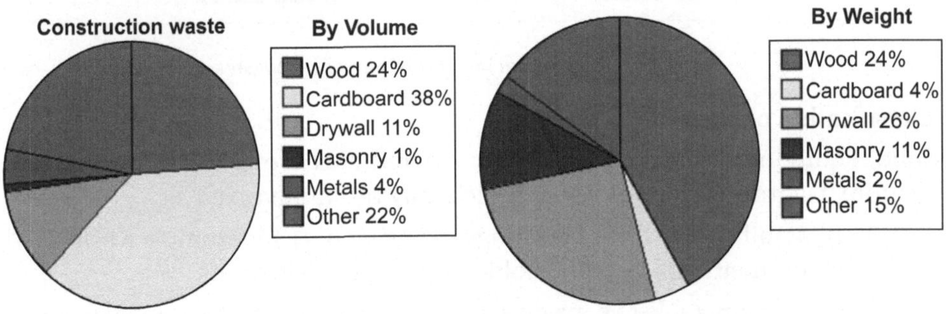

Fig. 6.4: Volume and weight percentages of the construction and demolition wastes

Types of hazardous waste in feeding industries to building and materials. The most common examples of industrial hazardous waste include:

- Acid and alkali wastes mainly generated from surface treatment and metal finishing processes, production of chemicals, paper, petrochemicals and pharmaceuticals.
- Sludge from industrial waste water treatment containing heavy metals such as lead, mercury, hexadecane chromium, zinc, copper, nickel, cadmium, arsenic. These are generated from a wide range of processes most commonly from chlorine production, pigment and paint manufacture, textiles, wood preservation, metal plating, tanning, smelting and refining of metals.
- Slag containing heavy metals from metal smelting furnaces, most commonly from smelters of lead, aluminum and copper.
- Oil wastes such as used lubrication oils, hydraulic fluids generated in almost all industrial plants from machinery repair and maintenance.

- Halogenated solvent wastes most commonly generated by metal cleaning, textile and leather de-oiling processes.
- Non- Halogenated solvent wastes, such as spirit, toluene, benzene, xylene, ethanol most commonly generated by the manufacturing of paints, inks, adhesives and resins.
- PCBs (polychlorinated biphenyl) present in electrical capacitors, vacuum pumps, plasticizers, fire retardants, cutting oils and hydraulic fluids.
- Empty chemicals and oil containers, any materials contaminated with chemicals or oil (rags, sand, etc.). These examples of industrial wastes might not be recognized as being hazardous by generators, despite the fact that they possess one or more hazardous characteristics[(12), (23)].

Wastes in Feeding Industries to Construction Sector

In this section, the type and amount of wastes and pollutant resulting from the most important mining industries are discussed. Such as Iron extraction, steel industries, Aluminum industries, cement industries, cook industries and phosphates industries[(13):(20)]. The amount and kind of wastes specially hazardous wastes resulting from production of one tone are mentioned. The most important industries are analyzed and the contribution of each product in building sector are shown in figure 6.5 this diagram illustrates a variety of common building applications for industrial materials. Note that the availability of specific industrial materials can vary regionally.

Cook Industry

Cook industry is one of the most harmful feeding industries. It is feeding industry in steel making, painting and chemical industries. Table 6.1 shows the liquid wastes resulting from cook industry, while table 6.2 shows the solid wastes resulting from cook industry in (kg/ton).

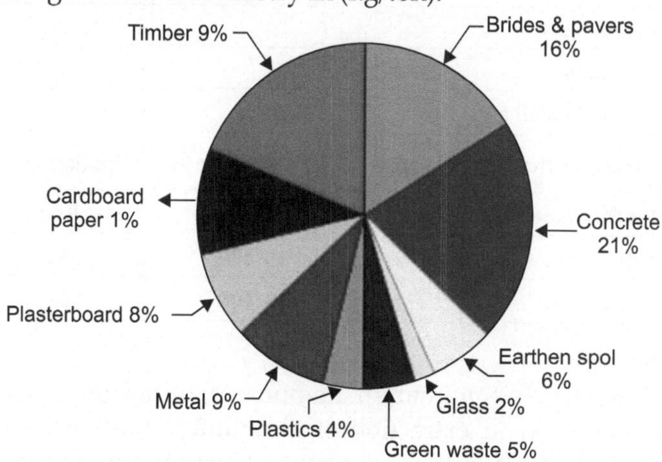

Fig. 6.5: Volume percentages of the materials used in construction and building sectors.

(A) Production of cook

Table 6.1: The liquid wastes resulting from cook industry

Contents	Amount (kg/ton)
Ammonia	0.990
Cyanide	0.05
Phenols	0.19
Sulphuric	0.18
Suspension products	0.04

Table 6.2: The solid wastes resulting from cook industry (kg/ton)

Steps	Waste particles	Carbon mono oxide	Organic compounds	Nitrogen oxides
Crushing	0.37	-	-	-
Heating	1.75	-	-	-
Extraction	0.58	0.03	1.25	0.02
Handling	0.03	-	-	-

Iron Industries

Iron industries are the most important industry in different constructions applications, Table 6.3 The particles resulting from preparation of 1 ton of iron ores. The type and amounts of wastes is completely different when manufacturing steels from scrape at casting ships as shown in table 6.4.

Table 6.3: The particles resulting from preparation of 1 ton of iron ores

Operation	Particles generated (kg/ton)
Transportation from mining	0.05
Crushing	0.1
Dry grinding	40
Wet grinding	–
Drying of grinded ores	9

Table 6.4: The wastes in production of iron in casting ships (kg/ton)

Product type	Slag	Sands	Iron
Molds	142	600	33
Final products	134	600	32

Aluminum Industry

Aluminum industry has minimum amount of hazardous wastes because of electrical cells used in extraction of aluminum. Table 6.5 shows wastes in Aluminum industries, but the amount of wastes are strong function in manufacturing method as shown in Table 6.6.

Table 6.5: Wastes in Aluminum Industries

Operation	Amount (kg/ton)	Notes
Production of alumina from bauxite	2000	
Production of Aluminum from alumina	66	Cyanide and fluoride compounds, and dusts
Production of Aluminum from scraps	traces	Very small particles

Table 6.6: Wastes Dependence on the Method of Manufacturing

Operation	Particles (kg/ton)
Biro furnaces	7.3
Bush furnaces	0.9
Reflective furnaces	2.2

Cement Industry

Cement industry contains all types of hazardous wastes and in all forms such as solid, liquid and gaseos. Table 6.7 and table 6.8 show solid and liquid wastes per ton respectively.

Table 6.7: Solid Wastes in Cement Industries

Operation	Particles (kg/ton)
Dry grinding	187
Dry method in clinker production	57
Wet method in clinker production	51
Clinker grinding	21

Table 6.8: Liquid Wastes in Cement Industries

Contents	Particles (kg/ton)
Soluble particles	6.66
Suspended particles	0.19
Alkali particles	1.38
Potassium	3.3
Sulphuric compounds	6.67

Gases resulting from fuel burning Sulphur oxides, nitrogen oxide- carbon oxides.

Phosphate Industry

Phosphate industry causes the air pollution Table 6.9 shows gas wastes in Phosphate industry, this industry have a lot of applications in chemicals necessary for building and construction industry in all stages from soil treatment to finishing and painting.

Table 6.9: Gas Wastes in Phosphate Industry

Contents	Particles (milligram / liter)
Chlorides	1574
Sulphates	2186
Hg	0.0001
Cadmium	0.0005
Nickel	0.2
Zinc	5
PH	6.5:8.5
Suspended particles	30
Dry particles (Cr, Cu, Zn, Hg, Pb)	95ppm

Glass Industry

Finally the kind and amount of wastes resulting from glass industries are also discussed because the glass industries will become one of the most important industries in Egypt in the near future. Egypt is very rich in highly qualified types of sands. The dependence of pollution up on the method of treatment and the kind of the process appears clearly. Table 6.10 shows the wastes in Glass industries and classify them according composition and/or physical properties.

Table 6.10: Wastes in Glass Industries

Wastes	Percentage % in mixture	Notes
Liquid wastes	20	Suspension particles from silica-calcium carbonate-sodium carbonate
Solid wastes	5:40	Glass particles reduced to 5% in automatic method while 40% in manual or blowing methods
Gases	20	Silicon oxides-lead oxides-Nitrogen oxides-sulphur oxides-selenium

Results and Discussion

Reduction or elimination of wastes resulting from the building and construction sector are the most important aim in green building procedure, it can be done by recycling of wastes or replacement of hazardous material to eliminate wastes from sources as follow:-

Material Recycling

A practice that can be encouraged at the building site by using separate containers for various materials. Reusing or recycling C&D materials (Construction and demolition) on site can reduce material hauling and disposal costs. These savings, applied to the total project cost, make it possible to do more work with the same budget. In addition, C&D materials (Construction and demolition) recycles will often charge less to accept recyclable materials that have already been separated from non-recyclable materials, so they make good economic sense for builders and project owners. Fig. 6.6 shows flow chart illustrating the main requirements of the waste classifications. Prior to the final disposal of hazardous waste off-site, waste generators are required

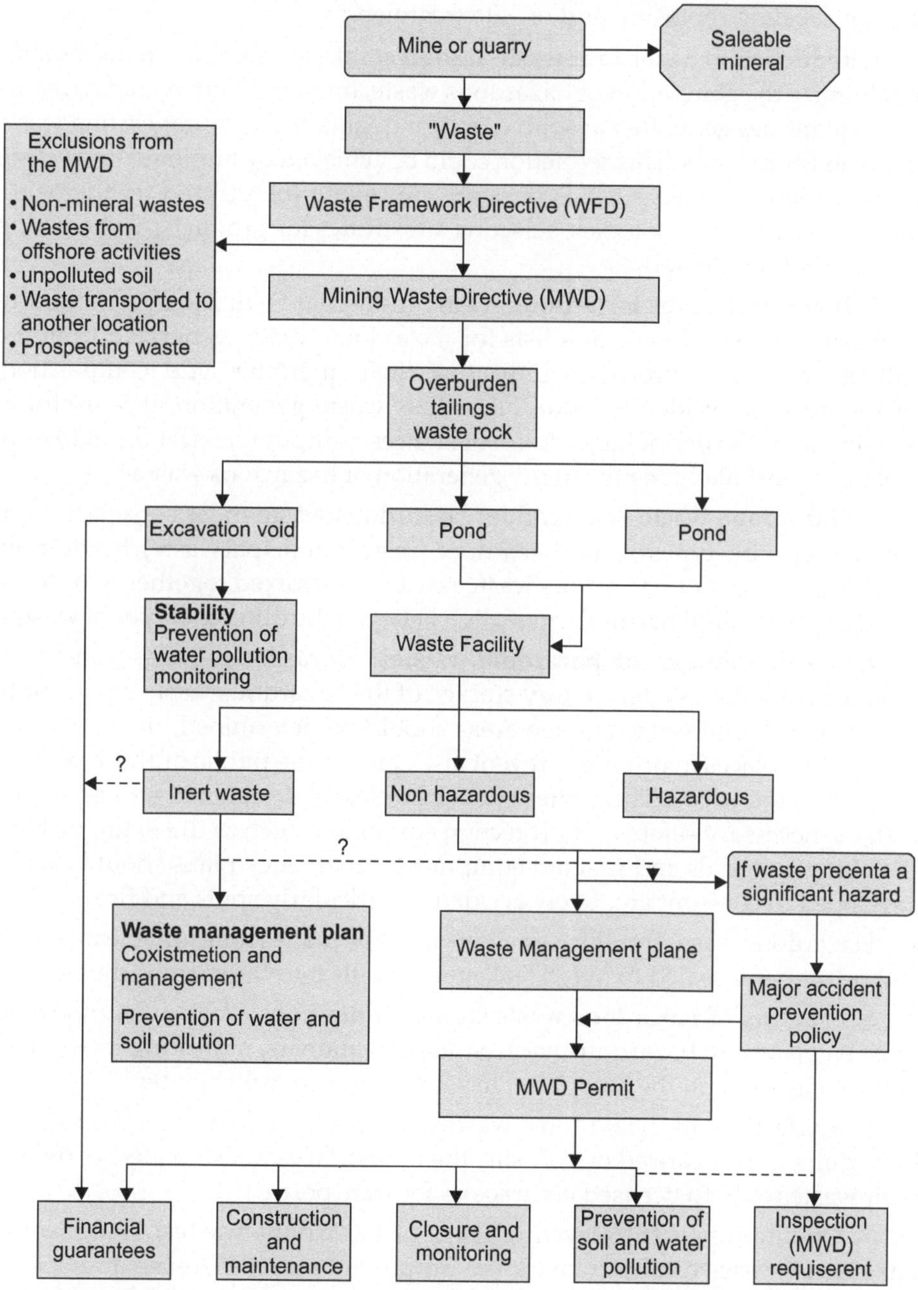

Fig. 6.6: Flow chart illustrating the main requirements of the waste classifications

to implement the necessary procedures to ensure the proper management of such waste within their industrial establishment, in order to comply with the requirements of Law 4/1994 and its Executive Regulations. Such procedures involve the reduction of hazardous waste at source, identification, safe on site storage, labeling reporting and on-site treatment: -

1. Reduction of hazardous waste at source: Take all necessary requirements to minimize the generation of hazardous waste, quantitatively by reducing the waste quantities generated at source, and/or qualitatively, by generating waste that is less hazardous. This reduction could be achieved by implementing waste minimization schemes, such as ones for improving the utilized technologies, adopting cleaner technologies, selecting substitutes for products, and/or using less harmful raw materials.

2. Identification of hazardous waste: Industrial facilities are required to establish complete description lists for hazardous wastes generated from the different industrial processes indicating their quantities and composition, for the purpose of identification hazardous waste generation, it is useful to keep in mind, the use of hazardous substances as input material for industrial processes most likely results in the generation of hazardous waste.

3. Hazardous waste segregation: Hazardous waste must be separated at source from other types of non-hazardous waste (municipal waste). In addition, the different types of hazardous waste must not be mixed together in order to avoid any undesired harmful interaction between the different types of wastes.

4. On-site storage of hazardous wastes: Hazardous wastes generators should ensure the safe temporary storage of the hazardous waste on-site until final disposal. The waste storage areas should be determined, they are away from public places in order to prevent any harm to the public or those persons exposed to the waste. These sites should be clearly designated and equipped with the necessary safety and protection equipment such as fire extinguishers, absorbing materials and first aid equipment. Emergency plans should also be developed to confront any likely accidents particularly spills and fire.

Hazardous waste storage containers must be made from suitable materials and be properly sealed to avoid leakages of spills into the surroundings.

5. Labeling of hazardous waste storage containers: Clear signs and labels must be placed on hazardous waste storage containers, indicating the content of the container and the associated hazards, if improperly handled.

6. Collection of hazardous wastes: In cases of treatment/disposal of hazardous wastes carried out off-site, the industrial establishments are deliver their wastes only to licensed contractors for transport.

7. On-site treatment/recycling/reuse of hazardous wastes: Treatment of hazardous wastes can be done for the purpose of recycling/reuse or disposal. If treatment is carried out on-site, approved treatment system and the technical specifications of the treatment units and their operational programs must be recorded.

8. Hazardous waste register: All establishments handling hazardous wastes are required to keep a record of the generated wastes, the method of disposal and the parties who will receive this waste must be registered.

Data must be included in the hazardous waste register:-

- Name and address of the establishment
- Name and job title of the person responsible for filing the register
- The period covered by the current data
- A comprehensive list of the types and quantities of hazardous wastes resulting from the different activities
- Method of disposal of the resulting hazardous wastes
- The parties contracted with to receive the hazardous wastes
- Date on which the form is filled
- Signature of the officer in charge.

Material Replacements

Some industrial materials, such as fly ash and slag cement used as supplementary cementations material in concrete, offer significant performance benefits over virgin materials. Other industrial materials, such as foundry sand, perform just as well as—and in some cases better than—virgin materials in building applications. Coal bottom ash used as bedding material for green roofs are lighter weight than alternatives, an important quality in this application. Fig. 6.7 shows waste reduction and elimination scheme

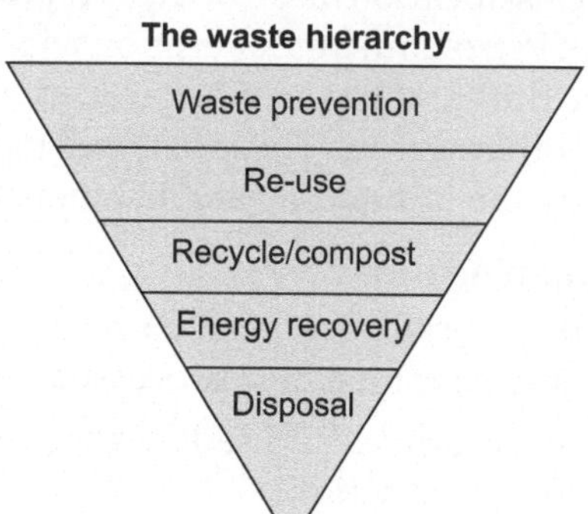

Fig. 6.7: Waste reduction and elimination scheme

Green Building

Green or sustainable building is the practice of creating and using healthier and more resource-efficient methods of construction, renovation, operation, maintenance, and demolition. Designing with industrial materials and recycling

C&D materials (Construction and demolition) generated from projects leads to more sustainable buildings. Most green building certifications give points for these practices; two of the best-known certification systems are the U.S. Green Building Council's Leadership in Energy and Environmental Design (LEED) green building rating system and the Green Building Initiative's Green Globes TM green building rating system.

Legal Framework for Hazardous Waste Management in Egypt

Law 4/1994 for the environmental and its Executive Regulations (ER) present the primary overall legal framework for the management of hazardous waste. In addition, Laws 93/1962 and 48/1982 specify the limits for hazardous wastewater discharge into the public sewers and River Nile and waterways, respectively.

According to Law 4/1994. It is prohibited to import hazardous waste or allow its entrance into Egypt. Moreover, Egypt is a party of the Basel Convention on The Trans-boundary Movement of Hazardous Waste. In this respect, the export of this type of waste from Egyptian industrial establishments, for the purpose of treatment or recycling, is to take place only upon the approval of the Egyptian Environmental Affair Agency (EEAA).

Under development is a system for permitting of industrial establishments generating and handling hazardous waste, following the stipulation of law 4/1994 and its ER. This is carried out by the Ministry of Industry in cooperation with EEAA, and is expected to become operational in the near future. Granted permits would include details of on-site management practices, and would present a further requirement for compliance, in addition to those presented above, which are currently used as the basis for the enforcement of law 4/1994. The hazardous waste classification lists being prepared by the Ministry of Industry, and Ministry of Petroleum in cooperation with EEAA and the Ministry of Health, determine the different types of hazardous wastes generated within the industrial sector and other sectors. These lists will facilitate the identification process of such wastes by the industrial establishments.

Conclusions and Recommendations

1. Many industrial materials are used to replace non-renewable virgin materials that must be mined and processed for use.
2. Conserves natural resources and reduces the energy use and pollution associated with these activities.
3. Substituting coal fly ash (an industrial material) for portland cement in concrete saves the energy and greenhouse gas emissions associated with producing cement.
4. The beneficial use of industrial materials results in less material being sent to disposal facilities, which saves landfill space and further reduces greenhouse gas emissions and other pollutants.

Waste management activities that can be implemented immediately by the industrial establishments

1. Identification of generated hazardous waste.
2. Segregation of hazardous waste at source.
3. On-site safe storage.
4. Proper labeling of hazardous waste registration.
5. Hazardous waste minimization.
6. Training and awareness for workers handling these wastes.
7. Sending used wastes to recycling companies.
8. Using wet, electrical, or less pollutant methods in manufacturing.
9. Recycling of wastes in production areas.
10. Use filters for air purifications according to national standards automation for process.
11. Following the standard roles in waste management for hazardous and non-hazardous materials.

REFERENCES

1. Metal handbook, Vol. 2,P S, Cambridge University press,1980.
2. R.W. Perry. "Perry's chemical engineers handbook", 1984.
3. Ibid, Trans. "AFS " vol. 2,P. 33, 1980.
4. J.V. Dawson, BCJRAL Trans. AFS, vol. 10, No. 1, 1962.
5. C.S.Rao [Environmental Pollution Control Engineering] wilily eastern limited new age international limited 3rd reprint, 1999.
6. Ianl.Pepper, Charles P.Gerba and Mark L.Brusseau, [Pollution Science] Academic Press, Inc, 1996.
7. A Kamala and D.L Kant Rao [Environmental Engineering] Tata Mc Graw –hill publishing co limites, 1994.
8. Book of ASTM STANDARS, Part 27: Plastics – General Methods of Testing, Nomenclature, American Society for Testing and Materials, 1969.
9. John Delmonte: [Plastics in Engineering], Penton Publ. Co., Cleveland, Ohio, 1949.
10. Charles A. Harper: [Handbook of Plastics and Elastomers], Mc Graw-Hill Book Co., New York, 1975.
11. W.B.White: in "Encyclopedia of Material Characterizations: Surface, Interface, Thin Films, (ed.C.Bundle), Letchworth, Butterworth-Heineman. Bunce N., "Environmental Chemistry" Wuerz Publishing Ltd., Winnipeg, Canada, 1991.
12. Cope C.B., Fuller W.H., and Willets. S.L, "The Scientific Management of Hazardous Wastes", Cambridge University Press, Cambridge, 1983.
13. Dohlido J.R., and Best G.A. "Chemistry of Water and Water Pollution" Ellis Harwood, New York, 1993.
14. Hesketh H.E., Cross F.L., and Tessitore J.L "Cleaning and Destruction of Hazardous Wastes" Economic Publishing. Lancat-er, Pennsy, 1990.

15. Jack man A.P. and Powell R.L., "Waste Treatment Technologies" Noyes Data Corporation, Park Ridge, New Gersy, 1991.
16. La Grega M.D., Buckingham P.L, and Evans J.C., "Hazardous Waste Management", Mc Graw-Hill, New York, 1994.
17. Wong L.K., and Wong M.H.S., "Hand book of Industrial Waste Treatment" Marcel Decker, Inc., New York, 1992.
18. Egyptian pollution Project "Hazardous Waste Management" EPAP Technical Information Sheet 3, 2001.
19. Egyptian Environmental Policy Program, Technical Information Sheet, 2002.
20. E.I.Kazantsev "Industrial Furnaces", 1st English Edition, Mir Publishers Moscow, 1977.
21. A.M.Mikhailov "Metal Casting", 1st English edition, Mir Publishers Moscow, 1989.
22. Hassell Kenneth A [Biochemistry and Uses of Pesticides], 2nd Ed, VCH Publishers, Inc., New York, 1991.
23. Gross, Douglas, [Managing Hazardous Wastes Containing Heavy Metals], SciTech Publishers Matawan, NJ, 1990.
24. R. R. Pawar, and V. T. Deshpande, Acta Crystallogr. 1968, 24A, 316.
25. D.R. Lide, (ed.) in Chemical Rubber Company Handbook of Chemistry and Physics, CRC Press, Boca Raton, Florida, USA, 79th Edition, 1998.
26. I.S. Butler and J.F. Harrod in Inorganic Chemistry, Principles and Applications Benjamin Cummings, California, USA, 1989.
27. H.J.M. Bowen in Environmental Chemistry of the Elements, Academic Press, London, UK, 1979.
28. A.M. James and M.P. Lord in Macmillan's Chemical and Physical Data, Macmillan, London, UK, 1992.
29. P.A. Cox in The Elements: Their Origin, Abundance, and Distribution, Oxford University Press, Oxford, UK, 1989.
30. Recommendations of Court Scientific Research Bulletin, Center for the Study and Management Consulting, Environment and Development, vol 9, November 1999.
31. Ahmed said Eldemerdash, Plastics in Human Service, Akra series, Publisher Dar Elmaref, Cairo, Egypt, 1981.
32. Recommendations of the International Conference to Reduce the Environmental Risks, Cairo University, Sep. 2000.
33. Recommendations of the International Conference on Environment and Development in the Arab World, Assiut University, Mar 2002.

7

Qualitative and Quantitative Analysis of Hot Rolled Ductile Cast Iron as Composite Structure in Building Elements

ABSTRACT

Being based on ideas about the structure of cast iron as a composite material and analyzing the bonding of discontinuities at the graphite-metal matrix interface, the qualitative and quantitative analysis was done for Hot rolled ductile cast iron as composite structure have graphite nodules as reinforced element. The analysis was done at different hot rolling condition and different cooling rates, the shape and distribution of the graphite nodules in the matrix were evaluated quantitatively, different parameters such as shape factor, volume fraction, mean free path and number of nodules per unit length and per unit area. The directionality resulting from rolling was taking into consideration so the measurements were done in the longitudinal and transverse directions. The measurements related to the matrix such as grain size, number of grain per unit area and inter granular surface ration were evaluated in the transverse and longitudinal direction also. The difference between the structure on the surface attached to rolling mill and the structure inside the samples were determined. This work aim to study the applications of Hot rolled ductile cast Iron in the building elements based upon structure which affect properties.

Keywords: *DCI, hot rolling, quantitative measurement, qualitative analysis.*

Introduction

Iron castings, as objects of art and weapons of war have been produced for more than 2000 years. Compared with steel, ductile cast iron has generally inferior ductility, weld-ability, toughness and fatigue resistance however, it has superior cast-ability (high Ca and Si), machine-ability, wear, corrosion resistance and damping capacity. In a sense, the iron foundry industry produces an invisible yet vital product, since most iron castings are further processed, assembled, and then incorporated as components of other machinery, equipment, and consumer items.

The term "cast iron" refers not to a single material, but to a family of materials whose major constituent is iron, with important amounts of carbon and silicon. Cast irons are natural composite materials whose properties are determined by their microstructures - the stable and metastable phases formed during solidification or subsequent heat treatment. The major microstructure constituents of cast irons are: the chemical and morphological forms taken by carbon, and the continuous metal matrix in which the carbon and/or carbide are dispersed. The following important microstructure components are found in cast irons carbides, Graphite, Ferrite, Pearlite, Martensite, Austenite and Bainite. Cast iron having a spheroid or nodular graphite structure were developed nearly 75 years ago, and referred to as ductile cast iron. Figure 7.1 shows the time - temperature transformation diagram (TTC) for Cast Irons.

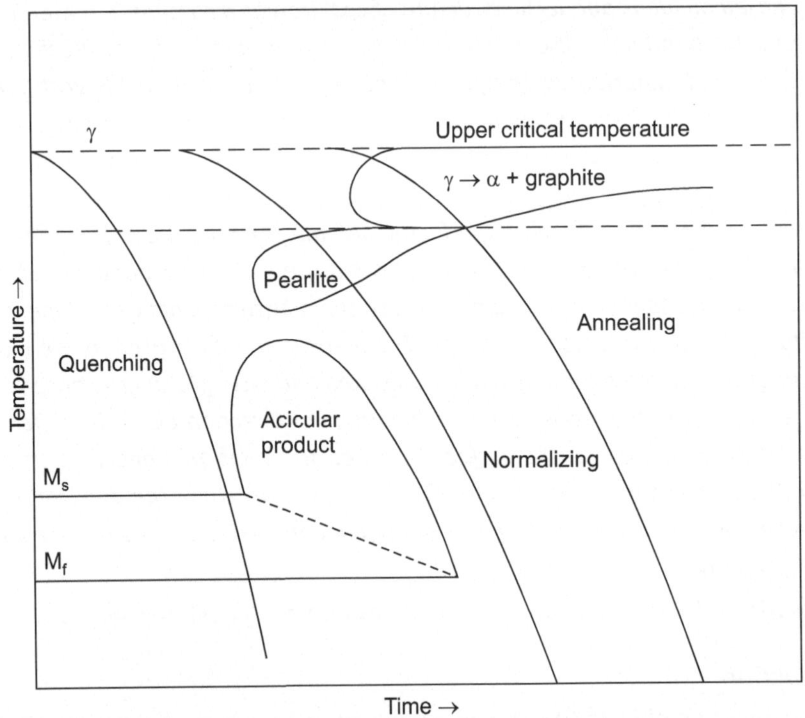

Continuous cooling transformation (CCT) diagram showing annealing, normalizing, and quenching, M_s = martensite start temperature, M_f = martensite finish temperature.
Source: J.R. Davis, Ed., cast Irons, ASM Speciality Handbook, ASM International, 1996, p 192

Fig. 7.1: The time - temperature transformation diagram (TTC) for Cast Irons

Ductile iron should be considered as a family of materials offering a wide range of properties depending on the chemical composition and heat treatment and the consequent microstructure modifications. Matrix microstructure importance is emphasized by the use of matrix names to commonly designate the different types of ductile irons

(a) Ferritic DCI: this DCI is characterized by a good ductility and impact resistance; ultimate tensile and yield strength are equivalent to a low carbon steel.

(b) Pearlitic DCI: a pearlitic DCI is characterized by high strenght, good wear resistance and reduced ductility and impact resistance.

(c) Ferritic-pearlitic DCIs: these are the most common DCI; properties are intermediate between ferritic and pearliticgrades and good machinability is obtained with low production costs.

(d) Austenitic DCI: this DCI shows a high corrosion and oxidation resistance, with good strength and dimensional stability at high temperature.

(e) Martensitic DCI: these DCI are obtained controlling both the chemical composition (to prevent pearlite formation) and the heat treatment (quench and temper): very high strength and wear resistance are obtained, but with lower values of ductility and toughness.

(f) Bainitic DCI: this DCI is obtained controlling chemical composition and/ or heat treatment: the result is a hard and wear resistant material.

(g) Austempered DCI (also ADI): ADI are obtained after an austempering heat treatment, with very high tensile strength values (twice than a pearlitic DCI), high elongation and toughness.

The importance of ductile cast iron can be appreciated from production statistics, which represent 21% (by weight) of all ferrous castings produced in the world. After more than fifty years, ductile iron should be considered as a family of materials offering a wide range of properties depending on the chemical composition and heat treatment and the consequent microstructure modifications. Matrix microstructure importance is emphasized by the use of matrix names to commonly designate the different types of ductile.

II. EXPERIMENTAL WORK

A. Material

The ductile cast iron used in this work is obtained from El-Nasr Casting Company. The slab cut from centrifugal casting pipe with 1000 mm diameter and 10 mm thickness, which consider as the main commercial product in the Company. The chemical composition of the ductile cast iron is shown in table 7.1.

Table 7.1: The Chemical Composition of the Ductile Cast Iron

Contents	C	Si	Mg	S	Mn	Fe
Percentages %	3.68	2.1	0.0042	0.017	0.35	Balance

B. Treatment before Rolling

- Slices were double annealed (L.H.T) to 900°C and hold for 2 hr prior to furnace cooling to 700°C, then held at this temperature for 3 hr before the furnace cooling to the room temperature.

- Some of the slices were feritizing annealed (F.H.T) at 920°C for 30min then furnace cooled for 30min Annealing: Full feritizing Annealing used to remove carbides and stabilized Pearlite, heat to 900°C, holding long enough to dissolve carbides, then cooling at a rate of 85°C/h to 705°C, and still air cooling to room temperature. It improves low temperature fracture resistance but reduces fatigue strength.

C. Preheat before rolling

- The L.H.T specimen is soaked at 950°C for one hour before rolling, while the F.H.T specimen is soaked at 900°C for one hour before rolling.

D. Rolling process

Rolling was carried out on the slices in the circumference direction of the pipe by using a laboratory two - high reversing mill with 320mm diameter rolls and 450mm length. The slices were heated to a temperature range between 900°C and 950°C there soaked for one hour at this temperature. Table 7.1 shows the rolling conditions of DCT. The rolls speed was 25m/min. Reduction in cross sectional area was carried out on 2 to 4 passes. Some of the rolled strips were air cooled A.C, while the others were furnace cooled, F.C at 700°C.

Table 7.2: Show Rolling Condition

Specimen Number	Before rolling			After rolling		
	FHT	LHT	Soaking Temperature °C	Hot Rolling Reduction %	Cooling rate (After rolling)	Rate Sec^{-1}
11	XX		900	36	A.C	7.82
31	XX		900	42	F.C	8.68
32	XX		900	50	F.C	10.06
42	XX		900	26	F.C	6.13
43	XX		900	26	F.C	6.13
52		XX	950	46	F.C	9.23
53		XX	950	44	F.C	9.11
54		XX	950	50	F.C	10.06
62		XX	950	51	F.C	10.35
63		XX	950	48	F.C	9.75

E. Heat Treatment

All specimens were double-heat-treatment annealed (DHTA) by heating in the muffle furnace to 900°C : 910°C and holding for 3hr then furnace cool to 700°C and holding at this temperature for 3 hours and then furnace cool to room temperature.

F. Metallographic Examination

The specimens were prepared for examination first by grinding on different grades of silicon carbide "SiC" papers coarse grinding followed by fine grinding at 180, 240, 320, 400, 600, 800,1000 and 1200 finally polishing was conducted with Alumina powder (3 μm) size. The details of the microstructure were revealed after etching by standard etching solution of the alloy selected. All specimens had to be etched and polished several times to obtain best results and to produce a uniform level of sample examination. The surfaces of the samples before and after rolling and heat treatment were examined using an Olympus optical microscope Model BHM at selected magnification. The details of the microstucture were revealed after etching in 3% nital solution. The etching process was done by emerging the surface of the samples in nital solution. Specimen must be etched and polished several times to obtain best results and produce a uniform level of graphite matrix.

Quantitative Metallography Measurements

A quantitative analysis of the microstructures was produced carried out over four (4) fields across the surface to indicate:

(1) The volume fraction V_f of each phase (count analysis was applied).

Point Fraction (P_p) for a specific phase *a*, is the number of points that lie in the phase *a* per test point. It is calculated through the Point Counting Technique, by dividing the number of intersection points that lie in phase *a* by the total number of intersection points of the grid. We can see this from equations and

$$P_{P_\alpha} = \frac{1}{n^2}\left(\sum_{j=1}^{n}\sum_{i=1}^{n} I_{(\text{Point }(j,i)\,\in\,\text{Phase }\alpha)}\right), \tag{1}$$

$$I_{(\text{Point }(j,\,i)\,\in\,\text{Phase }\alpha)} = \begin{cases} 1 & \text{Point }(j,\ i) \in \text{Phase } \alpha \\ 0 & \text{Otherwise} \end{cases}, \tag{2}$$

where P_{P_α} is the point fraction of phase *a*, *n* is the number of intersection points per row or column, *j*, *i* are the iterators over the row and the column respectively. *I* is Indicator function which evaluates to one if the intersection point (*j*, *i*) is in the phase α.

(2) Average grain size by linear intercept technique.

N_t is the total number of grains in a single phase. It is calculated from equation (3).

$$N_t = N_w + \frac{1}{2}N_i \tag{3}$$

where N_w is the number of grains completely in the field of view of the microscope (within the micrograph) and N_i is the number of grains intercepted by the border of the microscope or the micrograph.

(3) Average particles radius D_A using number of modules per unit area and can calculated as follows:[(118)]

$$D_A = \left(\frac{4V_f}{N_g}\right)^{\frac{1}{2}} \quad (4)$$

N_A is the number of spatial objects per unit area. Its measurement unit is M^{-2}. It is calculated by determining and A_t, which is the total area viewed by the microscope (the area of the micrograph).

$$N_A = \frac{N_t}{A_t} = \frac{1}{\bar{A}} \quad (5)$$

where $\bar{A}$ is the mean area of the grains.

N_L is the number of segments of test line that lie within the phase α per unit length of the test line

L_A, The Lineal Fraction, is the total length of lineal intersections of a test line with the grains of the specified phase α. Lineal Fraction is equivalent to zero, if the line does not intersects with any grain of phase α. It equals one, if the line totally passes in the phase α.

(4) Inter nodule spacing (MFP) by measuring P_L no of particles per unit length and sustain in the equation

$$MFP = \frac{1 - V_f}{P_L} \quad (6)$$

Average Size, $\bar{L}_3$, is the mean intercept length. It represents the average dimension (length) of a collection of grains or particles. It is independent of grain shape. The subscript 3 indicates that this quantity represents volume or three-dimensional value. It is calculated from

$$\bar{L}_3 = \frac{L_L}{N_L} = \frac{\sum_{i=1}^{N}(L_3)}{N} \quad (7)$$

where L_L is the lineal fraction of the grains, N_L is the number of intersection line portions, L_3 is the length of the test line portion, and N is the number of features (grains, or phases).

Equation can be used for both grains and phases. When it is used with grains of a single phase microstructure, $\bar{L}_3$ represents a basic measure of the grain size.

Assume that the number of grains of the same phase is n, and the test line length equals l.

$$\bar{L}_3 = \frac{L_L}{N_L} = \frac{\frac{n}{n}}{\frac{n}{l}} = \frac{l}{n} \tag{8}$$

(5) The shape factor by using equation:

$$S.F. = \frac{2}{3}\left(\frac{P_L}{V_f N_g}\right) \tag{9}$$

V_f volume fraction of secondary phase
N_g average grain size number
D_A Average particles radius
P_L no of particles per unit length
MFP Inter nodule spacing
S.F the shape factor

Metallographic Relations

These are the basic equations and their relations:

$$V_v = A_A = L_L = P_P \tag{10}$$

$$Sv = \frac{4L_A}{\pi} = 2P_L \tag{11}$$

$$L_V = 2P_A \tag{12}$$

$$P_v = \frac{1}{2}L_V S_V = 2P_A P_L$$

Quantities, on the left hand side of equations from (10) to (13), are spatial quantities, which have a high value to calculate and are difficult to calculate on the other hand. Quantities, on the right hand side, can be easily measured from a two dimensional sections of the micrograph. Thus, it can be find out the values of the left hand side quantities.

The following terms were determined according to ASTM E112 :-

1. Average grain size number by linear intercept technique.
2. Average grain diameters using number of modules per unit area
3. Average intercept distance μm
4. Area of average grain section $mm^2 \times 10^{\wedge 6}$
5. Average number of grains per $mm^3 \times 10^{\wedge 6}$
6. Nominal grains per mm^2
7. Nominal grains per mm^2 at 100x

Calculations were carried out in several areas in each specimen investigated at 100x projected on a screen measuring 500 mm^2. The measurement is an average of over five readings for each condition. The scattering value for each specimen was +1%. All calculations were measured around a circle to consider all directions 360°.

It is common to express the grain size by this equation:

$$N = 2^{(n-1)} \tag{14}$$

where: n is the number of grains per square inch at magnification of 100x.

Results and Discussions

A. Microstructures Qualitative Analysis

Figure 7.2 represents the microstructure of heat treated specimens after rolling which divided into two main groups surface specimen and inside specimen.

Heat treatment produce a full ferritic matrix the ferrite grain is elongated in the rolling direction, and also the graphite flattened as the amount of reduction increases. Heat treatment does not eliminate directionality (anisotropy remain) but only decompose the cementite (carbides) which lead to reduce strength and improve ductility and impact properties necessary for machining rolled material into gears.

The ferrite grain size becomes finer with the graphite nodule diameter decreases. When the microstructure is very fine, the inter-granular fracture can be eliminated due to elongation increases with decreasing ferrite grain size.

The above (40%) reduction graphite start to break and the shape ratio of graphite decreases with increase in the reduction percentage because the formation of secondary graphite. Figure 7.2 also shows that above 40%. The ferrite grain size decrease is dropped due to enhance nucleation due to decrease in M.F.P and increases stress concentration.

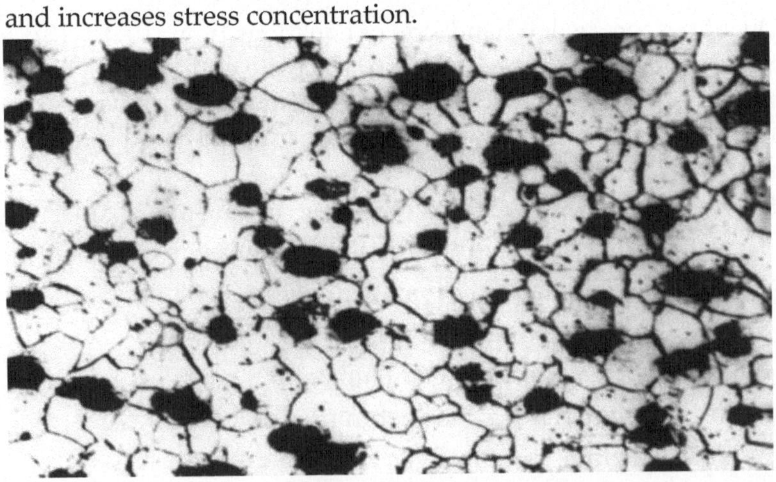

(A) FC, FHT, 26%

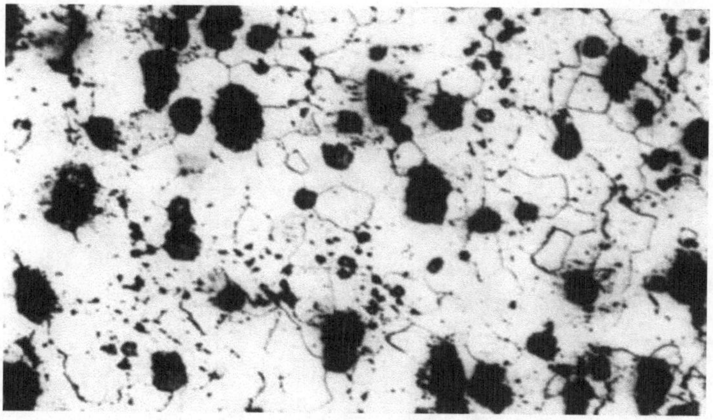

(B) FC, FHT, 50%

A and B Compare between maximum percentage reduction 50% and minimum percentage 26%

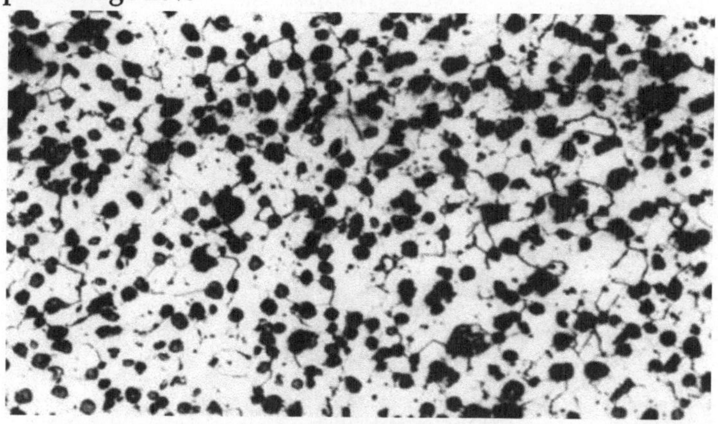

(C) AC, FHT, 36%inside

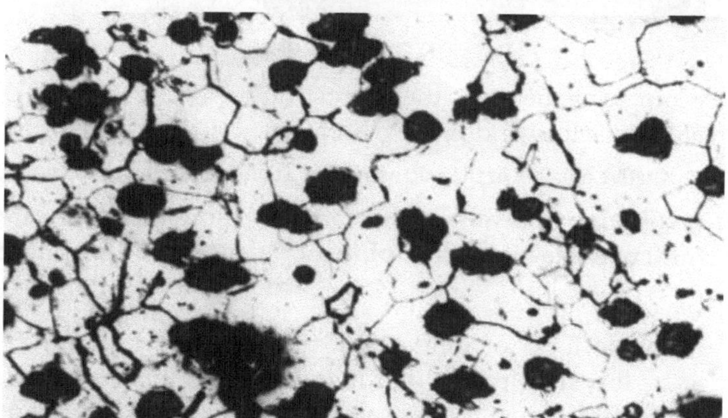

(D) AC, FHT, 36% surface

C& D Comparing between the surface and inside structure for the same sample at the same condition

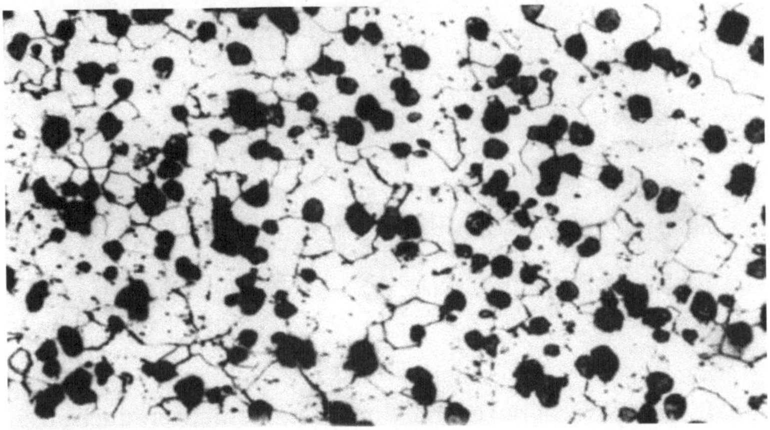

(E) FC, FHT, 42%inside

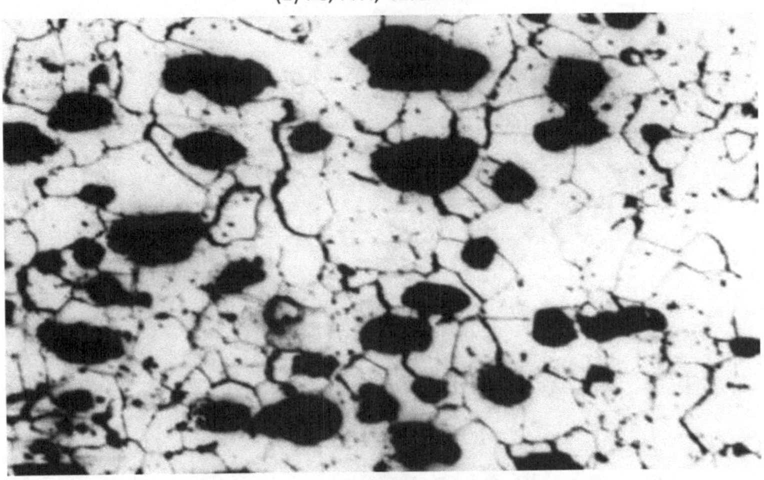

(F) FC,LHT,44%, inside

E& F Comparing between the microstructure changes inside the structure when treated in factory and in the laboratory

Fig. 7.2: Qualitative analysis of the microstructure at different rolling and cooling conditions

The qualitative analysis of the samples show that their are two main constituent ferrite matrix and graphite nodules (secondary phase) :

Graphite

This is the stable form of pure carbon in cast iron. Its important physical properties are low density, low hardness and high thermal conductivity and lubricity. Graphite shape, which can range from flake to spherical, plays a significant role in determining the mechanical properties of cast irons. The figures below show that graphite flakes act like cracks in the iron matrix, while graphite spheroids act like "crack arresters", giving the respective irons dramatically different mechanical properties. Table 7.3 show the quantitative analysis of the graphite (secondary phase) which include the following terms:-

Vv = graphite volume fraction

NA = Number of nodules per unit area

PL = Number of Nodules per unit length

DA = Average graphite diameter (mm)

MFP = Mean free path ledge to edge spacing

Ferrite

This is the purest iron phase in a cast iron. In conventional Ductile Iron ferrite produces lower strength and hardness, but high ductility and toughness. In Aus-tempered Ductile Iron (ADI), extremely fine-grained acicular ferrite provides an exceptional combination of high strength with good ductility and toughness. Table 7.4 shows the quantitative analysis of the ferrite phase which include the following terms:-

Vx = Ferrite volume fraction.

NLT = No of grain in the transverse direction.

NLL = No of grain in the longitudinal.

NL = Average no of grains per unit length.

TL = Measured value in the transverse and longitudinal direction.

Grain size is the most common and important term in the quantitative analysis of any structure, table 7.5 shows the quantitative metallographic terms related to grain size and grain distribution which include the following terms:-

NA = Number of ferrite grains per unit area.

G = Grain size number.

d = Average ferrite grain diameter.

S.F = Shape factor calculated.

Cxx = Intergranular surface ratio.

r_o/r = Ratio between radius of nodules in the longitudinal and transverse direction.

Table 7.3: The Quantitative Measurements Related to Microstructure Analysis of the Graphite (Secondary Phase) at Different Rolling Conditions

No	Vv	NA	DA	PL	MFP
11S	3269	143.02	0.020162	37.6	0.01783
11l	21.32	25.752	0.032897	18.2	0.043711
31S	26.71	950.54	0.019217	34.2	0.02143
31l	23.16	440.19	0.024569	23.6	0.032326

32S	25.64	262.08	0.0363825	17.3	0.042983
32I	108.59	417.39	0.023881	73	0.039396
42S	23.4	494.67	0.024454	24.95	0.030701
42I	23.56	196.56	0.39051	16	0.047775
43S	22.92	313.04	0.030607	19.86	0.038812
43I	21.15	155.3	0.043071	13.96	0.058483
52S	20.35	203.83	0.035614	16.1	0.04947
52I	20.51	359.14	0.027047	21	0.037852
53S	17.63	240.74	0.030452	17.6	0.046801
53I	13.46	235.39	0.026851	17.4	0.049736
54S	18.91	184.43	0.0365	15.77	0.053104
54I	15.89	220.83	0.030638	16.8	0.050065
62S	19.74	399.58	0.024884	22.6	0.035513
62I	19.73	410.1	0.02447	22.85	0.035348
63S	25.41	504.75	0.02548	25.2	0.029599
63I	22.86	417.39	0.02630	23.06	0.033457

Table 7.4: The Quantitative Measurements Related to Microstructure Analysis of the Ferrite (Matrix) at different Rolling Conditions

No	Vx	L	T	NL	NT	NL average
11S	67.31	37.67	24.5	67.49	66.33	66.91
11I	78.68	28.75	18.38	44.06	42.57	43.32
31S	73.29	33.5	23.33	55.12	58.0129	56.57
31I	76.29	30.25	21.13	47.81	50.47	49.14
32S	74.36	28	14.25	45.41	34.92	40.17
32I	81.41	30.13	20.13	44.38	45.06	44.85
42S	76.6	30.75	27.25	48.41	52.93	50.67
42I	76.44	22.5	17	35.49	40.52	38.01
43S	77.08	30.75	22.63	48.11	53.5	50.81
43I	78.85	18.67	14.67	28.55	33.9	31.32
52S	79.65	24.38	19.13	36.91	43.77	40.34
52I	74.49	31	21.5	47.03	49.29	48.16
53S	82.37	22.75	16.88	33.31	37.34	35.33
53I	86.54	27	20.25	37.62	42.64	40.13
54S	81.09	33.98	18	53.51	40.45	37.98

54I	84.11	24	18.13	34.41	39.28	36.85
62S	80.26	36.7	23.8	55.14	54.04	54.59
62I	80.77	32.75	20	48.9	45.12	47.01
63S	74.59	30	21.83	48.5	53.33	50.82
63I	77.14	28.28	20.17	44.68	47.65	46.17

Table 7.5: The Quantitative Measurements Related Grains Size and Grains Distribution at different Rolling Conditions

No	NA	G	d	dr	dl	ro/r	S.F	Cxx
11S	3581.29	7.1	0.31	16	24	1.5	0.8245	0.7807
11I	1500.51	7.6	0.026	28	92.1	1.04	1.2936	0.828
31S	2558.01	8.3	0.020	16	26	1.625	0.9776	0.7679
31I	1930.38	8	0.022	2	35	1.522	1.1593	0.8063
32S	1768.57	7.3	0.029	32.1	47	1.46	0.545	0.8228
32I	1608.82	7.7	0.075	25	39	1.56	1.4467	0.7959
42S	2049.87	8	0.022	24	37	1.542	1.1412	0.8024
42I	1150.73	7.7	0.030	33	50	1.515	1.1731	0.8261
43S	205.11	8	0.022	26	41.3	1.58	1.1665	0.8368
43I	774.28	6.7	0.035	42	62	1.476	1.2591	0.8173
52S	1292.44	7.3	0.079	45	62	1.378	1.3261	0.8336
52I	1854.49	7.8	0.024	26	40	1.538	1.2705	0.8210
53S	995.04	7	0.037	26	41	1.577	1.552	0.8006
53I	1283.29	7.3	0.029	33	50	1.515	2.028	0.8218
54S	1149.1	7.2	0.030	36	55	1.528	1.4188	0.8326
54I	1081.3	7.1	0.031	33	50	1.515	1.7069	0.8144
62S	2383.81	8.2	0.021	25	38	1.57	1.3741	0.8285
62I	1765.09	7.8	0.024	30	45	1.5	1.405	0.8045
63S	2069.2	8	0.022	26	32	1.731	1.0507	0.8016
63I	1703.2	7.8	0.024	26	41	1.577	1.1827	0.8607

From the above determination of the size, shape and distribution of the hot rolled ductile cast Iron samples, the quantitative metallographic of the sample transform description into quantity the most significant factors affect the structure in this study are the rolling condition specially the percentages reduction and the cooling rates. The heat treatment conditions of the experiments have also significant effect, there is significant difference between the foundry heat treated (FHT) and the laboratory heat treated (LHT) samples. Figures 7.3, 7.4 and 7.5 show the effect of rolling percentages on the volume fraction , average graphite diameter and shape factor at different conditions in the study range respectively.

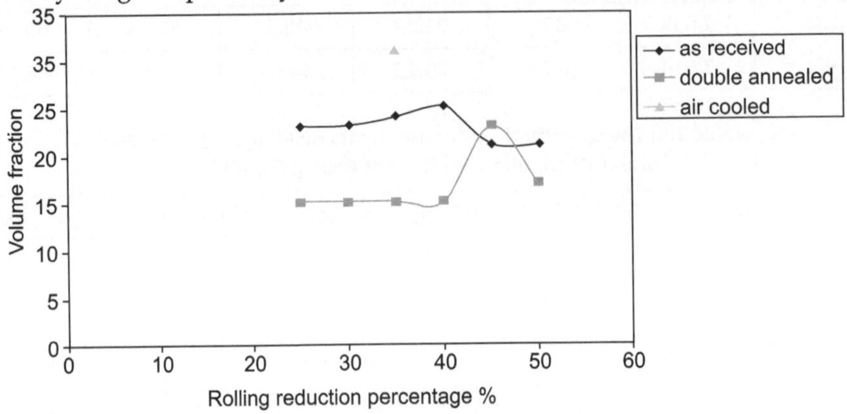

Fig. 7.3: The effect of reduction percentages on volume fraction of secondary phase (graphite) at different conditions

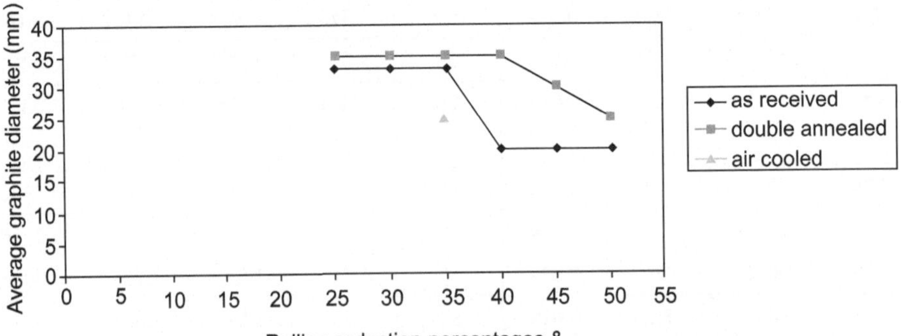

Fig. 7.4: The effect of reduction percentages on average diameter of the secondary phase (graphite) at different conditions

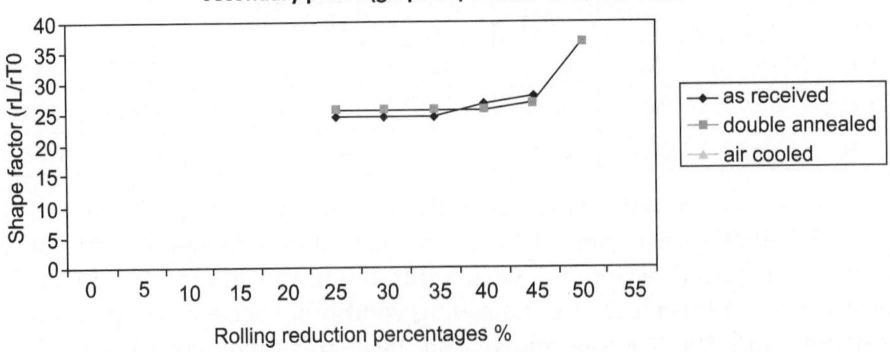

Fig. 7.5: The effect of shape factor of the secondary phase (graphite) at different conditions

All of theses value is the average of 4 photograph of each specimens. For each value determined with scattering not more than + 3%.The ferrite grain size : According to ASTM (7.5 : 7.8). The graphite diameter is vary according ASTM (7.2 : 7.7)

Conclusions

1. Hot rolled ductile cast iron is composite structure with ferrite softer matrix and secondary phase distributed through the matrix
2. Graphite nodules are deformed by hot rolling into lens shaped disks. Noduality increases linearly with the increase of the amount of deformation by rolling.
3. Flattening of graphite nodules were higher at the surface than inside shortness the distance between vicinity of graphite nodules are occured
4. Ferrite grain size was dropped sharply with increasing rolling reduction which may be attributed to enhance of nucleation process.
5. High reduction amount cause the accumulation of deformed graphite
6. The shape factor of graphite in ferrite matrix rolled alloys increases as the amount of reduction increases.
7. Further deformation leads to the fragmentation of graphite and creation of secondary nodular graphite.

REFERENCES

1. Michael, L. He. "Metallographic Interpretation of Steel Forging Defects." Microscopy Society of America, 2007.
2. Kay Geels Kay Geels "Metallographic and Materialographic Specimen Preparation, Light Microscopy, Image Analysis and Hardness Testing", in collaboration with Struers A/S, ASTM International 2006.
3. Metallography and Microstructures, Vol. 9, ASM Handbook, ASM International, Materials Park, OH, 2005.
4. G.F. Vander Voort , Metallography: Principles and Practice, ASM International, Materials Park, OH, 1999.Vol. 03.01 of the ASTM Standards covers standards devoted to metallography (and mechanical property testing)
5. G. Petzow, Metallographic Etching, 2nd Ed., ASM International, 1999.
6. http://en.wikipedia.org/wiki/Adaptive_thresholding
7. http://www.metallography.com/grain.htm.
8. http://www.scirp.org/journal/PaperInformation.aspx?PaperID=29418
9. H. Mohamadzadeh, H. Saghafian and Sh. Kheirandish, "Sliding Wear Behavior of a Grey Cast Iron Surface Remelted by TIG," Journal of Materials Science & Technology, Vol. 25 No. 5, 2009, pp. 622-628.
10. M. A. Shaker, "Note on the Effect of Nodularization Characteristics on the Workability of Quench-Hardened and Tempered Cast Irons," Journal of Materials Processing Technology, Vol. 32, No. 3, 1992, pp. 545-552. doi:10.1016/0924-0136(92)90252-N
11. V. Singh, "Pysical Metallurgy," Standard Publishers, 2005, pp. 459-462. [4] C. Meric, S. Sahin, B. Backir and N. Koksal, "Investigation of the Boronizing Effect on the Abrasive

Wear Behavior in Cast Irons," Materials & Design, Vol. 26, No. 9, 2006, pp. 751-757. doi:10.1016/j.matdes.2005.01.018

12. O. Aponbiede and N. M. Okelekwe "The Effect of Chloride Salts on the Mechanical Properties of Gray Cast Iron," Journal of Emerging Trends in Engineering and Applied Sciences, Vol. 2, 2011, pp. 256-259.
13. K. Edalati, F. Akhlaghi and M. Nili-Ahmadabadi, "In- fluence of SiC and FeSi Addition on the Characteristics of Gray Cast Iron Melts Poured at Different Temperatures," Journal of Materials Processing Technology, Vol. 160 No. 2, 2005, pp. 183-187. doi:10.1016/j.jmatprotec.2004.06.007
14. Bocus S. and Zaldarys G.: "Production of Ductile Iron Casting with Different Matrix Structure", Materials Science (Medziagotyra) Vol. 11, No. 4, Pp 307-310, 2010.
15. Charles .V.W: ASM Handbook, Volume 1, Properties and Selection: Irons, Steels, and High Performance Alloys Section: Cast Irons, 2005.
16. Jezerski J. and Bartocha D.: "Properties of Cast Iron Modifying with Inoculants" Journal of Archieving in Materials and Manufacturing Engineering, Vol. 22. No. 1, pp 25-28, 2007.
17. Bockus S,Zarldarys D,Production of Ductile Iron Casting with different Matrix Microstructure, Material Science, vol 16,No 4 2010
18. Zhou W., Zhu H., Zhang D, Zheng H., Hua Q. and Zhai Q:" Niobium Alloying Effectin High Carbon Equivalent Grey Cast Iron China Foundry Vol. 8., No. 1, Pp. 36-40,2011
19. Agbu S: "The Iron and Steel Industry and Nigeria's Industrialization" Exploring Cooperation with Japan, No 418, Pp. 1-146, 2007.
20. Rivera G.L, Boeri R.E, Sikora J.A," Solidification of Grey Cast Iron", Acta Materialia Inc. Pp 331-335, 2004
21. Alp.T, Yilmaz F. and Wazzan A.A: "Microstructural characteristics-Property relationships in cast irons", the six Saudi engineering conferences, Dhahran, Vol. 5 Pp.281-295, 2002.
22. Seidu S.O, Ogunniyi I.O: "Control of chilling tendency in grey cast iron reuse", Materials Research, Vol.16(1), Pp. 145-149, 2013.
23. Kalinin V. T., KHrychikov V. E., Krivoshev V. A. and Menyando E. V.: "Theory and Practice of Cast Iron Inoculation by Ultra and Nanodispersed Materials" Metallurgical and Mining Industry Vol. 2, No. 5, Pp. 341-347, 2010.
24. ASM Metal Handbook Properties and selection irons, steel, and high-performance alloys (cast Iron), Vol.1 Pp 35-37, 2005
25. ASM Metal Handbook Casting, Vol. 15, Pp.1372-1375, 1988.
26. Krause, D. E.: "Gray Iron-A Unique Engineering Material" Gray, Ductile, and Malleable Iron Castings-Current Capabilities, ASTM STP 455, American Society for Testing and Materials, Philadelphia, Pp. 3-28, 1969.
27. Elkem AS Foundry: "Overview of the Alloying Elements and their Effect in Grey Iron" Technical Information 12A and 12B, No. 3, Pp 1-8, 2011.
28. Pluphrach G.: Study of the Effect of Solidification on Graphite Flakes Microstructure and Mechanical Properties of an ASTM a-48 gray Cast Iron using Steel Molds, Songklanakarin Journal of Science and Technology, Vol.32(6), Pp.613-618, 2010.
29. Dioszegi A, .Fourlakidis.V, Svensson I.L, Microstrocture and Tensile properties of Grey Iron, Research report 04:1 ISSN. 1404-0018, School of Engineering Jonkoping University Sweden, 2004
30. Nakae H, Shin H., Effect of Graphite Morphology on Tensile Properties of Flake Graphite Cast Iron, Materials Transactions, Vol.42, 7,Pg. 1428-1434,2001

8 The Effect of Laser Irradiation on the Mechanical Properties of Ti6Al4VELI

ABSTRACT

In these work, new technique for Laser irradiation of Ti6Al4VELI which is a-b structure was done at room temperature in the normal atmosphere without any external media, the effect of laser irradiation on the Ti6Al4VELI the chemical composition of the alloy before and after laser irradiation were recorded by Energy dispersive X-ray " EDX" technique. The variation in mechanical properties due to laser irradiation at different wavelengths were measured by determination of the variation of modulus and hardness at maximum load with number of pulses. The wear rate was measured for the Ti6Al4VELI before and after laser irradiation at 5000 pulses where the maximum improvement in the hardness occur at all wavelengths in the current study, it improves surface mechanical characteristics. The effect of laser irradiation on the structures was studied by SEM, the quantitative analysis was done at all irradiation conditions. Laser treatment is suitable for both field works and industry. The improvement in mechanical properties occurs due to microstructure changes without significant change in chemical composition. The efficiency and life time of the alloys were increased, it is patent number 24014 in Egyptian patent office.

Keywords: *Surface treatment, Titanium, Mechanical properties, Laser irradiation.*

Introduction

Titanium can exist in two crystal forms. The first is alpha, which has a hexagonal close-packed crystal structure, and the second is beta, which has a body-centered cubic structure[1],[2]. In unalloyed titanium, the alpha phase is stable at all temperatures up to 1620°F (880°C.) where it transforms to the beta phase. This temperature is known as the beta transus temperature.The beta phase is stable from 1620°F. (880°C.) to the melting point[3].

As alloying elements are added to pure titanium, the elements tend to change the temperature at which the phase transformation occurs and the amount of each phase present[4],[5]. Alloy additions to titanium, except tin and zirconium, tend to stabilize either the alpha or the beta phase. Elements called alpha stabilizers stabilize the alpha phase to higher temperatures and beta stabilizers stabilize the beta phase to lower temperatures[6],[7].

The classification of the titanium according to chemical composition means studying the effect of alloying elements on the microstructure[8],[9]. Alloying elements generally can be classified as α and β stabilizers. Alpha stabilizers such as Aluminium and oxygen, increase the temperature at which the α phase is stable. Beta stabilizers such as Vanadium and Molybdenum, result in stability of the β phase at lower temperatures. This transformation temperature from $\alpha + \beta$ or from α to all β is known as the β transus temperature. The β transus is defined as the lowest equilibrium temperature at which the material is 100%β[10],[11].

The β transus is critical in deformation processing and heat treatment. Below the beta β transus temperature, Titanium is a mixture of α+ β if the material contains some β stabilizers; otherwise it is all α if it contains limited or no β stabilizers [12]:[14]. The β transus is important. Because processing and heat treatment often is carried out with reference to some incremental temperature above or below the β transus. Alloying elements that favor the α crystal structure and stabilize it by raising the β transus temperature include Aluminium, gallium, Germanium, Carbon, Oxygen, and Nitrogen[15].

High strength alloys: Ti-6Al-4V Grade 5 is the black horse alloy in various engineering applications due to its light weight and high durability, this alpha-beta alloy is the workhorse alloy of the titanium industry [16],[17]. The alloy is fully heat-treatable in section sizes up to one inch and is used up to approximately 400°C (750°F). Since it is the most commonly used alloy - over 70% of all alloy grades melted are a sub-grade of Ti-6Al-4V - its uses span many aerospace engine and airframe components uses and also major non-aerospace applications in the marine, offshore and power generation industries in particular [18].

The addition of 0.05% palladium, (Grade 24), 0.1% ruthenium (Grade 29) and .05% palladium and 0.5% nickel (Grade 25) significantly increases corrosion resistance in reducing acid chloride and sour environments, raising the threshold temperature for attack to well over 200°C (392°F). Ti-6Al-4V ELI (Grade 23) The essential difference between Ti-6Al-4V ELI (Grade 23) and Ti-6Al-4V (Grade 5) is the reduction of oxygen content to 0.13% max in Grade 23. This confers improved ductility and fracture toughness, with some reduction in strength. Grade 23 has been widely used in fracture critical airframe structures and for offshore tubular[19]. Mechanical properties for fracture critical applications can be enhanced through processing and heat treatment. Grade 29 also having a lowered level of oxygen will deliver similar levels of mechanical properties to Grade 23 according to processing. Grade 23 was used in our study and irradiated by lasers in the normal atmosphere, figure 8.1 **Phase diagram and crystal structure of Ti6Al4VELI**[20],[21].

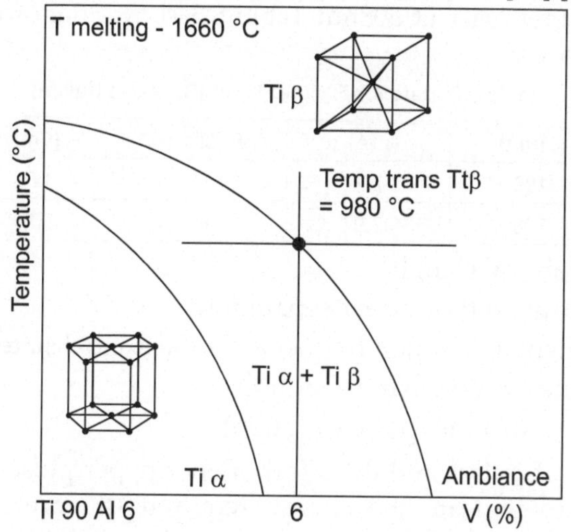

Fig. 8.1: Phase Diagram and Crystal Structure of Ti6Al4VELI[7]

Experimental Work

Materials

The alloys used throughout this work was supplied by Sandvik Co, France in the form of bars of **Ti6Al4VELI**. Table 8.1 shows the chemical composition of the alloy used.

Table 8.1: The Chemical Composition of Ti6Al4VELI (Grade 23)

Type Analysis			
Carbon (Maximum)	0.08%	Titanium	Balance
Aluminium	5.50 to 6.50%	Vanadium	3.50 to 4.50%
Nitrogen (Maximum)	0.05%	Iron (Maximum)	0.25%
Oxygen (Maximum)	0.130%	Hydrogen (Maximum)	0.013%
Other, Total (Maximum)	0.40%		

*Other, Each (Maximum) = 0.1%

**For AMs 4930rev. D, Hydrogen = 0.0125% and Yttrium = 0.005%.

Laser Surface Irradiation

The surface irradiation of the alloys was studied. Samples used in this investigation were in the standard size for every test according to ASTM. All the experiments were performed at room temperature in air at atmospheric pressure; it was shown elsewhere[10] that the presence of air has no measurable influence on the process of irradiation by UV laser[11]. The irradiation is done on one side of the sample and covers all the surface area of the sample. The main goal of this work is optimize condition for laser irradiation of the samples by Excimer laser at 308nm Table 8.3 shows data for used rare gas halide Excimer laser.

Table 8.2: Data for Excimer Laser (Rare Gas Halide)

Gas type	λ (nm)	r (A)	w (Cm^{-1})	σ (Cm^2)	τ (ns)
ArF	193	2.2	–	12	4.2
XeCl	308	2.9	194	50	11

λ = transition wavelength
r(A) = equilibrium inter-nuclear separation
ω = fundamental vibration frequency of the excited state
σ = stimulated emission cross section
τ = radiative life time (pulse duration)

The number of pulses and the effect of energy per pulse on the hardness were recorded to indicate the energy required (fluence) to improve the mechanical properties. In the shape of a rectangle with width (w = 4 mm) and length (l = 10 mm) was used in the laser process the power density ranges from (0.75 W/Cm^2 to 0.1 W/Cm^2) without any focusing. The laser irradiation condition is listed in Table 8.3.

Table 8.3: Laser Irradiation Conditions

Type	Wavelength nm	No. of pulses	Energy per pulse mJ	Repetition rate (Hz)
Excimer	UV 308.6	0, 2000, 5000, 10250, 15000, 50000	6	200
Excimer	UV 193	0, 2000, 5000, 10250, 15000, 50000	6	200

duration time = 6nano second & total energy = energy per pulse*number of pulses.

Excimer laser irradiation is performed directly in the air and without any intermediate media, figure 8.2 shows schematic presentation of the laser irradiation process.

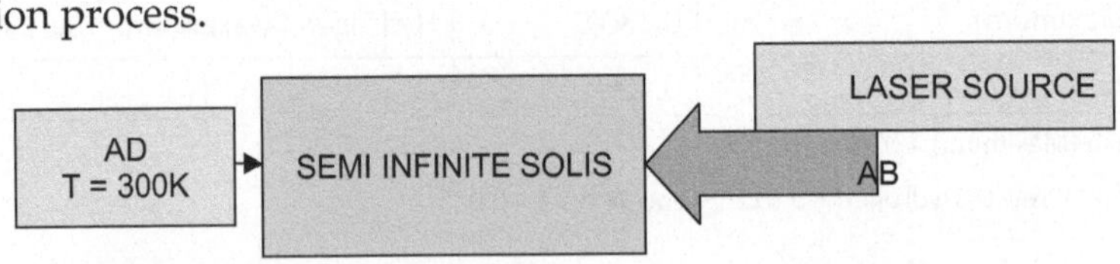

Fig. 8.2: Schematic Presentation of the Laser Irradiation Process

Energy Dispersive X-ray " EDX"

The quantitative method of elemental analysis of the samples has been examined at the Chemical labs of the ministry of Telecommunication in Egypt by SEM JSM-T200 at 25KV acceleration voltage, 20mm working distance, and magnification 200x, (1peak omitted 0.02 KeV). Each value is at least an average of 2 readings

Mechanical Measurements

Superficial Hardness

The hardness of the specimens were measured at the Mechanical Engineering department at AUC by using Superficial Rockwell hardness tester with ball diameter 1/16″ at load 30Kg. Each hardness value is at least an average of 5 readings and they are good to ± 4%.

Wear and Friction Coefficient

A pin-on-disk wear test (ASTM G 99) was selected to measure the wear before and after laser irradiation at El-Nasr Automotive Co in Egypt. A pin with a round tip is positioned perpendicular to a flat disk. A ball, rigidly held is often used as the pin specimen. The test machine rotates the disk at 60 to 600 rpm. The wear path is a circle on the disk surface. Surface finishes of 32 μ in (AA) or less are typically used. Test results are usually reported as volume loss per cubic millimeter for the pin. The test has been done under load of 1Kg. Each value is at least an average of 3 readings.

Scanning Electron Microscope (SEM)

The specimens were examined by scanning electron microscope (SEM) operating at a nominal accelerating voltage of 30kv. Specimen preparation is very simply accomplished by cutting a thin slice of the specimen containing the surface of interest, chemical and electro etching were done at standard conditions, the samples were inserting into the specimen chamber for direct examination of the laser irradiation effects on the structure.

Quantitative Metallography Measurements

A quantitative analysis of the microstructures was produced carried out over four (4) fields across the surface to indicate:

The volume fraction V_f of each phase (count analysis was applied).

Average grain size by linear intercept technique.

Average particles radius D_A using number of modules per unit area and can be calculated as follows:

$$D_A = (4\ V_f / N_g)^{1/2} \quad (1)$$

V_f volume fraction of secondary phase

N_g average grain size number

D_A Average particles radius

Results and Discussion

Energy dispersive X-ray "EDX"

To study the effect of laser irradiation on the Ti6Al4VELI the chemical composition of the alloy before and after laser irradiation were recorded by

Energy dispersive X-ray "EDX" technique. Table 8.4 shows EDX analysis of Ti6Al4VEL samples before and after laser irradiation at optimum conditions, change in chemical composition due to laser irradiation is relatively very small and the slight change in chemical composition does not affect the properties. Figure 8.3a and figure 8.3b show the spectrum of EDX analysis; the distribution relatively unchanged in case of Ti6Al4VELI. The slight change in some elements is due to diffusion of some elements in solid state as a result of laser irradiation and formation of new microstructures. In general laser irradiation does not produce any significant effect in the elemental distribution and no reasonable change in the chemical composition but some elements such as Ba (barium) may immigrate due to diffusion of elements resulting from the ability of this element to absorb laser irradiation at specified wavelengths[10].

Table 8.4: EDX Analysis of Ti6Al4VEL Samples Before and After Laser Irradiation at Optimum Conditions

Element	Before		After	
	Element %	Atomic %	Element %	Atomic %
Ti	72.31	80.53	72.61	80.55
Al	3.52	6.96	3.53	6.94
V	4.75	4.97	4.99	5.21
Ba	19.43	7.55	18.87	7.30

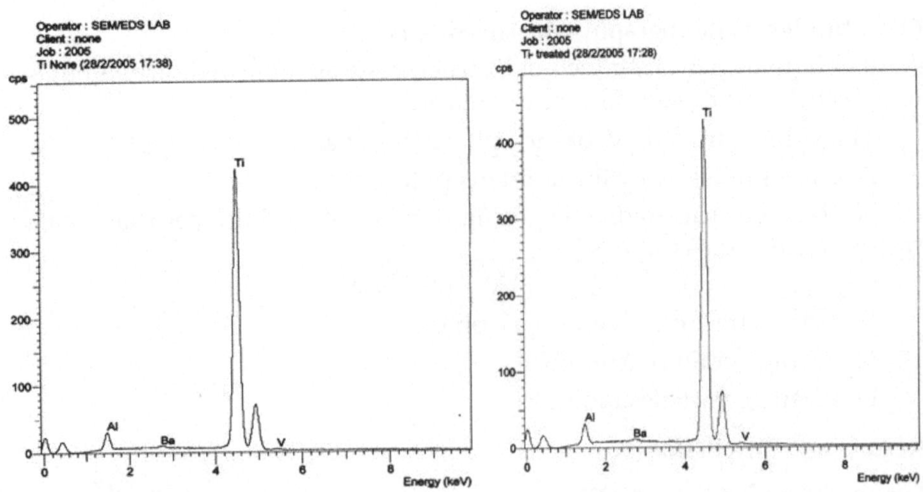

(a) Before laser irradiation (b) After laser irradiation

Fig. 8.3: EDX Energy dispersive x-ray of Ti6Al4VELI

Mechanical Tests

Hardness

The variation in mechanical properties due to laser irradiation at different wavelengths were measured. Figure 8.1 and figure 8.2 show the variation of modulus and hardness at maximum load with number of pulses.

Fig. 8.4 shows the variation of Hardness at maximum load with number of pulses at 308nm, the value of modulus increased until 5000 pulses. The decreasing rate in modulus after 5000 pulses have sinusoidal behavior, while remain constant when the number of pulses were more than 10250 pulses.

The variation of hardness at maximum load with number of pulses at 193nm laser irradiation was shown in Fig. 8.5. The hardness value is increase slightly to reach its maximum value in the range between 5000 and 10250 pulses, after that the hardness was decreased slight with increase in the number of pulses.

When the number of pulses increased the hardness value decreased due to sample burning.

The effect of the number of laser pulses on the hardness of **Ti6Al4VELI** was irradiated at 193nm and 308nm have almost similar behavior. The beam energy at 193nm pulses is larger than the beam energy at 308nm. According to the energy equations and principles, low wavelengths means higher frequency and higher amount of energy absorbed. The improvement at 308nm is better in some points due to change in the grain size and distribution of $\alpha + \beta$ structure which will be explained in terms of microstructure change. The initial microstructure of the irradiated alloy (the room temperature microstructure) plays the significant role in that case. The decrease in hardness of **Ti6Al4VELI** after laser irradiation is due to the formation of higher energy phases but these phases have lower hardness.

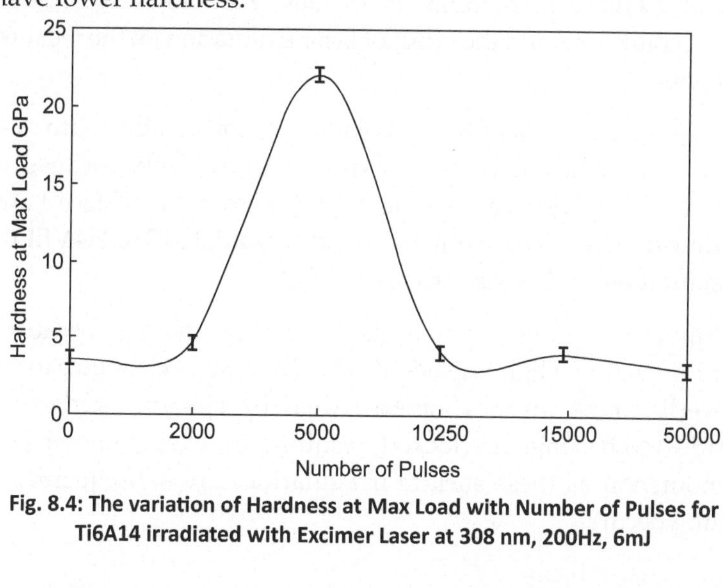

Fig. 8.4: The variation of Hardness at Max Load with Number of Pulses for Ti6A14 irradiated with Excimer Laser at 308 nm, 200Hz, 6mJ

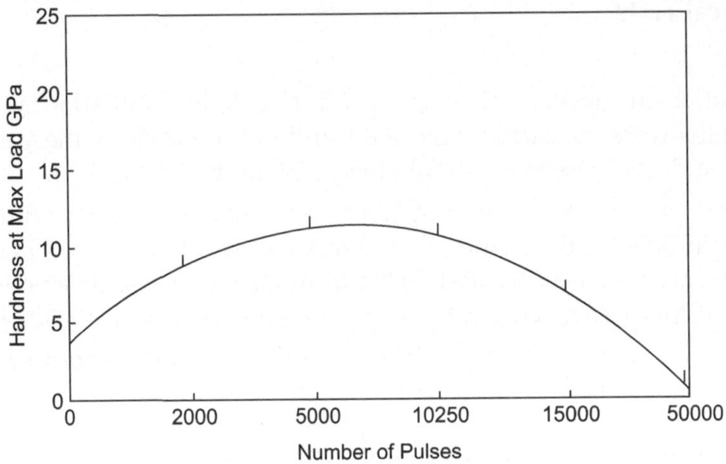

Fig. 8.5: The variation of Hardness at Max Load with Number of Pulses for Ti6Al4VELI irradiated with Excimer laser at 193nm, 200 Hz, 6mJ

Wear Resistances

The wear rate was measured for the **Ti6Al4VELI** before and after laser irradiation at 5000 pulses where the maximum improvement in the hardness occur at all wavelengths in the current study. Increasing the surface load between sliding surfaces has been found to cause a proportional increase in material wear rates.

Increasing the sliding distance of an assembly will cause a roughly proportional increase in material loss. Table 8.4 shows wear variation at constant test conditions and the effect of laser irradiation on the wear resistance improvements.

Wear resistance generally increases proportionally with increasing surface hardness (which may be very different from bulk hardness). Surface deformation during wear causes a localized increase in surface hardness on work-hardened metals. This explains why the irradiated **Ti6Al4VELI** are more wear resistant than un-irradiated **Ti6Al4VELI**.

Very smooth surfaces promote cold welding (galling) because of high molecular interaction. High finishes also lack adequate clearance to store wear debris. Overly rough finishes increase wear by allowing surface asperities (irregularities) to become interlocked, resulting in what is known as a "stick-slip" phenomenon as these surface irregularities are subsequently worn off when sliding occurs.

Table 8.4: Shows the improvement in wear characteristics for Ti6Al4VELI before and after laser irradiation

Materials	Weight before (gm)	Weight after (gm)	Δw (gm)	Wear volume (cm^3)	Wear coeffi-cient	Wear rate (cm^3/mm)	%Impro-vements
Ti6Al14VELI	77.52	77.5	0.02	0.004165	43.9804	2.0835E-7	
Ti6Al4VELI Irradiated	77.7	77.7	0	0	0	0	100%

Scanning Electron Microscope (SEM)

The effect of laser irradiation on the structures was studied by SEM before and after irradiations at 5000 pulses because these value introduce significant improvement in properties. Fig. 8.6 shows SEM of **Ti6Al4VELI** at 2000X before and after laser irradiation by Excimer laser 308nm, 200Hz, 5000 pulses, 6 mJ, (a) Before irradiation and (b) After irradiation, the qualitative analysis of the samples show significant increase in the grain size due to laser irradiation.

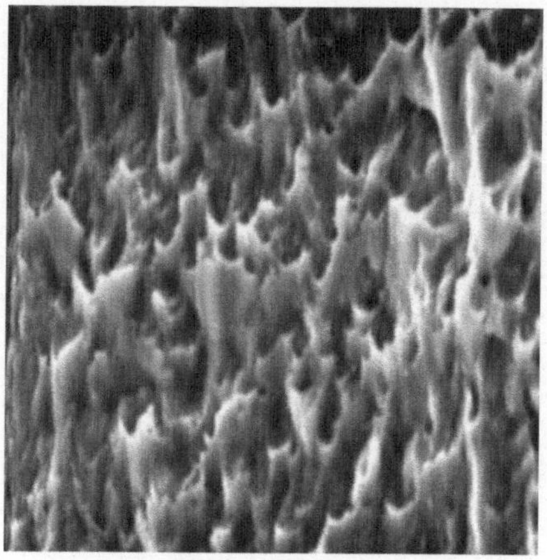

(a) Before laser irradiation

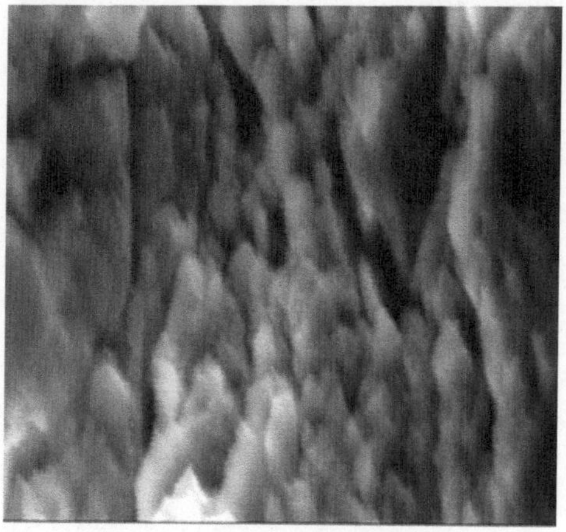

(b) After Laser irradiation

Fig. 8.6: SEM of Ti6Al4VELI at 2000X before and after laser irradiation by Excimer laser 308nm, 200Hz, 5000 pulses, 6 mJ

Qualitative analysis for the samples grain size at all number of pulses in the study range, all micro grain size measurements were calculated according to ASTM standard, grain size number, average diameter of the grain, average intercept distance, average number of the grains per unit and average number of the grains per unit volume and nominal grain at standard magnification were evaluated before and after laser irradiation at different number of pulses as shown in table 8.5.

The relation between the grain size number and average grain diameter as function of the number of pulses were plotted in figure 8.7 and 8.8 respectively. the grain size number decreased while average grain size increased gradually with increase in the amount of laser energy photons absorbed and reach maximum size of the grains at 5000 pulses, when the number of pulses increased over 5000 pulses the average grain size decreased due to the effect of secondary phase as shown in figure 8.1. β phase have BCC structure and less grain size than a structure which is HCP structure.

Table 8.5: The Qualitative Analysis of Samples before and after Laser Irradiation

Micro-grain size measurements	Before irradiation	2000 pulse	5000 pulse	15000 and 10250 and 5000 pulse
ASTM grain size number	10	9.5	7.5	10
Diameter of average grain mm	11	13	27	11
Average intercept distance mm	10	11.9	23.8	10
Area of average grain section $mm^2 \times 10^{-6}$	126	178	0.713×10^{-3}	126
Average number of grains per $mm^3 \times 10^{-6}$	0.566	0.336	0.029630	0.566
Nominal grain per mm^2	7940	5610	1111	7940
Nominal grain per mm^2 at 100x	512-645	362	71.68	512-645

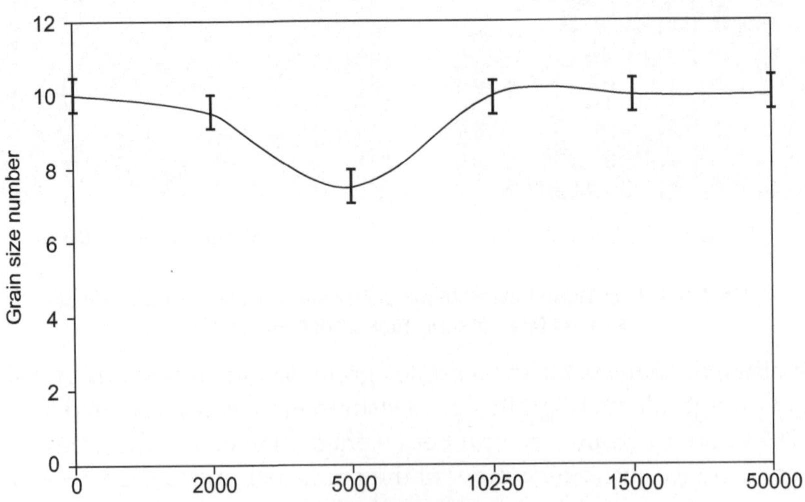

Fig. 8.7: The relation between Number of Pulses and Grain size Number for Ti6A14VELI irradiated by 308 nm, 6mJ, 200 Hz

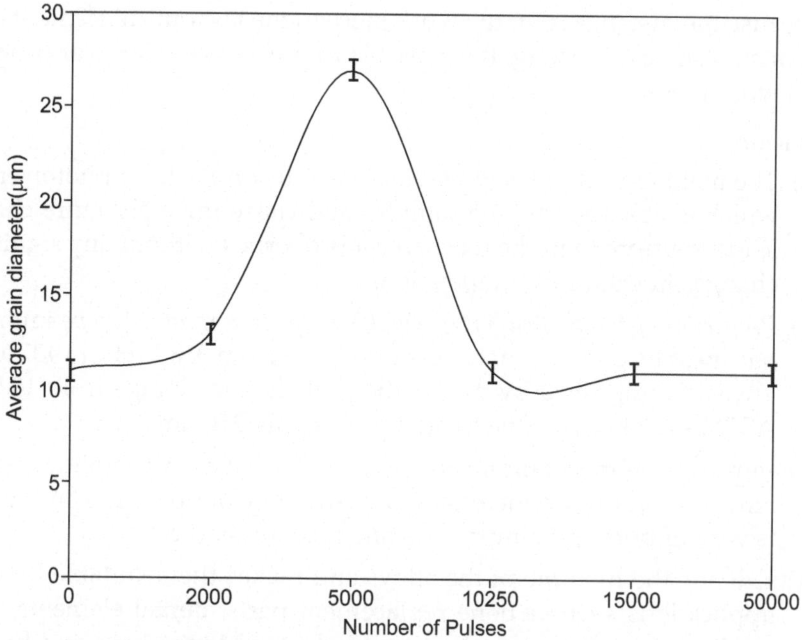

Fig. 8.8: The relation between Number of Pulses and Average Diameter of the Grain (mm) for Ti6A14VELI irradiated by 308 mm, 6mJ, 200 Hz

Comparing Laser Treatment with Conventional Methods

Commercially pure titanium and many alloys generally have a limited response to heat treatment and work hardening; strength and surface hardness can be obtained from the heat treatable meta-stable beta alloys but compressive surface treatment such as solution treated, annealing and aging is normally beneficial, but surface treatment is normally beneficial for the various reasons given over, table 8.6 indicates the extent to which typical alloy Ti6Al4VELI will respond to heat treatment.

Table 8.6: The treatment of Ti6Al4V Grade 5 by conventional methods [18]

Alloy	Heat Treatment	Annealed or solution treated hardness HV	Heat treated and aged hardness HV	Comment
Grade 5	750°C 1 hr WQ	275-300	350-400	Limited in effect with sections above 20 mm
Ti-6Al-4V	500°C 2 hrs. AC			

Ti6Al4VELI is the black horse alloy in the modern engineering industries, the major advantages of laser surface hardening include close control of the power input comparing with conventional methods; the high power density provided by the laser, which in turn maximize the total energy input and, the ability of the laser to reach normally inaccessible areas on the work-piece surface. Because no vacuum or protective atmosphere enclosure is needed, and because the distance from the work piece to the last optical element of the laser system can be quite long. It is possible to process very large or irregular-shaped work pieces.

Conclusion

(a) The main idea of the new method depends on the laser photon energy which is absorbed by the samples and cause microstructure changes leads to improve in the mechanical properties without any significant changes in chemical composition.

(b) *Properties of the treated* **Ti6Al4VELI** *alloys was recorded to be* improved hardness by 36% (the hardness improved from 318 MHV to 437 MHV) – wear is improved by 99.8%- the particle size change from 10 to 7.5 ASTM - thickness of the treated part is only 250 nm.

(c) Improve the mechanical properties of the **Ti6Al4VELI** alloys such as hardness and wear, increasing the efficiency of operation and lifetime is very important to improve economical feasibility.

(d) Extends the life time of the alloys and makes them suitable for many applications such as bone replacement parts, dental elements, space applications, marine applications, industrial spare parts and Increase the efficiency of surgical instruments.

(e) The new treatment method makes **Ti6Al4VELI** *alloys suitable for* Applications require long periods of operation and maintain the dimensions stability.

(f) Ti6Al4V is the black horse alloy in various engineering applications due to its light weight and high durability, the new method is addressing of the alloys and overcome the problems of relatively high prices.

(g) The new laser treatment technique has the following *industrial features comparing with conventional methods*:-

   (i) Processing is performed directly in the air and without any intermediate liquid or gas.

   (ii) New method does not use expensive chemicals such as surface coverage.

   (iii) New methods does not include any complex interactions, hazardous wastes or harmful gases may affect environment.

   (iv) Laser treatment process is relatively economic. It does not need a huge industrial equipment in a great place for the installation and operation of such equipment.

   (v) The main components in the new method are only the laser source and optical parts,it is considered as the only surface treatment method is done in the field.

REFERENCES

1. E. D'Anna, G. Leggieri, A. Luches, M. Martino, S. Luby, I. N. Mihailescu: Pulsed Laser Synthesis Of Titanium Silicides and Nitrides, Laser Assisted Processing SPIE. 1022 (1988) 130-135
2. V. Craciun, I. N. Mihailescu, I. Ursu, F. Craciunoiu, A. Corici, G. Leggieri, A. Luches, V. Nassisi, M. Martino: Multi-layer Metallization Structures with Titanium Nitride and Titanium Silicate Prepared By Multipulse Laser Irradiation, Applied Physics Letters 52 (1988) 1225-1227
3. I. Ursu, V. Craciun, I. N. Mihailescu, L. C. Nistor, A. Popa, V. S. Teodorescu, A. Luches, V. Nassisi, M. Martino, F. Cracinoiu, A. Corici, A. Andrei, G. Semenescu, G. Onicioiu: Diffusion Barrier With TiN/TiSi2 Prepared By Multi-Pulse Excimer Laser Irradiation, New Laser Technologies And Applications, Olympia, Editrice Compositor Bologna (1988) 195-203
4. E. D'Anna, G. Leggieri, A. Luches, G. Majni, M. Martino, P. Mengucci, I. N. Mihailescu: Multipulse Laser Synthesis of Metal Silicates, High Power Lasers and Laser Machining Technology SPIE 1132 (1989) 120-127
5. I. Ursu, I. N. Mihailescu, V. Craciun, A. M. Prokhorov, V. I. Konov, V. G. Ralchenko, S. A. Uglov, A. Luches, M. Martino, G. Leggieri, A. V. Drigo: Laser Scanning Synthesis of Surface Compound by Irradiation of Metals And Semiconductors in Chemically-Active Gases, Ernst Abbe Conf. On Optics Eac Jena (1989) 257-269
6. V. Craciun, G. Leggieri, A. Luches, M. Martino, I. N. Mihailescu, I. Ursu: Synthesis of Metallic And Semiconductor Nitrides By Multipulse Laser Irradiation of Solid Samples In Ambient Gases, Applied Surface Science 43 (1989) 304-307
7. V. Craciun, A. V. Drigo, G. Leggieri, A. Luches, M. Martino, I. N. Mihailescu, I. Ursu: Nitride Synthesis with UV-Pulsed Lasers: Applications in Microelectronics and Metallurgy, Energy Pulse and Particle Beam Modification of Materials, K. Hohmuth And E. Richter Eds., Dresden (1990) 57-65
8. E. Deanna, G. Leggieri, A. Luches, M. Martino, A. Perrone, A. V. Drigo, J. Zemek, I. N. Mihailescu: Nitride Layer Formation by Multipulse Excimer Laser Irradiation of Solid Samples, Laser Assisted Processing II SPIE 1279 (1990) 182-194
9. E. Deanna, G. Leggieri, A. Luches, M. Martino, Materials Processing with Pulsed Electron Beam, High Energy Density Technology in Materials Science, F. Garbassi and E. Occhiello Eds. , Kluwer Academic Publishers (1990) 89-103
10. V. Craciun, I. N. Mihailescu, Gh. Oncioiu, A. Luches, M. Martino, V. Nassisi, E. Radiotis, A. V. Drigo, S. Ganatsios: Direct Oxinitride Synthesis By Multipulse Excimer Laser Irradiation Of Silicon Wafer In Nitrogen Containing Ambient Environment, Journal of Applied Physics 68(5) (1990) 2509-2511.
11. V. Craciun, G. Leggieri, A. Luches, M. Martino, I. N. Mihailescu, E. Radiotis, I. Ursu: One-Step Surface Implantation and Reaction by Laser Irradiation of Multi-Structures Deposited On Si and Ge Samples, Vacuum 41 (1990) 912-914
12. E. D'Anna, A. V. Drigo, G. Leggieri, A. Luches, M. Martino, P. Mengucci, I. N. Mihailescu, A. Perrone, J. Zemek: Silicon Nitride Synthesis by Multipulse Laser Irradiation, Vuoto XX(2) (1990) 430-434
13. E. D'Anna, G. Leggieri, A. Luches, M. Martino, A. V. Drigo, G. Majni, P. Mengucci, I. N. Mihailescu: Nitridation of Titanium by Multipulse Excimer Laser Irradiation Applied Surface Science 46 (1990) 365-370

14. E. D'Anna, G. Leggieri, A. Luches, M. Martino, A. Perrone, G. Majni, P. Mengucci, A. V. Drigo, I. N. Mihailescu: Surface Nitride Synthesis By Multipulse Excimer Laser irradiation, Excimer Lasers And Applications III, SPIE 1503 (1991) 256-268
15. E. Deanna, G. Leggieri, A. Luches, M. Martino, P. Mengucci, I. N. Mihailescu: Synthesis Of Pure Titanium Nitride Layers By Multipulse Excimer Laser Irradiation, Quantum Electronics And Plasma Physics G. C. Righini Ed. (1991) 175-181
16. E. Deanna, M. L. De Giorgi, A. Luches, M. Martino, V. Craciun, I. N. Mihailescu, P. Mengucci: Titanium Nitride Titanium Silicate Structures Obtained by Multipulse Excimer Laser Irradiation, Laser Micro technology and Laser Diagnostics of Surfaces. I. Korotev and V. Y. Panchenko Eds. SPIE 1723 (1991) 14-20
17. V. Craciun, I. N. Mihailescu, G. N. Mihailova, A. S. Seferov, M. Bertolotti, A. Ferrari, A. Luches, G. Leggieri, M. Martino: Direct Laser Doping of Various Materials, Laser Micro technology and Laser Diagnostics of Surfaces SPIE 1723 (1991) 83-87
18. E. D'Anna, G. Leggieri, A. Luches, M. Martino, A. V. Drigo, I. N. Mihailescu, S. Ganatsios: Synthesis of Pure Titanium Nitride Layers by Multi-Pulse Excimer Laser Irradiation of Titanium Foils in A Nitrogen Containing Atmosphere, Journal of Applied Physics 69(3) (1991) 1687-1695
19. I. N. Mihailescu, V. Craciun, L. C. Nistor, V. S. Teodorescu, E. D'Anna, G. Leggieri, A. Luches, M. Martino, A. Perrone, A. V. Drigo, S. Ganatsios, J. Zemek: Direct Nitridation of Si Surface by Multi-Pulse Excimer Laser Irradiation in A Nitrogen Containing Ambient Gas, Journal of Applied Physics 70 (1991) 2123-2131
20. E. D'Anna, G. Leggieri, M. Martino, P. Mengucci, I. N. Mihailescu, J. Zemek: Surface Nitridation By Multipulse Excimer Laser Irradiation, Progress on Surface Science 35 (1990) 129-142
21. E. D'Anna, M. L. De Giorgi, G. Leggieri, S. Luby, A. Luches, M. Martino, P. Mengucci, I. N. Mihailescu: Surface Nitridation of Titanium by Direct Laser Irradiation, Laser Advanced Materials Processing (1992) 867-872.
22. Hebatalrahman, Patent Number 24014 in Egyptian Patent Office.

9

A New Method for Fabrication and Laser Treatment of Nano-Composites

ABSTRACT

A new method for manufacturing of nano-composites was invented; a new technique calls Composite material machine with four strokes was established. Composite material machine is a machine for manufacturing of both plastic and metals matrix composites independent on size, type, and volume fraction of fillers. The machine works in four strokes, each of which worked separately. It depends on the material. The four stokes can be controlled to work in schedule controlled by the main control unit connected to the computer, the machine also work manually. The final products were treated by laser irradiation to improve mechanical properties without any significant change in composition. The new technique is cheap, qualified and simple design. The technique was full automated and has been transferred to industry successfully.

***Keywords**: Fabrication, parameters, nanocomposite, laser irradiation, nano-particles, reinforcement.*

Introduction

Nanocomposites are materials that are created by introducing nanoparticulates (often referred to as *filler*) into a macroscopic sample material (often referred to as *the matrix*). This is part of the growing field of nanotechnology[1, 2]. After adding nanoparticulates to the matrix material, the resulting nanocomposite may exhibit drastically enhanced properties. For example, adding carbon nanotubes tends to drastically add to the electrical and thermal conductivity. Other kinds of nanoparticulates may result in enhanced optical properties, dielectric properties or mechanical properties such as stiffness and strength[3]. In general, the nano-substance is dispersed into the matrix during processing[3]. The percentage by weight (called *mass fraction*) of the nano-particulates introduced is able to remain very low (on the order of 0.5% to 5%) due to the incredibly high surface area to volume ratio of nanoparticulates. Much research is going into developing more efficient combinations of matrix and filler materials and into better controlling the production process[4, 5].

Historical Background

A. Applications of Nano-composite Materials

An important use of nano-particles and nano-tubes is in composites, materials that combine one or more separate components and which are designed to exhibit overall the best properties of each component. This multi-functionality applies not only to mechanical properties, but extends to optical, electrical and magnetic ones[6, 7]. Currently, carbon fibres and bundles of multi-walled CNTs are used in polymers to control or enhance conductivity, with applications such as antistatic packaging. The use of individual CNTs in composites is a potential long-term application. A particular type of nano-composite is where nano-particles act as fillers in a matrix; for example, carbon black used as a filler to reinforce car tyres. However, particles of carbon black can range from tens to hundreds of nanometres in size, so not all carbon black falls within our definition of nano-particles [8-10].

B. Laser Method

In 1996 CNTs were first synthesized using a dual-pulsed laser and achieved yields of >70wt% purity. Samples were prepared by laser vaporization of graphite rods with a 50:50 catalyst mixture of Cobalt and Nickel at 1200°C in flowing argon, followed by heat treatment in a vacuum at 1000°C to remove the C60 and other fullerenes. The initial laser vaporization pulse was followed by a second pulse to vaporize the target more uniformly[11]. The use of two successive laser pulses minimizes the amount of carbon deposited as soot. The second laser pulse breaks up the larger particles ablated by the first one, and feeds them into the growing nano-tube structure. The material produced by this method appears as a mat of "ropes", 10-20nm in diameter and up to 100μm or more in length. Each rope is found to consist primarily of a bundle of single walled nano-tubes, aligned along a common axis. By varying the growth temperature, the catalyst composition, and other process parameters, the average nano-tube diameter and size distribution can be varied. Arc-discharge and laser vaporization are currently the principal methods for obtaining small quantities of high quality CNTs. However, both methods suffer from drawbacks. The first is that both methods involve evaporating the carbon source, so it has been unclear how to scale up production to the industrial level using these approaches. The second issue relates to the fact that vaporization methods grow CNTs in highly tangled forms, mixed with unwanted forms of carbon and/or metal species. The CNTs thus produced are difficult to purify, manipulate, and assemble for building nanotube-device architectures for practical applications[12-14].

EXPERIMENTAL STUDY

(a) The System Descriptions

When the four stroke composite material machine is describe, it is not only machine for manufacturing of composites but it is a complete system for manufacturing include grinding of raw materials, addition of additive, mixing and manufacturing in four steps. The manufacturing parameters are indicated as temperature, Pressure, cooling rate, and time of application of force. Fig. 9.1 shows the main steps of manufacturing.

The unit Dimensions = Height 4.5m-* width 5m *length 7m

The machine operations follow the following steps:-

1. Grinding to prepare raw materials in nano-size
2. The nano-size particles moves on the belt to add additive and other reinforcement
3. All components was mixed in a multi-speed mixer
4. The powder mixture was added to the iron mold
5. The mold was heated and treated with lubrication before mixture added
6. The manufacturing cycle work in four steps heating, Pressing, cooling and extraction of final products
7. The electronic arm moves mold and mixture away from heaters to the cooling path and vise verse
8. The control unit was adjusted to control both manufacturing parameters and movement of the electronic arm.

Fig. 9.2 shows the workshop design and Fig. 9.3 shows the main parts of the four stroke composite material system. The system design was simple and abundant to be suitable for small investment and youth projects. The system is suitable for plastic matrix composite, metal matrix composite, powder metallurgy, recycling of powder waste and fabrication of thermoplastics and thermosets.

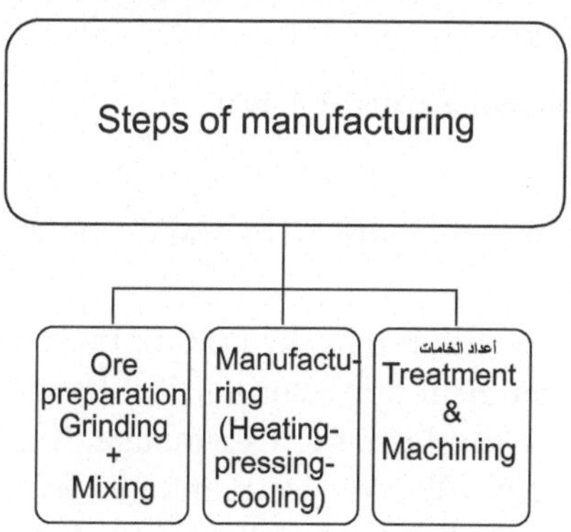

Fig. 9.1: Steps of Manufacturing

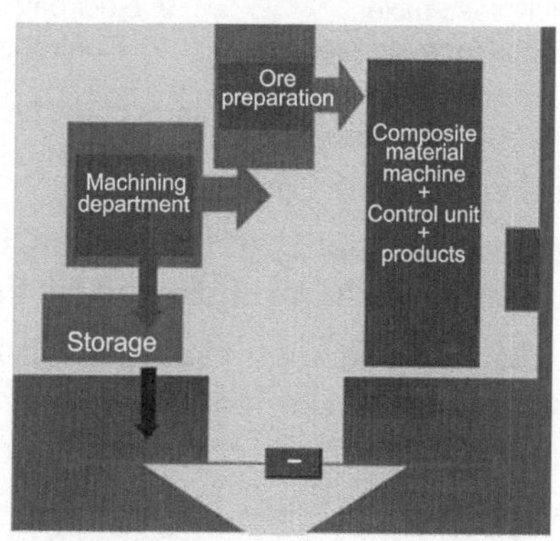

Fig. 9.2: The Workshop Design

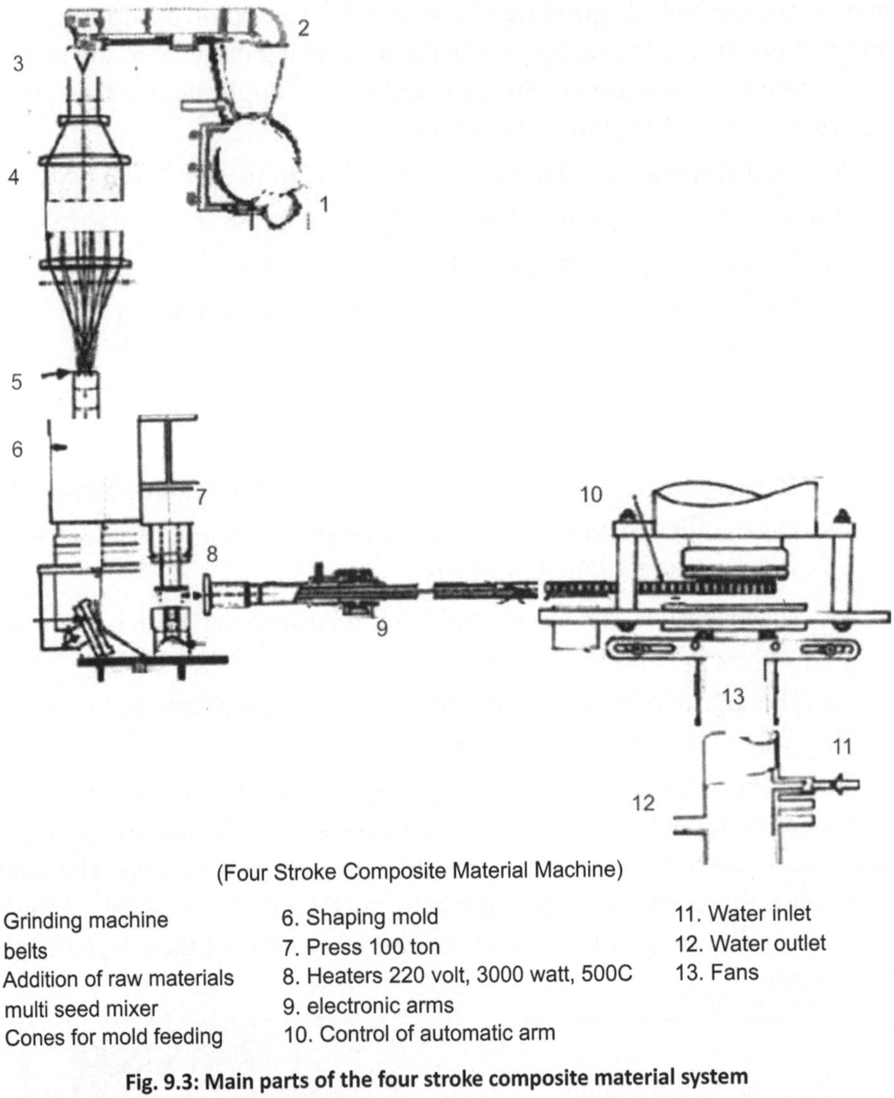

(Four Stroke Composite Material Machine)

1. Grinding machine
2. belts
3. Addition of raw materials
4. multi seed mixer
5. Cones for mold feeding
6. Shaping mold
7. Press 100 ton
8. Heaters 220 volt, 3000 watt, 500C
9. electronic arms
10. Control of automatic arm
11. Water inlet
12. Water outlet
13. Fans

Fig. 9.3: Main parts of the four stroke composite material system

(b) Fabrication of Composite

To prove the quality of the system, it was used to prepare FRP (plastic matrix composite) PMMA reinforced by fiber glass.

PMMA (poly methyl metha acrylate) are Considered as the material which have the best biocompatibility to be used in medical applications, but have a lot of disadvantages such as low hardness, low strength, high shrinkage, high water absorption and low thermal conductivity. These disadvantages have already overcome by making composite material consists of PMMA (poly methyl metha acrylate) as matrix and use fibre glass type E as reinforcement.

Type E fibre glass has a lot of characteristics because it is cheap, abundant and effective to overcome the disadvantages. Fibre glass was used in Volume fractions (zero %, 17 %, 35%, 50%, 65%) and the length to diameter ratio were (L/D = 1) (L/D=50). The manufacturing quality parameters are indicated as temperature, pressure, time of application of force and cooling rate. The material is treated using two different types of lasers such as Argon — ion laser with wavelength 514. 5nm and Nd — YAG with 355nmwavelength(third harmonic generation).

(c) Material Preparation

The material prepared by grinding and mixing for PMMA in the powder form which have diameter less than 100μm with short fibre type E-fibre glass which is mechanically cut to certain sizes. The fibre size which is recorded by length to diameter ratio L/d=50 Ownes Corning Co, 731ED 1/32" was chosen. The mixing of fibre with PMMA is done with certain volume fractions as mentioned above.

(d) Determination of Manufacturing Parameters

The manufacturing parameters were adjusted and the effect of temperature, pressure and cooling rates were recorded. Design and test of the new system were evaluated. The nano- composite material consists of poly methyl metha acrylate as matrix reinforced with fibre glasses as filler

The manufacturing steps may be summarized in the following steps:-

1. Grinding of PMMA by electrical blinder-and control the grinding time to be less than 1.5 min to avoid temperature rise and agglomeration of particles after that use mesh ≤ 300μm diameter for sieving.
2. Short fibre have used in powder form.
3. Mixing of the two powders.
4. Heating the mold.
5. Compress the mixture with (5:10 ton) hydraulic system.
6. Cooling the mold with water JET.

(e) Laser Irradiation

Samples used in this investigation were in a shape of disk of 25mm diameter and 7mm length. The irradiation is done on both sides of the samples and in different positions to cover all the area of the sample and achieve homogeneous surface suitable for testing. The different lasers irradiated samples at different conditions were examined before and after laser irradiation and the effect of laser was determined.

The type of laser used is Nd-YAG I used in the third harmonic (wavelength =355nm) which lies in the ultra violet (UV) region with power of bout 10milli watt, duration time 7nsec,repettion rate 17HZ and energy (40mmj/pulse) [6].

(f) Microscopic Examination

All specimens were prepared metallographically first by grinding on different grades of silicon carbide "SiC" paper coarse grinding and then fine grinding. The process had to be repeated several times to obtain best results and to produce uniform level of matrix. All of these pictures were carried out in several areas in each specimen by making negative at 500x by Olympus optical microscope

(g) Raman Spectroscopy

The behaviour of the material was studied by variation of the modes obtained from FT (IR) Raman spectrum. The results were obtained using Brucker FTIR Raman spectrometer using Nd-YAG laser power of 500MW as source of excitation. After irradiation the thin film of sample with different lasers, the spectra were obtained in the range 400 to 4000 cm^{-1}. The samples to be measured was fixed to holder and placed in front of the beam.[7]

Results and Discussions

(a) Fabrication Procedures

The fabrication quality parameters are indicated as follow:

1. Maximum fibre percentages to achieve success fabrication were (65%) increasing the fibre percentage up on this value will produce less qualified fabricated material.
2. Temperature is the most significant parameter in Fabrication. Over heating temperatures at all fibre percentage leads to dissociation of PMMA to monomers and different gases. As a result of low fabrication temperatures, viscosity becomes insufficient for deformation so the optimal deformation temperature is required to get viscous matrix suitable for addition of reinforcement.
3. The pressure required for deformation and time of force act were strong functions of both volume fraction and fibre percentages.
4. The fast cooling rate (water cool) may be recommended as the suitable Cooling rate regardless of fibre percentage and volume fraction.
5. The density of nano-composites will not be affected by laser irradiation.
6. Laser irradiation is used to improve the surface properties of the material as follow:

   A. The hardness will improved from (43 to 63) barcoul about (50%) when the exposure time increase from 21 nano second to 70 nano second and after that the hardness remain constant with increasing time.

B. The hardness improved with increasing fibre percentages and the maximum value was (60 Barcoul) at L/D = 1 and volume fraction 50%. This improvement increase with laser irradiation and reach its maximum at (80 Barcoul) with argon - ion laser at L/D =50 and volume fraction 50%.

C. The wear rate is improved with fibre percentage to reach (3.8m/m) at L/D = 50 and volume fraction 50%.

9. The wear rate and coefficient of friction were improved more with laser irradiation to reach 0.4m/m wear rate and 0.75 coefficient of fraction at argon irradiation (L/D =50 and volume fraction 50%)

10. Alkali resistance is excellent before and after laser irradiation and weight loss is less than 0.01% at exposure time more than 30000 hours

All of the above tests were done according to standard methods ASTM[3-7].

(b) Microstructure Analysis

The reinforcement strength to weight ratio and volume fraction have a significant effect on the manufacturing conditions and mechanical properties. Fig 9.4a and fig 9.4b show the microstructure of nano-composites when the length to diameter ratio equal 50, the fiber volume fraction is 17% and 50% respectively, fibers were distributed in random manner in the structure and cross linked together in different positions, this distribution prevents the crack propagation. In other words, the crack does not reach the critical size. Cross linking of reinforcement in the matrix is the main reason of improvement in the mechanical properties. When the volume fraction of fibers increased to 50%, the cross linking of fibers were increased, the crack propagation became very limited. The mechanical properties were improved as a result of increase in fiber volume fraction. In fig 9.4c and fig 9.4d show the microstructure of nano-composites when the length to diameter ratio equal 1, the fiber volume fraction is 17% and 50% respectively. When the fiber shape was circular the cross linking was relatively limited, when compared with the fibers in fig. 9.4a, that is the main reason for extra improvement in mechanical properties when the fiber size (length to diameter ratio) increased at the same volume fraction. When comparing fig 9.4d with both figure 9.4a and 9.4b, the random distribution of particles with high volume fraction 50% improves the mechanical properties and crack propagation theme better than fig 9.4c. The amount of cross linking was still lower than both fig 9.4a and fig 9.4b. The qualitative analysis of the microstructure of nano-composite explains the improvement in mechanical properties in terms of fiber shape, size and volume fraction. The laser irradiation effect was not detected by optical microscope so spectroscopic analyses of the samples were done.

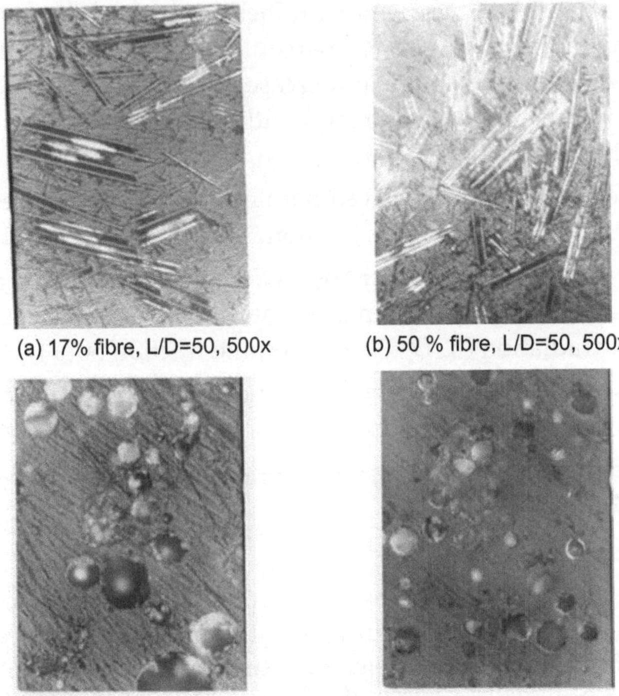

(a) 17% fibre, L/D=50, 500x
(b) 50 % fibre, L/D=50, 500x
(c) 17% fibre, L/D=1, 500x
(d) 50 % fibre, L/D=1, 500x

Fig. 9.4: The fibre impeded into the matrix before laser irradiation at 500x and at different percentages of fibres

(c) Raman Spectroscopy

Laser irradiation was a very good method for treatment of nano-composite without any change in morphology of the samples surface. Fig. 9.5 Raman spectrum of the nano-composite at different length to diameter ratio and different volume fractions before and after laser irradiation by Nd-YAG and Argon lasers. The spectrum was affect by laser type volume fraction of fiber, fiber shape and length to diameter ratio (fiber size). In quantitative analysis of the IR spectrum of the material each absorption band is characterized by four parameters

1. Band shape F(x)
2. Intensity of the band (integral intensity rather than peak depth)
3. Half band width of the band (the width of the band at its half depth)
4. The centre of mass of the band.

The complex behaviour reflecting two regions of dependence on the characteristics of lasers, which might be related to the structure changes and introduce the parameters characterizing the vibration motion of the vibrating groups such as the vibration activation energy in certain vibration energy levels.

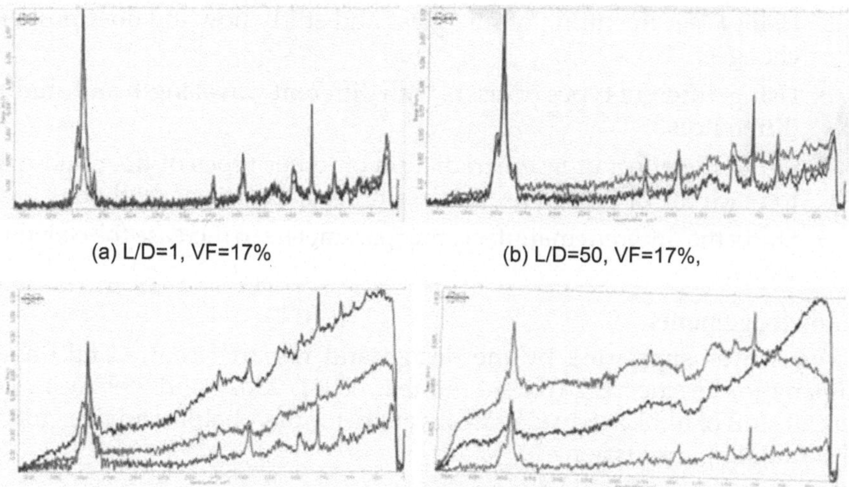

(a) L/D=1, VF=17% (b) L/D=50, VF=17%,

(c) L/D=1, VF=50 % (d) L/D=50, VF=50%

Fig. 9.5: Raman spectrum of the nano-composite at different length to diameter ratio and different volume fractions before and after laser irradiation by Nd-YAG and Argon lasers

Ar-treated

Non-treated

Nd-YAG-treated

Fibre is considered as the element that more affected by laser in the structure, the change in fibre shape leads to increase in the area exposed to lasers. Argon laser treated samples recorded higher peak values almost at all curves. The results were relatively compatible with the mechanical properties. The ability of material to absorb a certain laser wavelength is a property of the material as a function of laser type, wavelength, power and repetition rate.

Conclusions and Recommendations

Four strokes composite material machine is considered as economic and qualified method in production of nano-composites. The system is a multifunction system in compact design.

The initiative produces scientific contribution in a very specific field. The production of thermoplastic based composite material is a new trend all over the world, with these patents Egypt is one of the countries all over the world build and transfer new technology, the initiative produces 40 compounds contribute in more than 120 industries. Now shafts, gears, rods, chairs, tables, and electrical equipment are made from composites. Very small units for production of the parts mentioned above is established, this small unit works full automatic

The following Recommendation may be considered for future research:

1. Irradiation of fiber glass before manufacturing
2. Using laser in cutting of fiberglass and study how the fiber properties changes.
3. Using different types of lasers with different wavelength and study the differences.
4. Study the effect of laser irradiation on other types of fiber and matrix to reach the optimum properties and best treatment method.
5. Study the different manufacturing parameters to increase the economical value.

Acknowledgements

This work was supported by the design and research centre and Shoubra Company for engineering (patent number 20841, 23021 and 399/2004). I also thank all stuff of N.I.L.E.S in Cairo University for their helpful advice guidance and stimulating discussions.

REFERENCES

1. Bogomolov V N, Feoktistov N A, Golubev V G, Hutchison J L, Kurdyukov D. A, Pevtsov A B, Sloan J and Sorokin L M 1999 Proc. 7th Int. Symp. `Nanostructures: Physics and Technology', (St Petersburg, Russia) p 52
2. Bogomolov V N, Feoktistov N A, Golubev V G, Hutchison J L, Kurdyukov D A, Pevtsov A B, Schwarz R, Sloan J and Sorokin L M 2000 J. Non-Cryst. Solids 266 1081
3. Cardona M 1982 Light Scattering in Solids II ed M Cardona and G Guntherodt, Topic in Applied Physics vol 50 (Berlin: Springer) p 117
4. Davydov V Yu, Kitaev Yu E, Goncharuk I N, Smirnov A N, Graul J, Semchinova O, Uffmann D, Smirnov M B, Mirgorodsky A P and Evarestov R A 1998 Phys. Rev. B 58 12 899
5. Filip Van den Abeele, Joris Degrieck, Wim Van Paepegem, Experimental characterization and numerical modelling of impact damage in fibre-reinforced composites; Proceedings of the 12th European Conference on Composite Materials, Biarritz, France (*ECCM* 2006)
6. Patricia Verleysen, Joost Van Slycken, Filip Van den Abeele, Joris Degrieck, Advances in High Strain Rate Material Testing; Proceedings of the Ninth International Conference on Structures Under Schock and Impact, Wessex Institute of Technology, New Forest, UK (*SUSI* 2006)
7. Filip Van den Abeele, Joris Degrieck, Wim Van Paepegem, Impact Damage Model for Fibre-Reinforced Composite Materials; Proceedings of the 7th Congress on Theoretical and Applied Mechanics, FPMs-Faculty of Engineering, Mons, Belgium (*NCTAM* 2006)
8. C. Suryanarayana, Progr. Mater. Sci. 46, 1-184 (2001).
9. L. Takacs, Progr. Mater. Sci. 47, 355-414 (2002).
10. F.Kh. Urakaev, L. Takacs, V. Soika, et al., Russian J. Phys. Chem. 75, 1997-2002 (2001).
11. K. Tkácová, N. Stevulová, J. Lipka, V. Sepelák, Powder Technology. 83, 163-171 (1995).
12. J.Z. Jiang, R.K. Larsen, R. Lin, at al., J. Solid State Chem. 138, 114-125 (1998).
13. P.P. Chattopadhyay, S. Talapatra, S.K. Pabi, Mater. Chem. Phys. 68, 85-94 (2001).
14. P. Balaz, E. Boldizarova, S. Jelen, Hydrometallurgy. 67, 37-43 (2002).

10 Feasibility Study of Industrial Unit for Preparation and Recycling of Marble and Granite Wastes

ABSTRACT

In these work, Industrial unit for treatment of marble and granite wastes by physical methods was designed. It treats both wet and dry wastes. After treatment, wastes are used as filler or reinforcement for composite materials industries. Metal Molds are used in manufacturing for good surface finish and dimension stability. The molds have heaters and gas cooling system. Heating and cooling rates depends on the properties required in the final products. Final products have different shapes, properties, dimensions, thicknesses, lengths and colors. The unit treats the wastes of the natural marble and granite with all of their types and preparing them in a physical way in order to preserve their characteristics and keep them valid as products.

Keywords: *Feasibility study, wastes , marble, granite , recycling, preparation.*

Introduction

Mining wastes include waste generated during the extraction, beneficiation, and processing of minerals. Most extraction and beneficiation wastes from hardrock mining (the mining of metallic ores and rocks) and 20 specific mineral processing wastes are categorized as "special wastes" and have been exempted by the Mining Waste Exclusion from federal hazardous waste regulations under Subtitle C of the Resource Conservation and Recovery Act (RCRA). The mining industries based on cutting and forming marble and granite leads to environmental pollution problem, which is the greatest problem of the 20th century. The inhabitants of the industrial cities are suffering from the pollution resulting from the factories which causes huge amount of dust in the air of the surrounding areas specially the housing area[(1),(2)].

The remains of these products are not possible to get rid of them in the drains. Pollution is not only limited to the manufacturing area of marble and granite but the owners of the factories decided to export pollution to their neighbors, the owners of the factories get rid of the industry remains in the area down the slope of the mountain. The rest of cutting and sawing marble are mixed with the refrigerating water which forms a sticky liquid (alsahala), it does not have any significant use all over the world. Many workers have confirmed that factories owners insist to throw these remains behind in the direction of the housing area for a very important reason, (alsahala) after getting dry it becomes a solid ground, which permits the expansion of the factory space at the expense of the housing area[(3),(4)]. There is no drain neither sewage nor industrial that helps the drainage of the remains caused by the industry of marble in a safe way. (Sahala) has no economic value at all, carrying it far from the factories area is a big economic wastage because the percentage of water in it reaches 70%, it has a high density and leaving it in the open air for a long time exposed to the air turns it into fine dust. It has harmful effect on health, it affects the reserve of ground water and threaten their competitive edge[(5),(6)]. Fig. 10.1 Percentages of mining wastes relative to industrial wastes.

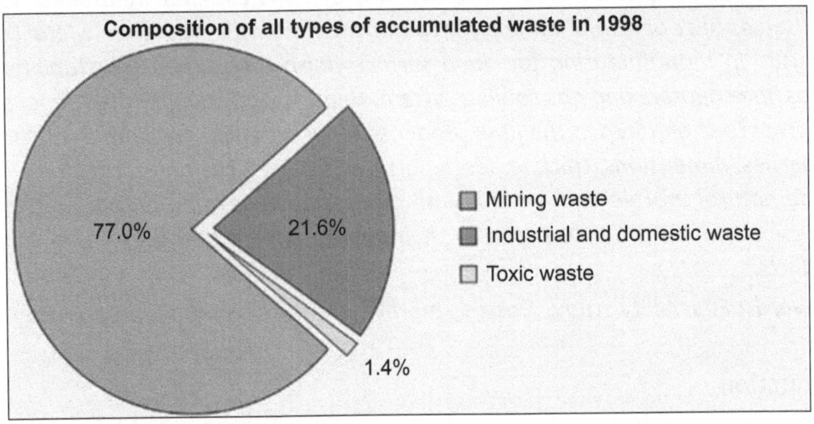

Fig. 10.1: Percentages of mining wastes relative to industrial wastes

The Industrial Uses and Applications

The project services more than 20 different industries; on top of them is the marble and granite industry. Egypt consumes annually about 20 million tons of the similar materials, like the materials used in the internal, external finishing processes and insulation and others, according to the lasts statistics of the Central Auditing Agency. Fig. 10.2 waste distribution in mining sites. The industry of the building materials is considered a feeding industry for several engineering industries, as follows:-

1. Manufacturing the tiles and the proof-sliding sheets of the insulating materials.
2. Finding a replacement from environment friendly materials for the combined additives, especially the fabricated fibers and the harmful asbestos.
3. Getting plastic based or metal matrix composite.
4. Manufacturing insulating materials with distinctive characteristics, It can be used in the external and external coverings due to the possibility of getting it in several forms and sizes.

5. The new composite is considered a type of the industrial marble with high quality and several industrial uses.
6. The industrial unit can be used in different forms and sizes, like using one unit for an industrial estate or small units for each set of factories.
7. The unit can be used for other industrial purposes like drying, grinding of other wastes.
8 It also can be used for dealing with industrial refuse of the building industry with all of its types and forms.
9. Finding an alternative of the metal coverings that can be used in office furniture, Some furniture parts, like tables chairs, sofa stands, the internal tiles and linings Segment.
10. Providing the building and construction sector with its needs of the building materials, fire resistance materials, chemical resistance materials and environmental resistance materials.
11. Containers, used for keeping gases and chemical materials, the project provides perfect products, like partitions of the operation rooms, and hanging ceilings.
12. Pipes, pipe links of gas, the organic liquids utensils, agriculture equipments, water pipes especially the hard water pipes or that which saturated with liquids(22),(23).

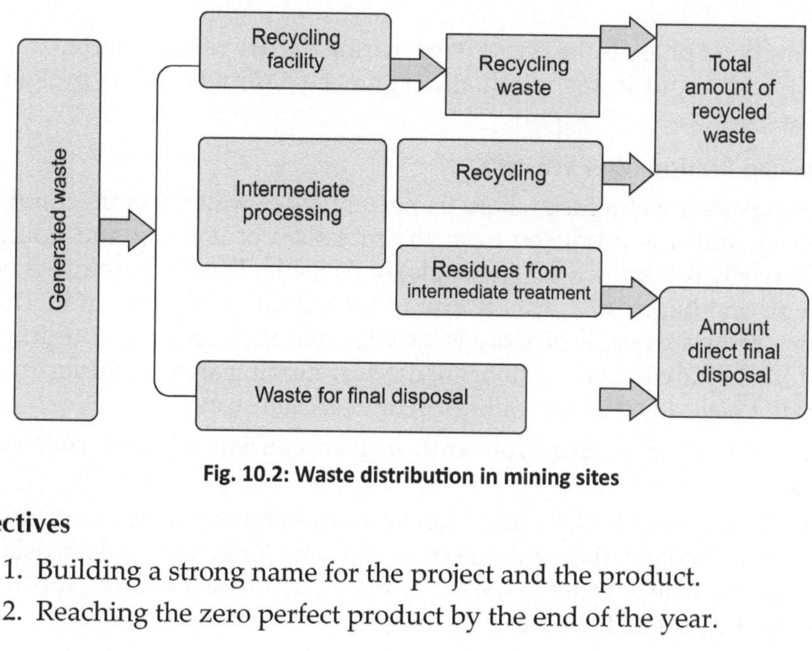

Fig. 10.2: Waste distribution in mining sites

Objectives

1. Building a strong name for the project and the product.
2. Reaching the zero perfect product by the end of the year.

3. Reaching the achievement of sale volume of 300,000 L.E. during the first year.
4. Providing job opportunities for a big number of youth and poor classes (80) persons, 40% of them are from women at least.
5. Achieveing the goals of recycling the refuse of the marble and granite industry.

Fig. 10.3 shows a chart of the objectives of recycling the marble and granite refuse.

Unit Description and Main Parts

The invention, subject matter of the project consists of a full automatic industrial unit that is operated to treat the natural marble and granite refuse, in all of their types. That is besides equipping it in a physical method to maintain its characteristics and making it suitable as a filling and strengthening material in the industry of the compound materials with a basis of metals or alloys. Fig. 10.4 shows the marble and granite wastes recycling unit[24]. The refuse of the natural marble ad granite refuse industry is divided into four main sections:

The First Section (Dry Wastes)

Dry refuse which results from the cutting and shaping processes of the marble and granite. It is known with marble fraction. It is of various shapes and sizes. This type of refuse is sometimes added to the mortar mixtures or the bricks industry, a substitution of pebbles or sand. This is considered as a waste of the economic value and the distinctive characteristics of the natural marble or granite.

The second phase is the phase of preparing the dry refuse (marble fraction) as the refuse is put in the automatic hammer phase where it is broken into suitable sizes.

The Second Section (Wet Wastes)

It is a type of the wet refuse where its percentage of water reaches about 70%. It is sticky and it is produced from the processes of leveling and polishing. Commercially is is known as (Al Sahala) or Al Sahla. The sticky refuse is heavy in weight and big in size. This is due to the existence of water in it. Thus, it is difficult to transport it or store it; besides that they are very soft granules. Therefore they are left on the floors of the surrounding areas in the factory and it does not have an economic value or commercial use at all.

The wet refuse preparation unit, in turn consists of three consecutive phases.

A. They start with the ventilation and turning over (A) as a current of air is pushed together with the continuous turning over for decreasing the percentage of water in the sticky material. This stage can be substituted by increasing the time of turning over.

B. The next phase is the drying phase, as the mixture is automatically pushed by a conveyor belt to the drying room which is fitted with heaters. The heaters are adjusted at 120°C centigrade degrees of a period of from three to four hours, for guaranteeing the drying process.

C. Sahal is got out of the dryer in the form of fragile masses which are transferred by a conveyor to the automatic turning over room as it is turned over and made in the form of powder suitable for sifting and mixing.

The third section (mixing and sieving)

The outcome of the two phases is collected in the automatic sieve. The mixture moves to the final drying and mixing phase. This phase is fitted with heaters at 120°C for a period of from 3 to 4 hours. This is for guaranteeing the final drying of the two mixtures.

The fourth section (manufacturing process)

The joining material is added by the upper hopper. The joining material consists of metal and plastic powders of the solid. The surface of the mould is leveled by the weight of the stumps and by using the automatic compression of the hydraulic pressure. The mixture is heated at the required temperature, according to its components. The heating rate depends on the type of the joining material, the stumps are fitted with upper and lower heaters, movable in a horizontal position in order to allow the movement of heaters to compress the mixture according to the thickness and type of mixture. It is also fitted with a tuber that allows passing the cooling gases upon desire for cooling the stumps. The new product is distinguished with the light weight and the ability to endure scratch and damping capacity comparing with the natural marble. It is also liable for the easy formation and is distinctive with different colors and shapes. The unit consists of several main parts. Fig. 10.5 shows float chart of the manufacturing process.

1. The wet refuse preparation unit.
2. The dry refuse preparation unit.
3. The bunker of the collection, final drying and mixture.
4. The metal molds.
5. The upper hammers.
6. The dual hydraulic compressors.
7. The horizontal upper and lower heaters.
8. The cooling gases tube and valves.

Operation and Maintenance Strategy

It is suggested to establish ten units in Shak Al Teaban district for absorbing the volume of refuse and facilitating the transport and circulation processes due to the difficulty of transporting the refuse to one place. Besides, the small size of the units facilitates the operation and maintenance processes, as it is planned in the periodic maintenance program the existence of a unit in the periodic maintenance and a unit the contingency maintenance and the existence of 8 continuous units at least in the work. Thus, the total of job opportunities is 80 units for the project, as a whole.

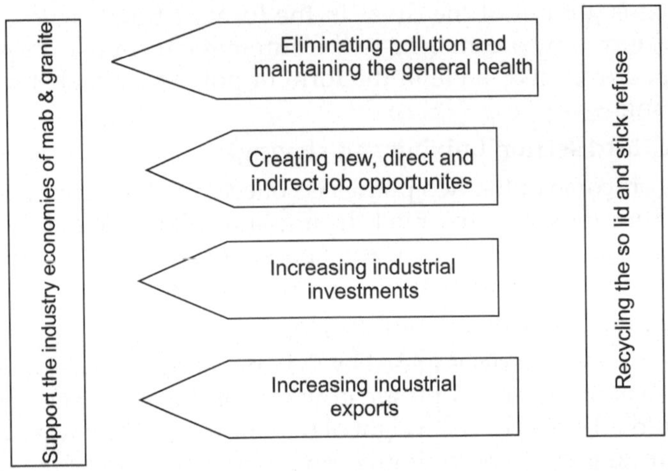

Fig. 10.3: A chart of the objectives of recycling the marble and granite refuse

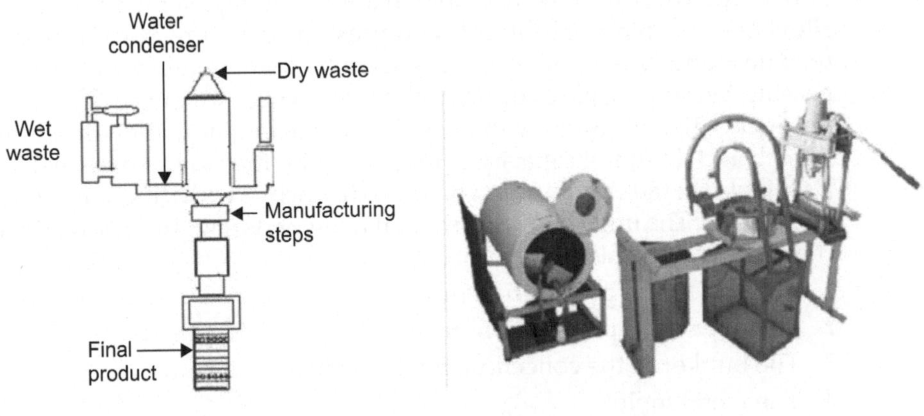

Fig. 10.4: The marble and granite wastes recycling unit

Market Analysis

A. Quality

Attention is given to the product together with focusing on the accuracy, dimensions stability, quality of design, strength, environmental resistance, conformity of colors and the dismantling and installation easiness.

B. The Price

The low price, together with the quality factors are desirable.

C. The Competition

Competition with the Local Product: No other similar product, except products made of plastic or metals that are less regarding the quality.

Competition with the Imported Product: There is a very expensive imported product and it is less regarding the characteristics as shown in table (1) the general characteristics.

The Beneficiaries from the Project

1. Customers who buy the production lines and machines.
2. The youths who have small enterprises.
3. The manufacturers of marble and granite who are interested to expand their products and improve the economical value of their enterprises
4. Direct and indirect employment opportunities. **Table 10.2 shows the manpower and employments in the project.**

Table 10.1: The General Characteristics of the Products

Characteristic	Hardness Shore D	Resistance of the organic dissolvers	Water absorption and the atmospheric factors resistance	Resistance of acids and alkaline
Value	60	Petrol resistor	Hot water and atmospheric factors resistor	Acids ad light alkaline resistor

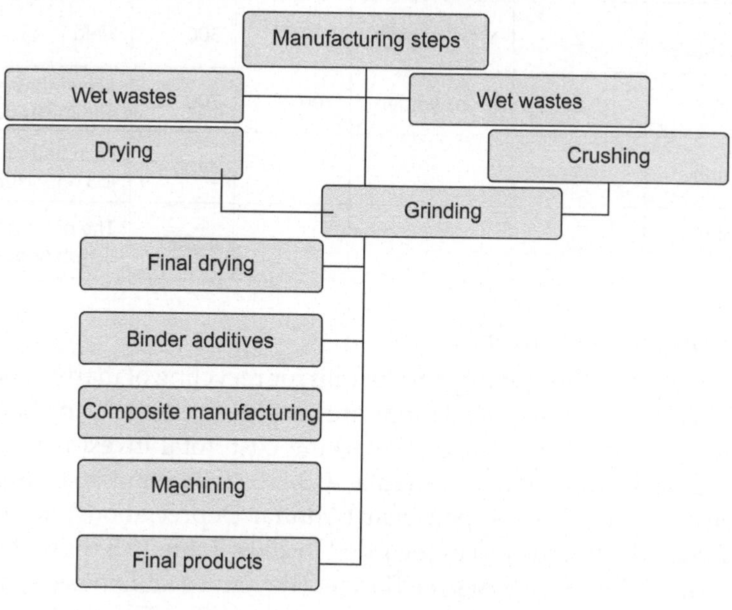

Fig. 10.5: Float chart of the manufacturing process

Fig. 10.6: Products from marble and granite wastes

Table 10.2: The Manpower and Employments in the Project

Job title	No. of employer	Gender	Monthly salary (L.E.)	Total (L.E.)	Nature of work
Engineer	1	Men/women	1000	1000	Production and quality supervisor
Technician	2	Men/women	600	1300	Operating the units
Maintenance technician	1	Men	400	400	Maintenance of the unit
Laborer	1	Men	300	300	Assistant works
Sale representatives	2	Men/women	250	500	Field
Accountant	1	Men/women	700	700	Accounting and administrative affairs
Total per unit	8			4200	Each unit provides 8 job opportunities
Project Total (10 units)	80			42000	The project provides 80 job opportunities

The Expenses and the Budget

The economical feasibility study for the unit for recycling of marble and granite wastes are calculated, The calculations are consider case study in Shak elsoban area in Tora, Egypt. The fixed cost, working cost, total investment costs and their distribution were shown in table 10.3, 10.4, 10.5 and 10.6 respectively. Operation Cost of a Stereotyped Year (Annual Depreciations) are shown in table 10.7 according to the prices recorded in 2009. Table 10.8 shows Direct and indirect costs. Table 10.9 shows the Budget (Revenues ad Expenses) according to the social fund for development roles and logistics. The total costs for the project is shown in table 10.10.

Table 10.3: Fixed Capital

Investment Factors	Investment Value	Total distribution of expenses
Land	0	
Buildings and constructions	0	
Machines. Equipment, installations	60400	
Equipment and furnishing	2000	
Means of transport	0	
Foundation expenses	1000	
Emergency reserve (10%)		
Total		63700
Total after increase		70 000
Minimum requirement		50 000

Table 10.4: Working Capital

Capital cycle (one month		
Raw materials – mediating raw materials	17445	
Wages and salaries	4200	
Power (electricity – fuel – utilities)	200	
Maintenance and spare parts	252	
Marketing expenses	100	
Building rents	400	
Insurance	15	
Emergency reserve (10%)	200	
Total		22812
total after increase		30 000
Minimum requirement		20000

Table 10.5: Investment Costs Total

Fixed assets	63700	
Working capital	22818	
Investment costs total		86512

Table 10.6: Distribution of Investments

Investment factors	Investment Value	Investment Distribution Total
Invested capital	17302	
Loan	69209	
		86209
		60000

Table 10.7: Operation Cost of a Stereotyped Year (Annual Depreciations)

Investment Factors	Investment Value	Percentage of Depreciation	Depreciation Value
Buildings and constructions	0	5%	0
Machinery and Equipment	60400	10%	6040
Requirements and furniture	2000	10%	200
Means of transport	0	20%	0
Foundation expenses	1000	10%	100
Emergency reserve	300	10%	30
Total			6370

Table 10.8: Direct and Indirect Costs

Investment Factors	Annual Investment Value	Total
Raw materials – mediating raw materials	209340	
Wages and salaries	50900	
Energy and utilities	2400	
Maintenance and spare parts	3020	
Marketing expenses	1200	
Building rents	4800	
Insurance	181	
Annual depreciations	6370	
Raw materials depreciations 2%	4178	
Loan interests 9%	6229	
Reserve	2400	
Operation costs total per a stereotype year		290527

Table 10.9: The Budget (Revenues ad Expenses)

Investment Factors	First year	Second year	Third year	Fourth year	Fifth year
Revenues	298200	340800	383400	404700	426000
Cash expenses total	224483	251074	277201	292882	309179
Net profits without the loan	73717	89726	106199	11818	116821
Loan installments	0	17302	17302	17302	17302
Net profit	73717	72424	88897	94516	99519
Cash flow	73717	146141	235038	329554	249072

Table 10.10: Total Investment Expenses for 10 Units

Fixed assets	63700	
Working capital	22812	
Investment expenses total per unit		86512
Investment expenses total of the project		865120
Minimum requirement		50 000
Maximum requirements		100 000

The Competitive Privileges

The competitive privilege of the products not only from the price, but also it depends on the characteristics of the products as follows:

1. Small weight regarding the solidity.
2. Big hypothesized age.
3. Easy shaping and relative operation with various colors and shapes.
4. Resistance to environmental conditions.

Technical Specification

Sustainability

The sustainability is considered the prevailing characteristic of the project. On the part of the financial aspect, establishing a group of small industrial projects for manufacturing the refuse of marble and granite depends at its beginning on a loan with an interest of 9% from the authorities responsible for financing the youth projects and paying attention to the small enterprises. Within a few months the project will be transferred to a project aiming at gaining profit. This is because the products obtained from it are economic and required commodities. It is expected that each project can cover all of its costs of equipment, machinery and raw materials, including the substitution and renewal, within a period from 5-10 years. This is besides achieving the economic feasibility and providing job opportunities. This is the first factor of the sustainability. The project provided the opportunity in an even way to all the girls and youths to start small enterprises. The second factor of the sustainability is the need of the society to replace a lot of the imported necessary commodities and replacing them with local ones. The dependency of the project on the available wealth sources in the surrounding environment is considered one of the sustainability factors. This is in addition that the project exploits the sources of the wealth in the best way than what actually exists. The most important factor of sustainability is that the project, originally, is based on scientific researches, developed technology and detailed economic feasibility study.

Risks and Probable Crises

(a) The high price of the imported raw materials.

Raw materials that should be imported from abroad. This leads to raising the prices of the products. This can be overcome by using local raw materials and technology in industrializing the unit.

(b) Crises Regarding the Pollution Resulting from the Industry Risks and the Environmental Laws, it can be overcome by achieving the following environmental and health conditions:

Public Conditions

- The required natural ventilation sources.
- Providing the required fire fighting equipment.
- Providing a permanent water source from the public net.
- The existence of a public net of the health/ industrial sewerage
- The Ministry of Environment should be communicated in order to assess the environmental effect of the project according to the suitable environmental classification model and the requirements of the environment law. The project is considered one of the new projects in the Egyptian industry. Initially, it could be classified in the grey list.

Special Conditions

- Providing the ventilation system and the automatic drawing for reducing the concentration of the emissions and maintaining the temperature in comfortable ranges.
- Safe disposal of the liquid refuse after treating it.
- Using the gloves, masks, protective glasses and ear plugs.
- Collecting the refuse, recycling and pressing it in the same project for producing other items.

(c) Problems connected with the truancy of the trained manpower.

It can be overcome by establishing a main training center connected with the project research center. This is for training staffs with high efficiency and also training them on the improvements which will be inserted on the production line.

In addition to the administrative difficulties, the lack of financing sources and the lack of the statistical data about the quantities and types of the marble and granite refuse.

Conclusions

The project produce significant contribution to the marble and granite industry can be summarized as follow:-

1. The first automatic industrial unit that deals with all types of the wastes, wet and dry marble and granite industrial refuse, and recycling them in order to get a final product in the same unit.
2. Using a physical method to treat the marble and granite refuse in order to maintain their natural characteristics.
3. Using the marble and granite refuse as a filling, strengthening and improving fillers in composite materials, as substitutions of the expensive additives.
4. Production of new composite materials in different shapes and colors which resisting scratch and environmental conditions
5. Production of composite materials that are suitable for insulation, lining and tiles.
6. Designing a complete production line (an industrial unit that performs the process of the physical treating of the marble and granite) and manufacturing new products.
7. Using the environmental pollutants in serving the environment itself to maintain the general health of the citizen and improve economics of the industry.
8. The new unit does not need skillful laborers and it can be established in the industrial zone of mining marble and granite. No Module is used in the packing and covering.
9. Production composite materials with electro-static features, resistance to bacteria and possibility of adding new distinctive features.

Recommendations

1. The continuous training for all the specializations by the accrued training centers.
2. Due to the importance of the data about the targeted markets, there is a great need for establishing an effective data base with continuous modernization.
3. The continuous coordination with the governmental and non-governmental boards and organizations.
4. Attempting to enroll in the supply records of the targeted places of the big and governmental companies and the decorations offices.
5. Working with the spirit of the team and the participation of workers in the material and spiritual successes. Securing the policy of satisfying the customers, the quickness of response for any remark and removing its causes, as a first priority for all the workers in the project, the continuous communication with the complaining and non-complaining customers.

REFERENCES

1. Ghosh, P. and A. K. Samanta. *J. Text, Inst., Part 188 (3)*, (1997) 209 12. Kwasnick, J. et al., *j Text. Inst., Part 1, 88 (3)*, (1997) 167.
2. Schmidt, A. X. and C. A. Marlies, *Principles of High Polymer- Theory and Practice*, McGraw-Hill, New York, 1948 Chapter 11.
3. Ghosh, *P., Polymer Science and Technology: Plastics, Rubbers, Blends and Composites*, Second Edition, Chapter 1 and 7, Tata McGraw-Hill, New Delhi, 2002.
4. Sett, S.K. and D. Sur, *J. Indian Fibre Text Res.*, 18 (1993)
5. Lewin, M., 'Chemical Processing of Fibres and Fabrics, Fundamentals and Preparation, Part B,' in *Handbook of Fibre Science & Technology*, Vol. 1, M. Lewin and S.B. Sello (Eds), Marcel Dekker, New York, 1984, Chapter 2.
6. Partridge, LK., *Advanced Composites*, Elsevier, Applied Science, London, 1989.
7. Mallick, P.K., *Fibre Reinforced Composites* Marcel Dekker, New York, 1988.
8. Shah, A.N. and S.C. Lakkad, *Fibre Sc. & Tech.*, **15** (1981)
9. Clark, B.A. and M.P. Ansell, *J. Mater. Sci.*, 21 (1986) 269.
10. McLaughlin, E.C., *J. Mater. Sci.*, **15** (1980) 886. 7. White, N.M. and M.P. Ansell, j. *Mater. Sci.*, **18** (1983) 1549.
11. Holmes M. and D.J. Dust, *GRP in Structural Engineering* Applied Science, London, 1983. Ghosh, P. and P.K. Ganguli, *Jute, Encyclopedia of polymeric Materials*, J.C. Salamone Ed., CRC Inc., New York, 5 (1996) 3504.
12. Kundu, B.C., K.C. Basak and P.B. Sarkar, *Jute in India*, Indian Central Jute Committee, Kolkata, 1959.
13. Nevell, T.P. and S.H. Zeronian, *Cellulose Chemistry and Its Application*, Ellis Horwood, Chichester, 1985, 22-26.
14. Sarkar, P.B., A.K. Majumder and K.B. Pal, *J. Text. Inst.*, 39 (1948) T-44. 11. McGregor, E.A. and C.T. Greenwood, *Polymers in Nature*, John Wiley, Chichester, 1982, Chapter 7.
15. Sarkar, P.B., *J. Indian Chem. Soc*, (1931) 397; 10 (1933) 263; 11 (1934) 5, 8, 407, 12 (1935) 168, 470, 542, 547.
16. Sarkar, P.B., *Sci. & Culture, 1* (1935) 60, 3 (1937) 411, 485, 551.
17. Gravitis, J. and P. Erins. *J. Appl. Polym. Sci.*, Appl. Polym Symp., 37 (1983) 421.
18. Staudinger, H., Ber 53B (1920) 1073.
19. Carothers, W. H. and J. W. Hill, *j Am. Chem. Soc.*, 54 (1932) 1559.
20. Ghosh, P. and N.R. Bose, *J. Appl. Polym. Sci.*, **58** (1995) 2177. 10. Ghosh, P. and P.K. Ganguli, *J. AppL Polym. Sci*, 52 (1994) 77.
21. Kesser, T.D.J., *Polypropylene*, Reinhold, New York, (1960).
22. Lewin, M. and J. Preston, *High Technology Fibres, Part A*, Marcel Dekker, New York (1985) 357.
23. Datye, K. V. and A. A. Vaidya, *Chemical Processing of Synthetic Fibres and Blends*, John Wiley & Sons., New York, 1984.
24. Hebatalrahman Patent 745/2008, Egyptian patent office,2008.

11

Study of the Manufacturing Parameters Affect the Fabrication of Nano and Micro Composites

ABSTRACT

In this research the fabrication quality parameters of micro and nano composites will be mentioned. The manufacturing parameter such as temperature, pressure, and cooling rate were studied. Poly methyl metha acrylate reinforced by fiber glass was considered as case study in the current work. The effect of fiber size (length to diameter ratio) and fiber volume fraction were evaluated. The fabrication temperature of the composite was evaluated. The factors affecting the heating rate such as power, volt and furnace efficiency were studied. At the end of research, the results and discussions explain the main parameters affecting fabrication of nano and micro composites.

Keywords: *Nano, Composite, thermoplastics, temperature, pressure, cooling rate, manufacturing, techniques.*

Introduction

Polymer nanocomposite have attracted great attention due to the unique properties introduced by nanofillers, which typically refer to carbon blacks, silicas, clays or carbon nanotubes (CNT). The polymer matrix acts as a supporting medium and the improvement in the properties of nanocomposites generally originates from the nature of these nanofillers[(1),(2)]. The term reinforcement is normally used to denote the increase in rigidity and strength achieved by dispersing inorganic fibers or particulates fillers in the polymer matrix[(3):(7)].

Effectiveness of Fiber in the Composite

The effectiveness of fibers or reinforcements in the composite depends mainly on three factors[(8),(9)]. **First,** it must have good bond strength between the polymer matrix and the fibers, this is usually achieved by coating the fiber with a material which bonds well to both fiber and polymers[(10)]. **Second,** the effect of fiber concentration on the properties of the composites[(11) : (16)].**Third,** The effect of fiber size in the other words, the effect of length to diameter ratio[(17):(20)].

In general, the fibers are assumed to be homogeneous, much stiffer than the polymer matrix, regular spaced, perfectly aligned or randomly distributed. The polymer matrix is assumed to be homogeneous and isotropic linear elastic[(21),(22)]. The interface between the fiber and the polymer matrix is an anisotropic transition region which must provide a stable bond between them[(23),(24)].

Solvent casting, melt mixing and coagulation methods are the common fabrication methods for nano-composites, some researches use combined methods, such as solvent casting in conjunction with sonication followed by melt mixing. For example the combination of solvent casting and melt mixing[(25),(26)] for SWNT/PMMA composites with considerable improvement in nano-tube dispersion[(27),(28)]. PMMA was dissolved in organic solvent that was also used to disperse additives and after that it cast into a dish. In situ polymerization method has also been used to make nano-tube-based nano-composites starting with nano-tube and monomers[(29),(30)]. The most common in situ polymerization methods involve epoxy in which the resin (monomer) and hardeners are combined with additives or reinforcement prior to curing (polymerization)[(31),(32)]. Its resin can be cross-linked after mixing with hardener[(33),(34)].

The development of nanotechnology is closely related to the new economy and high technology products towards 21st century[(35)]. As a new material, the nano-particle has certainly caught the imaginations of researchers around the world. Although the production technologies of nano-particles have had significant progress in the past few years, the commercial applications of nano-particles are often limited by the cost, handling, and safety issues[(36), (37)]. To address these application problems, a proprietary mechanic-chemical bonding technology has been developed to fabricate nano-composite powders. It can create nano-scale multifunctional composite materials contributing to the development of advanced materials and devices for rechargeable batteries, fuel cells, ceramics, metals, superconductors, cosmetics and pharmaceuticals. The technology is an enabling technique to broaden the applications of nano-particles. In these work, new method was developed, the nano materials can be bonded together using mechanical energy without any binders in a dry process[(37)].

Experimental work

I. Materials

The matrix is polymethyl metha acrylate (PMMA. It is thermoplastic prepared from monomer (methyl methacrylate) by additional polymerization process; polymer was in the granule form with 5mm diameter.

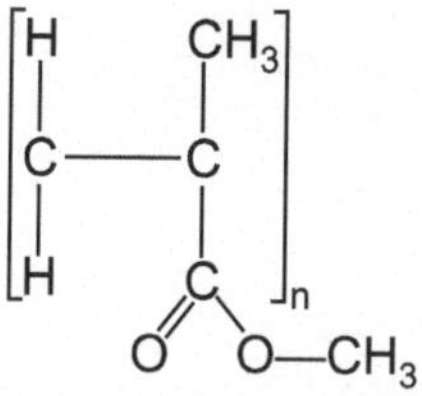

Fiberglass (brand milled fibers) are glass filaments coated with a specific sizing to enhance resin compatibility and hammer milled to a specified bulk density. Fibers are hammered milled to an average fiber length. Average fiber length is determined by the input glass and process conditions. In the current work, milled fibers are made from "E" (electrical) glass which conforms to MIL-R- 60346C specification with average bulk density 0.55g/cm^3 in floccular and powder form with length to diameter ratio (L/d=50 and, L/d=1) respectively.

II. Preparation of Material

Grinding

A blinder with variable speeds is used to change the pieces of thermo-plastics into powder form, The blinder speed is about 15,500 rpm, work at 200 volt - 50 Hz, and the grinding time is about 90 sec. Switch off for cooling is lasted about 180 sec to prevent the agglomeration of the particles and achieve reasonable degree of quality in grinding. The retained granules after sieving will be returned to blinder.

Mixing

Automatic mixing for thermoplastic in the powder form with short fibers at different aspects ratio was done. The amount of material required was calculated by changing the volume fraction percent into weight percent (L/d=50 and, L/d=1) respectively.

Composite Material Preparation

A methodology for design of new composite material is based on strength to weight ratio, manufacturability, and cost requirements are presented. Simple method for manufacturability and cost elements are developed and combined to produce a new technique of manufacturing of thermoplastic based nano-composites. This work establish very small setup for production of the thermoplastic based composites, this small unit become more suitable for determination of the best fabrication parameters at certain composition figure 11.1 show the experimental setup for manufacturing of nano-composites (a) fabrication test machine and (b) automatic blinder (mixing and grinding). The manufacturing quality parameters were determined as temperature, pressure, cooling rate and holding time (time of application of force).

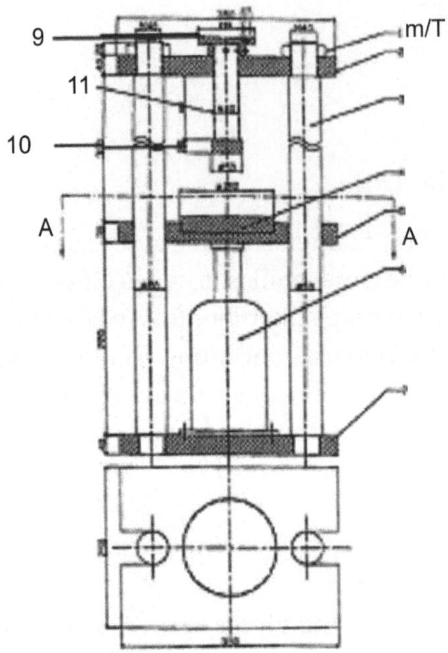

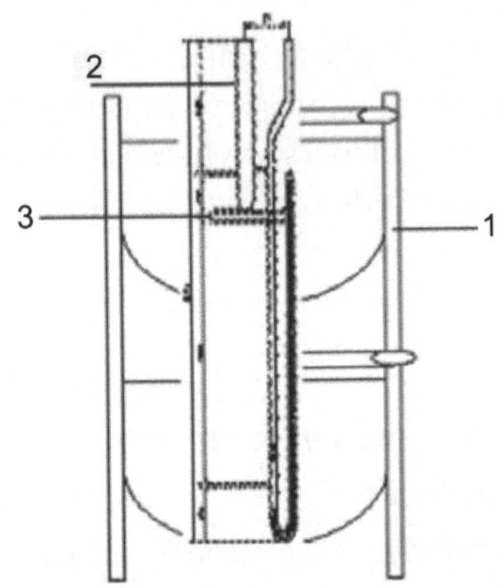

(a) Fabrication test machine

1. Nuts for fixation
2. Fixed arm of the pressing
3. Upper part of mold
4. Lower part of mold
5. Fixed rod
6. Pressing body
7. Lower bed
8. Pressing part
9. Manometer
10. Thermocouple
11. Stop watch

(b) Automatic blinder (Mixing and Grinding)

1. Fixation element
2. Mixing chamber
3. Sieving

Fig. 11.1: Experimental set up used in fabrication of nano-composites

The material was prepared by grinding and mixing of thermoplastic in the powder form. The mixing of fiber with thermoplastics and other modifiers was done. The process is done with certain volume fractions depend on the properties required in the final product. Equation number (1) and equation number (2) show the role of mixture to indicate respectively the density and the weight, the composite material was prepared in the solid form, it had different characteristics depends on the fiber percentages (volume fraction of fibers) and fiber size (length to diameter ratio).

$$\rho_c = \rho_f V_f + \rho_m V_m \tag{1}$$

$$W_C = W_f V_f + W_m V_m \tag{2}$$

Where

V_f = volume fraction of fiber
V_m = volume fraction of matrix
r_f = density of fiber
r_m = density of PMMA
W_f = weight percent of fiber
W_m = weight percent of PMMA

Fabrication Tests

The factors affect fabrication of nano-composites were determined by the following fabrication tests, all factors were fixed while only one factor changed. The fabrication conditions of the polymer matrix were (T = 240°C, P = 160 kg/cm^2) so this values were considered as indication values in the experimental tests. The tests were divided into four categories. First, the effect of cooling rates. Second, the effect of fabrication temperature. Third, the effect of the fabrication pressure. Fourth, the effect of fabrication time. Fig. 11.2 show the manufacturing parameters which affect the fabrication of polymer based composites. Fig. 11.3 shows The manufacturing steps of nano-composites materials. Table 11.1, 11.2, 11.3 and 11.4 show the fabrication tests.

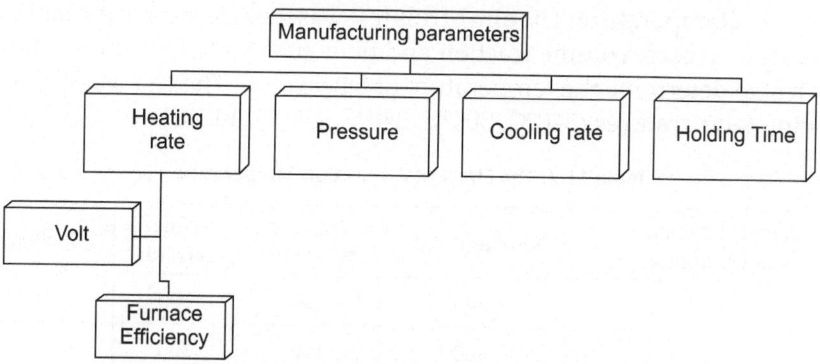

Fig. 11.2: Schematic diagram of the manufacturing parameters

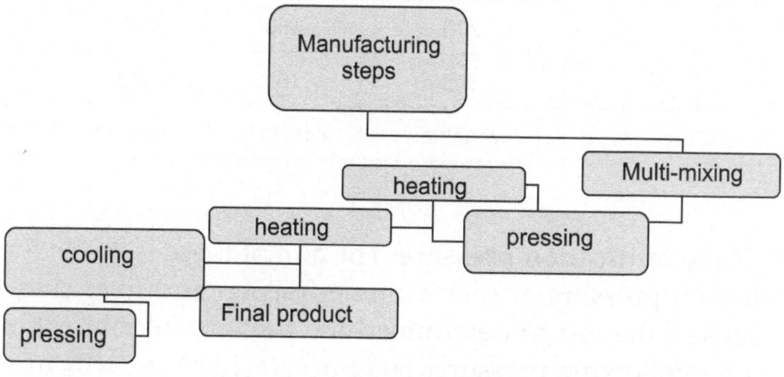

Fig. 11.3: The manufacturing steps of nano-composites materials

Test 1

The suitable cooling rate: The aim of these test was the selection of the best cooling rate, table 11.1 show the steps of the test to determined the cooling rate, the test was done at the following cooling rate ranges :-

1. Sow cooling rate mold cool (M.C)
2. Medium cooling rate air cool (A.C)
3. Fast cooling rate water cool (W.C)

Table 11.1: The Effect of Cooling Rates

Factors affecting manufacturing	Temperature°C	Pressure N/m^2*10^5	Time seconds	Cooling rate
Values recorded during experimental work	300	160	300	M.C
	300	160	300	A.C
	300	160	300	W.C
states	constant	constant	constant	variable

Test 2

The effect of temperature: The aim of this test was the selection of the fabrication temperature at each volume fraction and fiber size, table 11.2 shows the steps of the test to determine the temperature of fabrication. The test was done at the following temperatures (340°C, 300°C, 240°C, 200°C, 140°C).

Table 11.2: The Effect of Fabrication Temperature

Factors affecting manufacturing	Temperature°C	Pressure N/m^2*10^5	Time seconds	Cooling rate
Values recorded during experimental work	340	160	300	W . C
	300	160	300	W . C
	240	160	300	W . C
	200	160	300	W . C
	140	160	300	W . C
states	variable	constant	constant	constant

Test-3

The effect of the fabrication pressure: The aim of these test was the selection of the fabrication pressure at each volume fraction and fiber size, table 11.2 show the steps of the test to determined the pressure of fabrication The test was done at the following pressures 50 N/m^2*10^5,100 N/m^2*10^5,160 N/m^2*10^5, 300 N/m^2*10^5, 500 N/m^2*10^5

Table 11.3: The Effect of the Fabrication Pressure

Factors affecting manufacturing	Temperature°C	Pressure N/m^2*10^5	Time seconds	Cooling rate
Values recorded during experimental work	240	50	300	W . C
	240	100	300	W . C
	240	160	300	W . C
	240	300	300	W . C
	240	500	300	W . C
states	constant	variable	constant	constant

Test 4

The effect of time of application of force: The aim of this test was the selection of the minimum time required for fabrication time at each volume fraction and fiber size, table 11.4 shows the steps of the test to determine the time of fabrication. The test was done at the following desecrate times 30s, 60s, 90s, 120s, 150s.

Table 11.4: The Effect of Time of Application of Force

Factors affecting manufacturing	Temperature°C	Pressure N/m^2*10^5	Time seconds	Cooling rate
Values recorded during experimental work	240	160	30	W. C
	240	160	60	W. C
	240	160	90	W. C
	240	160	120	W. C
	240	160	150	W. C
states	constant	constant	variable	constant

all tests at different test conditions were repeated at different volume fractions of fibers 0%, 17%, 35%, 50%, 65%, and at different fiber sizes (length to diameter ratio) (L/D=50 and L/D=1), the average of three reading were recorded .

Results and Discussions

The suitable cooling rate is indicated from the first test, this test was done under constant temperature, pressure and fabrication time. Both air cool and furnace cool were failed, the samples were pores. The fast cooling rate (water cool) gave the best results. The same results were repeated at all volume fractions and all fiber sizes (length to diameter ratio). The cooling rate is a function of the matrix type, it independent of the amount of reinforcement and its size.

Temperature is the most important and the most effective factor in the fabrication of plastic based composites. The temperature increase when the amount of energy consumed increase the best fabrication temperature in the range from 300°C to 350°C, when the temperature increase the dissociation of the matrix occur, when the temperature decrease the fabrication quality also decreased. The temperature range is a strong function of the matrix, there is no significant changes can be recorded at any aspects ratio or at any concentration of fibers. Fig 11.4 show the heating rate as a function of the voltage change at constant current, While fig 11.5 show the variation of temperature with time during furnace heating, the heating rate and the time required to reach required temperature were depend on the furnace efficiency.

The effect of pressure was studied at constant temperature and holding time. The reading of the monometer was recorded at every volume fraction and aspect ratio. There was a significant increase in the fabrication pressure with the increase of the volume fraction of fibers fig 11.6 show The variation of fabrication pressure with volume fraction of fibers at different aspects ratio. The pressure required for fabrication was increased when the aspects ratio decreased, the decrease in fiber sizes need more force to get red of micro voids and pores. The decrease in fiber size from L/D=50 to L/D=1 lead to increase in the fabrication pressure about 50 MN/Cm^{2}.

The effect of fabrication time was studied at constant temperature and pressure. At relatively low concentration of fiber volume fraction in the range from 0% to 35% the holding time was constant at 240s at all aspects ratio considered in these work. At higher fiber concentrations in the range from 50% to 65%, The holding time increase with the decrease in the aspects ratio, the holding time increase about 60s to 120s when the fiber size dropped from L/D=50 to L/D=1 Fig. 11.7 show the variation of fiber volume fraction and fiber size with holding time during fabrication. The holding time was the less significant factor affect the fabrication of composites.

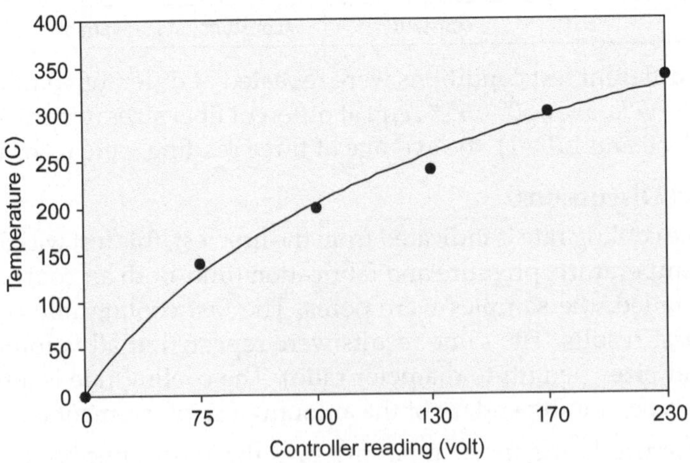

Fig. 11.4: Heating rate control

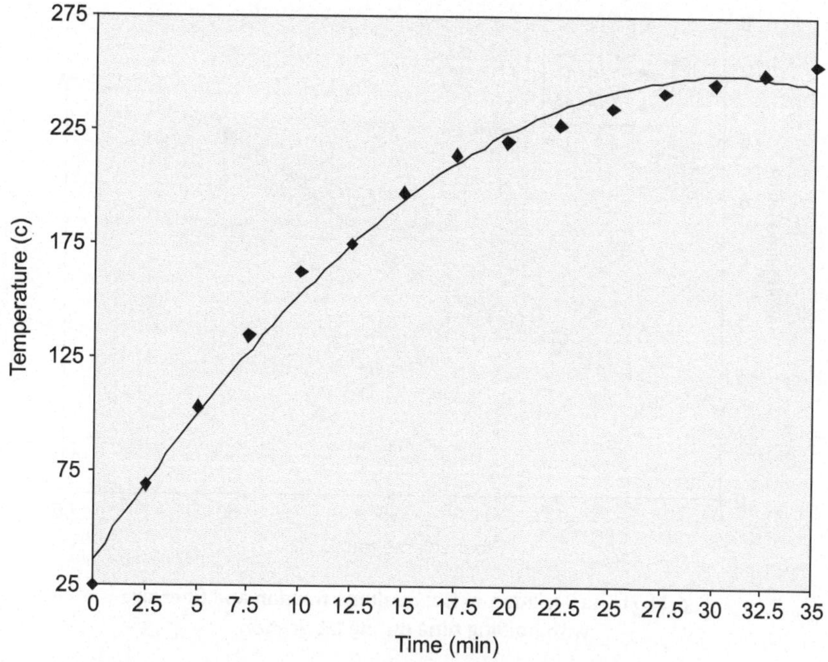

Fig. 11.5: The variation of temperature with time during furnace heating

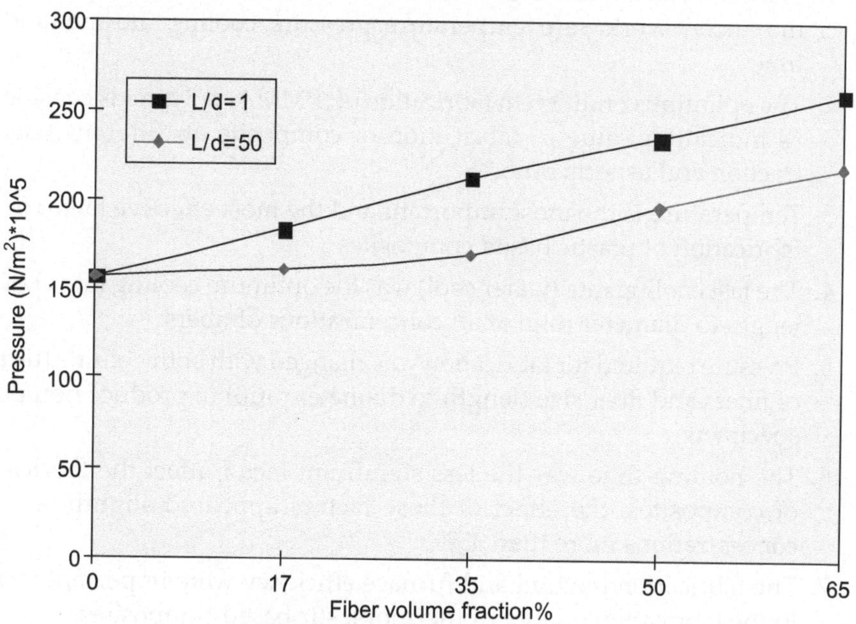

Fig. 11.6: The variation of fabrication pressure with volume fraction of fibers at different aspects ratio

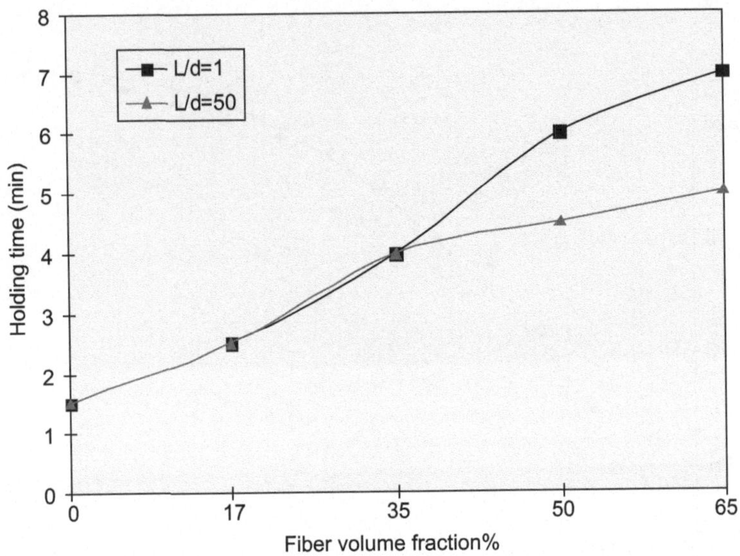

Fig. 11.7: The variation of fiber volume fraction and fiber size with holding time during fabrication

Conclusions

1. The main factors affecting the fabrication of nano-composites powders in the current work were temperature, pressure, cooling rate and holding time
2. The optimum condition in fabrication of (PMMA) polymer is considered as indication value in fabrication of composite at different volume fraction and aspects ratio.
3. Temperature is the most important and the most effective factor in the fabrication of plastic based composites
4. The fast cooling rate (water cool) was the optimum cooling rate at every length to diameter ratio at all concentrations of fibers.
5. Pressure required for fabrication was changed with both volume fraction of fibers and fiber size (length to diameter ratio) to produce non pores specimen
6. The holding time was the less significant factor affect the fabrication of composites, the effect of these factors appeared slightly at fiber concentrations more than 35%.
7. The fabrication method and furnace efficiency were important factors in the fabrication quality of thermoplastic based composites.
8. both cooling rate and temperature are factors related to matrix type regardless of the reinforcement type, size and volume fraction.

9. The new technique developed in these work was unique and suitable for a wide range of thermoplastic based, thermoset based and metal based nano and micro composites regardless of the reinforcement or filler type.

The new technique was registered as patent in the Egyptian patent office.

REFERENCES

1. D.R. Lied, (ed.) in *Chemical Rubber Company Handbook of Chemistry and Physics*, CRC Press, Boca Raton, Florida, USA, 79th Edition, 1998.
2. I.S. Butler and J.F. Harrods in Inorganic Chemistry, Principles and Applications, Benjamin Cummings, California, USA, 1989.
3. H.J.M. Bowen in Environmental Chemistry of the Elements, Academic Press, London, UK, 1979.
4. A.M. James and M.P. Lord in Macmillan's Chemical and Physical Data, Macmillan, London, UK, 1992.
5. P.A. Cox in *The Elements: Their Origin, Abundance, and Distribution*, Oxford University Press, Oxford, UK, 1989.
6. D.R. Lied, (Ed.) in *Chemical Rubber Company Handbook of Chemistry and Physics*, CRC Press, Boca Raton, Florida, USA, 79th Edition, 1998.
7. J. Selby, J. Chem. Ed. 1973, **50**, 306.
8. Environmental Applications and Impacts of Nanotechnology. Summary of Evidence presented to nanotechnology working group. The Royal Society and The Royal Academy of Engineering, December, 2003.
9. Nanotechnology - size matters. Building a successful nanotechnology company. A 3i white paper in association with the Economist Intelligence Unit and the Institute of Nanotechnology.3i (2002)
10. Statement on Nanotechnology. July, 2004. ICSTI
11. Anton et al The Global Technology Revolution:Bio/Nano/Materials Trends and their Synergies with Information Technology by 2015. RAND: Santa Monica, CA, (2001).
12. A Roadmapping Perspective: Science-Driven Technologies. September, 2002. The Albright Strategy Group.
13. BCC (2001). Proceedings of the 4th Annual BCC Conference Fine, Ultrafine and nanoparticles Oct. 14-17, 2001. Chicago, USA
14. Economic Perspectives of Nanotechnology: Enormous Markets for Tiny Particles. October, 2002. BASF Future Business GmbH
15. Technology Roadmap for Nanoelectronics. 2000. European Commission (EC)
16. Chemical Industry (2003). Chemical Industry R&D Roadmap for Nanomaterials by Design: From Fundamentals to Function. Chemical Industry Vision2020 Technology Partnership.
17. International Technology Roadmap for Semiconductors. 2004. The Royal Society & The Royal Academy of Engineering
18. Applications of Nanotechnology in Space Developments and Systems. April, 2003. VDI
19. Nanoscience and Nanotechnologies: Opportunities and Uncertainties. July 2004. The Royal Society.
20. Alexandre, Dubois-Polymer/layered Silicate Nanocomposites. Preparation, Properties and Uses of a New Class of Materials (2000)

21. International Technology Roadmap for Semiconductors. 2004. The Royal Society & The Royal Academy of Engineering
22. Polymer nanocomposites: from fundamental research to specific applications - ARTICLE Materials Science and Engineering: C, Volume 23, Issues 6-8, 15 December 2003, Pages 763-772 Hartmut Fischer
23. Jones, W.E., Jr.; Chiguma, J.; Johnson, E.; Pachamuthu, A.; Santos, D. Electrically and Thermally Conducting Nanocomposites for Electronic Applications. Materials **2010**, 3, 1478-1496
24. Jones, Wayne E., Jr.; Chiguma, Jasper; Johnson, Edwin; Pachamuthu, Ashok; Santos, Daryl. 2010
25. Rubbery and glassy epoxy resins reinforced with carbon nanotubes - ARTICLE Composites Science and Technology, Volume 65, Issues 11-12, September 2005, Pages 1861-1868 Luqi Liu and H. Daniel Wagner
26. M. Okamoto, Polymer/Clay Nanocomposites, "Encyclopedia of Nanoscience and Nanotechnology" (H. S. Nalwa, Ed.), Vol. 8, p. 1. American Scientific Publishers, Stevenson Ranch, CA, 2004
27. Polymer/layered silicate nanocomposites: a review from preparation to processing - REVIEW ARTICLE Progress in Polymer Science, Volume 28, Issue 11, November 2003, Pages 1539-1641 Suprakas Sinha Ray and Masami Okamoto
28. Zanetti M, Lomakin S, Camino G. Polymer Layered Silicate Nanocomposites. Macromol Mater Eng 2000; 279: 1-9
29. An overview on the degradability of polymer nanocomposites - ARTICLE Polymer Degradation and Stability, Volume 88, Issue 2, May 2005, Pages 234-250 Jitendra K. Pandey, K. Raghunatha Reddy, A. Pratheep Kumar and R.P. Singh
30. An analytical molecular structural mechanics model for the mechanical properties of carbon nanotubes - ARTICLE International Journal of Solids and Structures, Volume 42, Issues 11-12, June 2005, Pages 3075-3092 J.R. Xiao, B.A. Gama and J.W. Gillespie, Jr
31. Carbon Nanotubes: Properties and Application - REVIEW ARTICLE Materials Science and Engineering: R: Reports, Volume 43, Issue 3, 15 January 2004, Pages 61-102
32. Metal Handbook, Vol. 2, P S, Cambridge University press, 1980.
33. R.W. Perry. Perry's Chemical Engineers Handbook, 1984.
34. Ibid, Trans. AFS vol. 2, P. 33, 1980.
35. J.V. Daswon, BCJRAL Trans. AFS, vol. 10, No. 1, 1962.
36. Metal handbook, vol. 5 Cambridge University Presses, Cambridge, 1970.
37. Experimental trends in polymer nanocomposites - a review - REVIEW ARTICLE Materials Science and Engineering A, Volume 393, Issues 1-2, 25 February 2005.

12 Simplified Technique for Recycling of Micro and Nano-Composite with Industrial Wastes

ABSTRACT

In these work, the interest in composite materials to increase their participation in future lightweight structures for building applications in the next generation. Simplified methods for the recycling of composite materials and other industrial wastes were developed. The process should be automatic in all cases. First step is preparation of wastes from different industrial sources by grinding and mixing. Second step is manufacturing of certain iron molds with good inner surface finish, the molds were lubricated by specials oils. The rest step is the design of machine for remanufacturing of disposable material at certain conditions depends on the percentage of additives. all elements are exposed directly to be pressing and shaped by the usual procedures. Finally, each type of material takes a different recycling procedures.

Keywords: *Nano-composites, Recycling, Waste recovery, Manufacturing industries, Industrial waste.*

Introduction

Replacement of traditional metal components by composite plastics in applications such as bumpers, under bonnet components, body panels and exterior trim has significantly reduced the weight of the average car. Typically, 10% of a vehicle's weight (wt%) is made up of plastics and plastic composites, and for some lightweight vehicles this may be up to 20 wt%. Composites are increasingly used since they have the advantages of strength, durability and corrosion resistance together with low weight. Composites are composed of many different components, including glass fibre reinforcement, filler material and the thermoset or thermoplastic polymer, which is the matrix or continuous phase. The plastic polymer components commonly used include thermoset polyester, phenolic resin, epoxy resin, polypropylene and vinylester resin. It is the mixture of components embedded in the matrix that make composites difficult to recycle and the reason why such a high percentage is sent to landfill(1).

Fig. 12.1 shows the percentages of composite wastes in residual wastes as recorded in year 2003. Consequently, there is a need to identify novel process routes to enable the recycling of composite materials(2),(3).

Plastics form a fast increase percentage of the total solid wastes because their use is very important now in the modern life. Plastics basically consist of carbon, hydrogen and oxygen but they are not biodegradable(5),(6). Many varieties of plastics find their way into waste disposal streams but three types polyolefin, polystyrene, and poly vinyl chloride.

(PVC)-make up more than four-fifths of the total. One possible method of recycling plastics is to use it in the form in which it was first manufactured. I.e., by mixing the raw plastic during the production of new packs. However, there are problems due to a large number of Different grades of material within each major plastic type, and the grade employed depends on the characteristics required in the particular pack(7),(8).

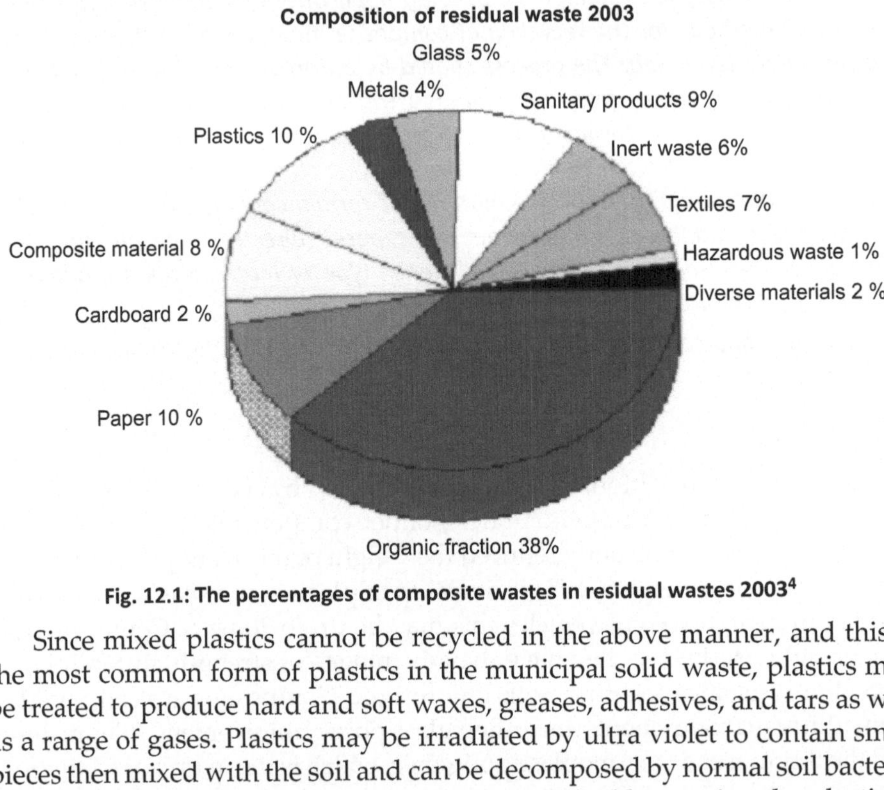

Fig. 12.1: The percentages of composite wastes in residual wastes 2003[4]

Since mixed plastics cannot be recycled in the above manner, and this is the most common form of plastics in the municipal solid waste, plastics may be treated to produce hard and soft waxes, greases, adhesives, and tars as well as a range of gases. Plastics may be irradiated by ultra violet to contain small pieces then mixed with the soil and can be decomposed by normal soil bacteria into basic chemicals, recycling may be accomplished by reusing the plastic in another form so our new composite material solve most of the problems of recycling plastics(9),(10).

Separation of the glass fibre from the filler was achieved using a drum carder machine, which gently separates the fibres from the friable char and filler matrix(11). The fibres can then be used as char-coated fibres to produce new composite plastic materials. Alternatively, the blackened glass fibre can be cleaned using low-temperature furnace oxidation to burn off the char to produce cleaned fibre. The recovered glass fibre, both cleaned and char-coated, were made up into test samples of a new composite by the industrial partners(12):(14). Test samples incorporating 25 wt% of the recovered glass fibre and 75 wt% virgin glass fibre were compared to a controlled sample containing 100 wt% virgin glass fibre[(15),(16)]. The results showed that up to 25 wt% of recycled fibre could successfully be incorporated into a new composite while still meeting manufacturers specifications[(17),(18)].

Slag is the most important waste in metals industries. The process of iron melting involves the formation of slag. The main sources of slag in a furnace are the refractory lining, coke ash and various oxides brought in during charging fluxes, scale and sand are formed in the furnace such as (FeO, SiO_2, MnO, etc.). Slag control for minimizing the melting temperature and viscosity of the slag is carried out by adding limestone[(19),(20)]. The basicity of the acidic slag are CaO/SiO_2=0.5-0.6. When higher amount of limestone added to the charge, the slag are basic CaO/SiO_2=1.5-2, When desulphurization reaction take place CaS and 20-30%FeO are found in the slag[(21)]. Fig. 12.2 shows useful ores and wastes during metals manufacturing.

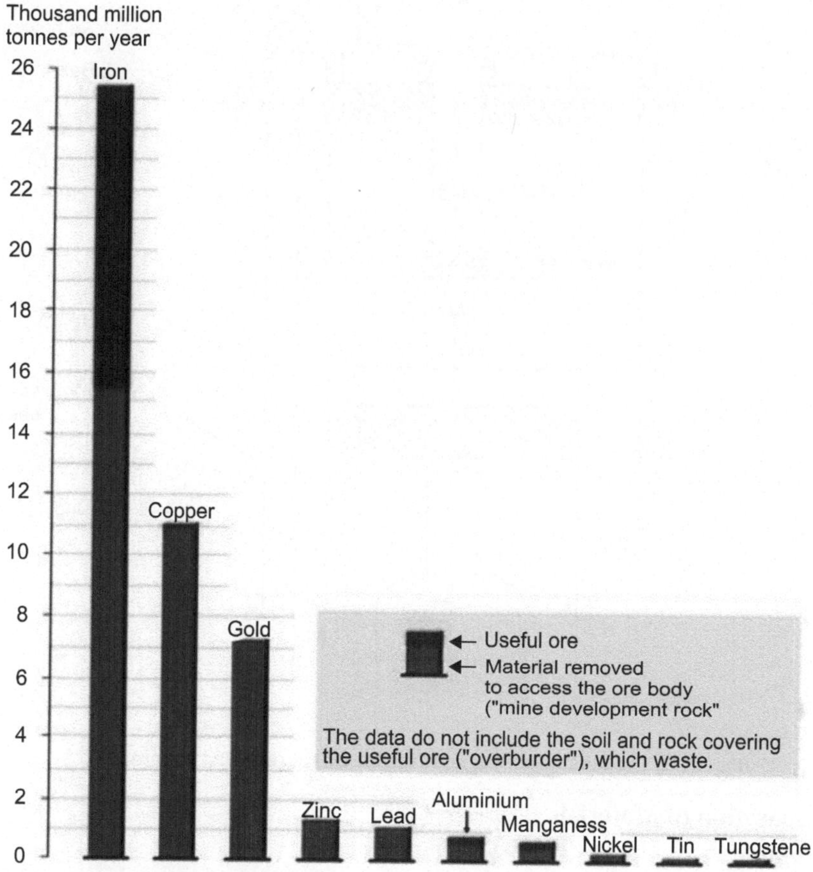

Source: Worldwatch institute, 1997 (Figures for 1995).

Fig. 12.2: Useful ores and wastes during metals manufacturing[(21)]

II. Experimental Work

A. Machine

New method for the recycling of composites reinforced by different types of additives and fibers, which is non-recyclable by traditional methods. Temperature controller is installed to maintain the temperature of the mixture constant. The compound formed maintain in the elastic form. it shredded to the appropriate sizes. Material is cooled after deformation by air stream. The resulting material is combined with thermoplastics or metals materials and manufactured under certain conditions of temperature and pressure appropriate to the type of matrix. Fig. 12.3 show the manufacturing utensils for waste recycling, the new technique has advantages such as simple design., good surface finish of the final product, low cost and the products resulting from the system have good surface finish.

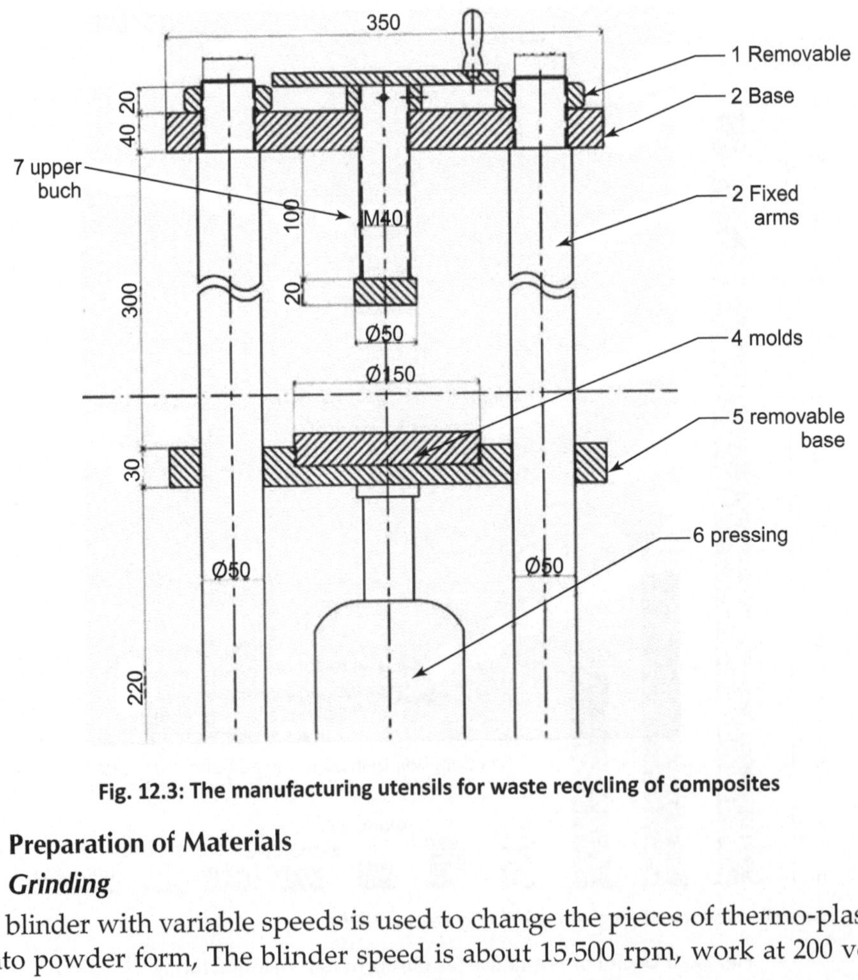

Fig. 12.3: The manufacturing utensils for waste recycling of composites

B. Preparation of Materials

1. Grinding

A blinder with variable speeds is used to change the pieces of thermo-plastics into powder form, The blinder speed is about 15,500 rpm, work at 200 volt -

50 hz, and the grinding time is about 90 sec. Switch off for cooling is lasted about 180 sec to prevent the agglomeration of the particles and achieve reasonable degree of quality in grinding. Powder size is less than or equal to 1mm.

2. Mixing

Mechanical mixing for thermoplastic with additives and wastes are done in the powder form (less than 1 mm diameter), slag, master patch, other modifier and a short fiber were added with different ratio the amount of materials are calculated by changing the volume fraction percent into weight percent.

3. Mold preparation

1. The mold is made from Iron in cylindrical shape as shown in Fig. 12.4, the inner surface of the mold is smooth and lubricated with certain types of oils.

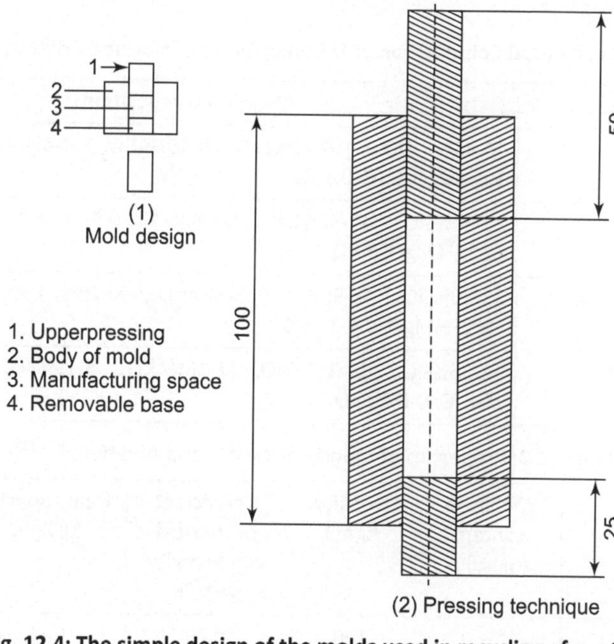

Fig. 12.4: The simple design of the molds used in recycling of wastes

2. The metals have high thermal conductivity and rapid cooling rates so the thickness of the mold should be sufficient to insure that the inner surface does not lose its temperature before the deformation is completed and prevent early solidification.
3. The body of the mold and the lower pressing are heated from room temperature and treated with special process combined between conventional method of heat treatment and laser surface treatment methods to increase ability to resist wear and friction while increase toughness.

4. Upper pressing may be made from the same treated iron or from special steel.
5. The pressure applied on the upper surface of the mold, tolerance between the upper pressing and the mold body allows the gases to escape away during pressing to avoid porous product, which drop the properties and work as crack initiation elements.

C. Materials Composition and Characteristics

This research deals with the industrial wastes from a new point of view, the desirable properties in this wastes is studied to benefit from this properties in production of new composite material. Table 12.1 shows chemical composition of different types of slag and additives, while table 12.2 shows physical and thermal characteristics of the additives and reinforcement used in the current work.

Table 12.1: Chemical Composition of Different Types of Slag and Additives[(22) : (26)]

Properties	Chemical compositions
Acidic slag	40-45% SiO_2, 18-25%CaO, 9-18%Al_2O_3, 4-8%FeO, 2-5%MnO, 1-4%MgO, 0.05-0.1%S)
Basic slag	25-30%SiO_2, 42-50%CaO, 6-8%AbO_3, 0.5-1%FeO, 0.7-1.5%MnO, 12.15%MgO, 0.9-1.1%S.
Desulphumiation slag	25-30%SiO_2, 42-50%CaO, 6-8%Al_2O_3, 30-20%, FeO, 07-1.5%MnO, 12:15%MgO, 0.9-1.1%S
E-type fiber glass	52-56%SiO_2, 16-25%CaO, 12-16%Al_2O_3, 8-13%BO, 1%Na_2O and 1%K_2O, 0-6%MgO

Table 12.2: Properties of Industrial Wastes and Additives[(21), (22)]

Slag	Moisture content (mass)%	Density Kgm3	Coefficient of thermal conductivity w/m°K	Heat capacity Kj/Kg°C	Notes
Boiler slag	–	100	0.29	0.75	
Lumpslag	–	2150	0.93	0.88	
Blast furnace	20-30%	700-400	0.3-0.35		At 25°C
Fiber glass Type E		550	0.04	21:25	

D. Raman Spectroscopy

The behavior of the material was studied by variation of the modes obtained from FT (IR) Raman spectrum. The results were obtained using Brucker FTIR Raman spectrometer using Nd-YAG laser power of 500MW as source of excitation. After irradiation the thin film of sample with different lasers, the spectra were obtained in the range 400 to 4000 cm^{-1}. The samples to be measured was fixed to holder and placed in front of the beam[7].

III. Results and Discussions

Composite Materials Properties

In this work a group of composite materials are prepared by changing the percentage of fibers and slag impeded in the matrix, the corresponding manufacturing conditions is adjusted. The values gives an indication about the different compositions which produce a significant improvement in the properties both temperature and applied pressure is changed at each compound. Fig 12.5 shows ideal packing fractions in practice these values can rarely be approached. In general the increase in fiber glass and additives volume fraction leads to change in structure as shown in fig. 12.6 while the

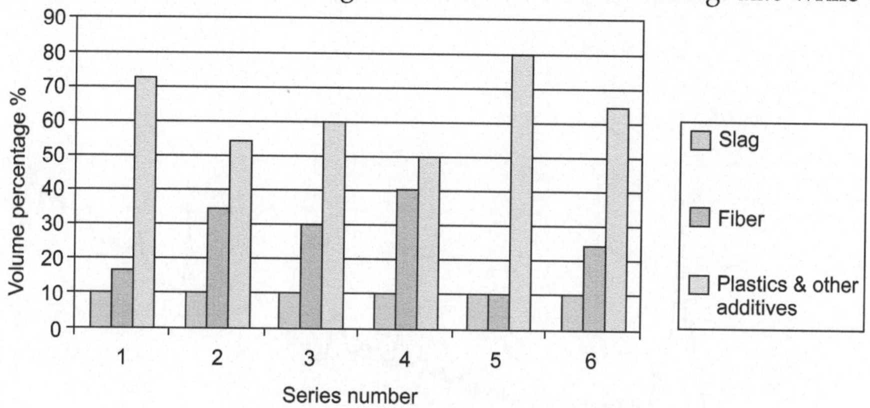

Fig. 12.5: The composition expected for differentseries of composite materials

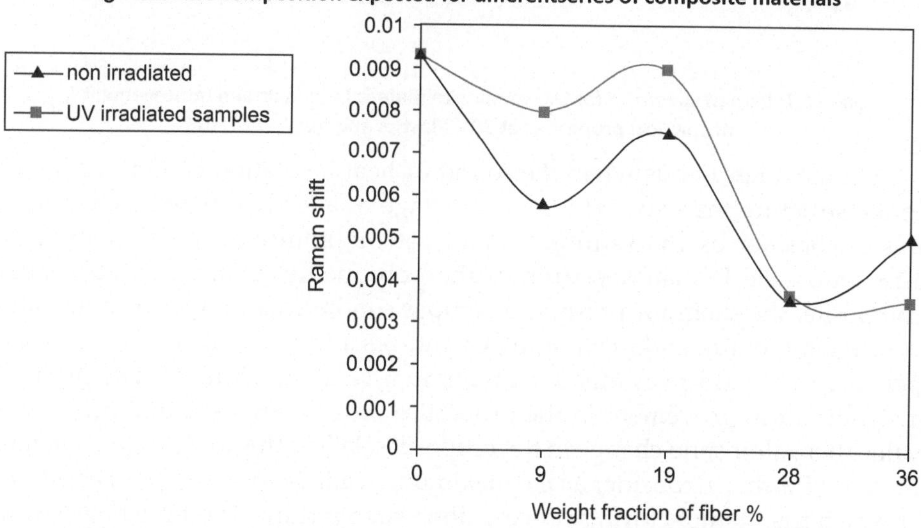

Fig. 12.6: Structure variation (raman shift) with variation in additives percentages

improvement in thermal and sound insulation related to the amount of slag impeded in the matrix. Theoretically the increase in strength is continue as the increase in the fiber percentages and additives is increased but in actual practical work the maximum limit of improvement in strength is at 50% fibers.

Spectroscopic analysis

Fig. 12.7 shows the laser Raman spectroscopy of the poly methyl metha acrylate matrix composite reinforced by short fiber glasses with length to diameter ratio equal L/D = 1, this condition produce the maximum improvement in the properties. Then the percentage fibers increases larger than this value, the matrix become unable to imbed more fibers and additive and the strength decreases.

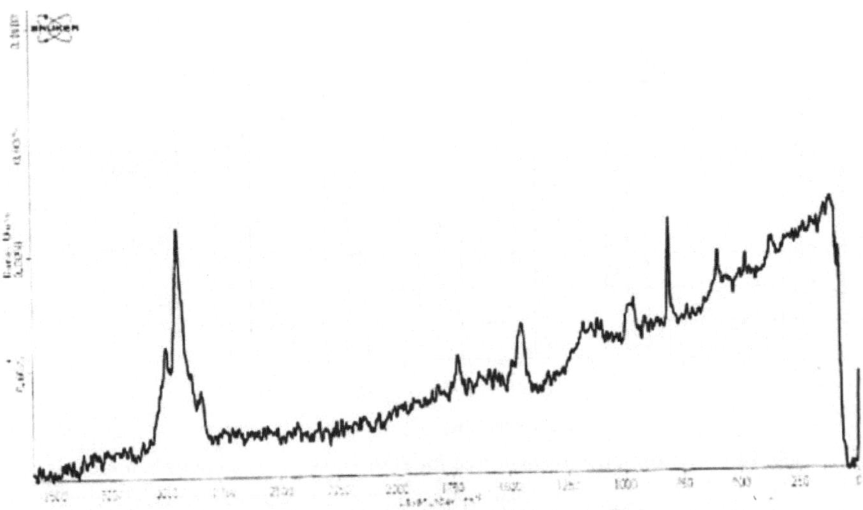

Fig. 12.7: Raman spectrum for the composite material at maximum improvement in mechanical properties at 50% Plastics and fiber size L/d=1

On the other hands when the sound or heat insulation is more preferred in the structure than strength the percentage of additives may reach to 65%, this is consider as the saturation limits of the additives in the matrix, fig 12.8 shows the Raman spectrum of the poly methyl metha acrylate matrix composite, the diagram produce a comparison between the two composites have the minimum and maximum percentages additives (fibers, slags, master patch). At 17% additives this is the minimum value of additives may produce a significant improvement in the properties of the composite and below this value there almost no change in the properties. When the additive percentages become 65% this is consider as the maximum available percentage of additives at which the manufacturing process done successfully. The raman spectrum show a significant difference in amplitude and in the structure at the two cases and this can produce explain for the difference in properties between the two compounds.

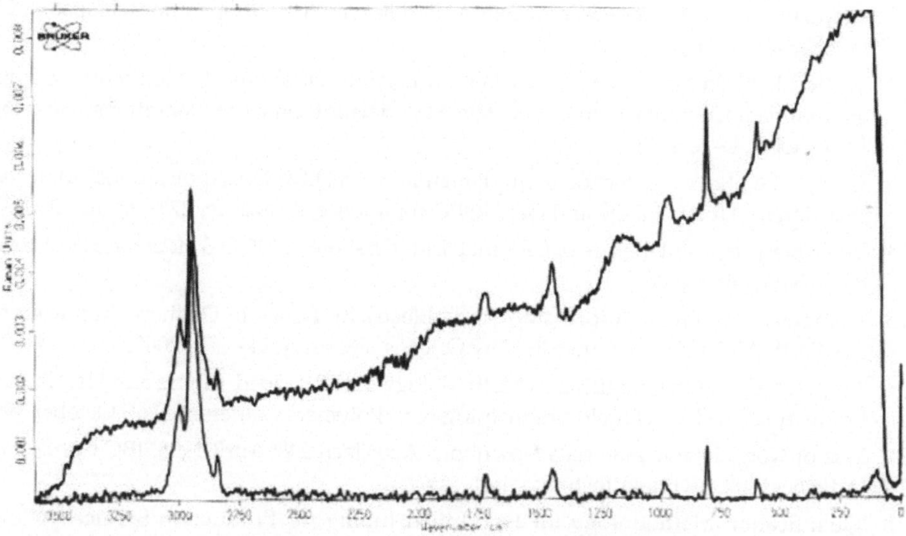

Fig. 12.8: Raman spectrum for the samples contain minimum percentages of additives 17% and Maximum percentage of additives 65%

Conclusions

1. The new technique for composite material recycling is simple, abundant and suitable for different types of industrial wastes such as slag and fiber wastes.
2. The properties of the final products depends on the volume fraction of additives (reinforcement) in the composite material structure
3. The new technique is economic because almost 70% of the contents are wastes, it combined more than one type of wastes
4. The manufacturing conditions depends mainly on the thermoplastic matrix at the same additive percent and volume fraction.
5. The control of additive percentages leads to a material with good insulations characteristics, impact resistance and relatively reasonable strength.
6. Slag are used as filling material to improve thermal characteristics of the composite without any pre-preparation or treatment.

REFERENCES

1. 'Performance of FRP Lined steel tubing in production environment,' P Medlicott, Fourth International Conference on Composite Materials for Offshore Operations. Houston, TX, October 4 – 6, 2005.
2. 'Static Electricity and the Use of GRP Materials Offshore', P Medlicott, Fourth International Conference on Composite Materials for Offshore Operations. Houston, TX, October 4 – 6, 2005
3. 'Composite Material Selection & Implementation in Oil & Gas Applications', Materials Selection for Upstream Oil and Gas" IQPC conference, Aberdeen, 27th January 2004.
4. 'Static Electricity and the Use of GRP materials Offshore', CMOO-3 Houston 31st October to 2nd November 2000.
5. 'Composite Materials: Addressing Static Electricity Issues in Offshore Applications' ETCE/OMAE 2000 Conference in New Orleans, February 14 - 17th, 2000.
6. 'Progress towards a Qualification Methodology for FRP Lined Tubing and Flowlines in Production Service", Oilfield Engineering with Polymers Conference 26th October 1998
7. 'Use of Non-Metallic materials Downhole' Aberdeen 24th April 1998. IBC Conference 'Advances in Downhole Technologies'.
8. 'Qualification Methodology for FRP Lined tubing for Production Service: A Joint Industry PROGRAM' 2nd International Conference on Composite materials for Offshore Operations (CMOO2), Houston, October 28-30 1997.
9. 'Using Composite Materials to Minimise Weight and Maintenance and Maximise Safety' Euroforum Offshore Platforms '96, London, 18-19th March 1996.
10. 'How can Composite Materials be Successfully Applied to your Current and Future Offshore Projects? IIR Conference Aberdeen, 15-16th November 1995.
11. 'Overviewing the Diverse Applications and Advantages of Composites in the Offshore Industry' IIR Conference Aberdeen, 7 - 8th December 1994.
12. 'GRP and HDPE: Alternative Solutions to Corrosion', UK Corrosion, London 19-21st October 1993.
13. M.l.Hair, [Infrared spectroscopy in surface chemistry], Marcel Dekker, New York,1967.
14. Metal handbook, Vol. 5, Gambridge university presses, Cambridge ,1970.
15. Bogomolov V N, Feoktistov N A, Golubev V G, Hutchison J L, Kurdyukov D. A, Pevtsov A B, Sloan J and Sorokin L M 1999 Proc. 7th Int. Symp. `Nanostructures: Physics and Technology', (St Petersburg, Russia) p 52
16. Bogomolov V N, Feoktistov N A, Golubev V G, Hutchison J L, Kurdyukov D A, Pevtsov A B, Schwarz R, Sloan J and Sorokin L M 2000 J. Non-Cryst. Solids 266 1081
17. Cardona M 1982 Light Scattering in Solids II ed M Cardona and G Guntherodt, Topic in Applied Physics vol 50 (Berlin: Springer) p 117
18. Davydov V Yu, Kitaev Yu E, Goncharuk I N, Smirnov A N, Graul J, Semchinova O, Uffmann D, Smirnov M B, Mirgorodsky A P and Evarestov R A 1998 Phys. Rev. B 58 12 899
19. Filip Van den Abeele, Joris Degrieck, Wim Van Paepegem, Experimental characterization and Numerical Modelling of Impact Damage in fibre-reinforced Composites; Proceedings of the 12th European Conference on Composite Materials, Biarritz, France (ECCM 2006)

20. Patricia Verleysen, Joost Van Slycken, Filip Van den Abeele, Joris Degrieck, Advances in High Strain Rate Material Testing; Proceedings of the Ninth International Conference on Structures Under Schock and Impact, Wessex Institute of Technology, New Forest, UK (SUSI 2006)
21. Filip Van den Abeele, Joris Degrieck, Wim Van Paepegem, Impact Damage Model for Fibre-Reinforced Composite Materials; Proceedings of the 7th Congress on Theoretical and Applied Mechanics, FPMs-Faculty of Engineering, Mons, Belgium (NCTAM 2006).
22. M. Okamoto, Polymer/Clay Nanocomposites, "Encyclopedia of Nanoscience and Nanotechnology" (H. S. Nalwa, Ed.), Vol. 8, p. 1. American Scientific Publishers, Stevenson Ranch, CA, 2004
23. Polymer/layered silicate nanocomposites: a review from preparation to processing - REVIEW ARTICLE Progress in Polymer Science, Volume 28, Issue 11, November 2003, Pages 1539-1641 Suprakas Sinha Ray and Masami Okamoto
24. Zanetti M, Lomakin S, Camino G. Polymer Layered Silicate Nanocomposites. Macromol Mater Eng 2000; 279: 1-9
25. An Overview on the Degradability of Polymer Nanocomposites - ARTICLE Polymer Degradation and Stability, Volume 88, Issue 2, May 2005, Pages 234-250 Jitendra K. Pandey, K. Raghunatha Reddy, A. Pratheep Kumar and R.P. Singh.

13

Risks Concerning Work in Building Materials Industries
(Case Study of Marble and Granite Mining Region in Tora)

ABSTRACT

The research addresses the risks related to building materials industries. Workers are exposed to risks in construction and building sites in general. As well as the risks connected with the manufacturing of marble and granite as one of building materials industries are discussed in the current work. It is considered as one of the feeding industries in the construction sector. Marble and granite mining area in Tora (Shak Elsoban) is considered as case study in these research. The risks that workers are exposed to in the site area are studied and analyzed with focus on the effect of these risks on the economies of the industry, which in turn affect the building materials industry. Study and analysis of identification and legalization of the risks related to working sites according to the practical are done. The study are depends mainly on the reality of the statistic data available about accidents and injuries types and effects. The research ends with a package of conclusions and recommendations which establish clear strategies to limit the risks of such an important industry with taking into account the economical factors.

***Keywords**: Risks, building materials, mining industries, pollution, wastes.*

Introduction

The term of industrial health is an important term which is developed in recent times to reflect factors of security and safety that should be made available in facilities during the performance of various industrial processes. It is consider health work conditions which are an important factor in economics of any industry[(1),(2)].

Industrial health is a science that deals with four main factors for prevention and improving the health and safety and raising the efficiency of workers in the areas of their professional work. Therefore, working conditions should be compatible with the requirements of the industrial health. The most important factors of industrial health are summarized as **enough space, healthy environment, lighting appropriate,** and **reducing noise.** At the start, it is important to understand the technique of manufacturing process and identify its major factors. Analyze and identify the interactive and reciprocal relationship between each factor to achieve a secure engineering product at all manufacturing stages. The selection of materials in accordance with international standard specifications criteria of quality and safety are the key element in achieving industrial safety during manufacturing process. The safe disposal of exhaust resulting from industry, turn over security of the commodity and product are essential parts of the industrial health concept and its achieving factors[3],[4]. One of the objectives of safety and professional health is to maintain elements of production in the forefront of which the human race. Legislation and laws give the right to the human being to get a safe working environment[5],[6]. The following table 13.1 shows the impact of the circumstances and factors in the work environment on the efficiency of performance, it record heat and humidity equations and the extent of their impact on the efficiency of workers in the industrial environment and their ability to complete the work[7],[8].

Table 13.1: The Impact of the Circumstances and Factors in the Work Environment on the Efficiency of Performance[9]

Temperature rest	Relative air humidity	The impact on human and efficiency
21°C	40%	The maximum rest
	75%	Work without feeling bored
	85%	Feeling bored
	91%	Tiredness and no rest
24°C	65%	No rest
	80%	Severe boredom
	100%	It is impossible to carry out the hard work
31°C	25%	Subliminal uncomfortable
	50%	Work is still possible
	65%	It is impossible to carry out the hard work
	80%	A rise in body temperature

It is already clear the importance of the existence of measurement devices in the work environment to maintain appropriate rates for work. According to the statistical data of the International Lab Organization in USA about two million people lose their lives because of accidents and work injuries. Workers are exposed to about 270 million work accident and 160 million diseases infection cases linked to the work annually[10],[11].

Work accidents and injuries have changed their form, but did not lose their destructive capability, work accidents and injuries still have heavy losses and damages

Whether the individual who was injured or his family or the institution he works for are affected by accidents and injuries of work direct and indirect.

In addition to the number of deaths and injuries mentioned above, it costs enormous economic losses. Work accidents and injuries were valued the costs of the year 2001 by 4% of the total world gross domestic product (GDP) which is evaluated to be more than the amount of $1251353 millions dollars as business interests. The world spends about $170.9 billion dollars annually on the effects resulting from accidents and work injuries according to what estimated by the department of Health and Safety in USA[12].

In Latin America alone costs of accidents and work injuries in the year 2000 were estimated to be about $ 76 billion dollars. The organization ISO has issued a new standard specification on technical terminology for the chain of standard specifications ISO 14000, this specification is expected to contribute in clarifying the definition of environmental terms and definitions. It will also help to facilitate explaining the activities of environmental management and uses of terms[13],[14].

This specification will also help all users of the chain of the international specifications ISO14000 and professionals working in the area of environmental management to safe money, time and efforts, which are wasted in the search for the meanings of environmental terms. This specification represent the fruit of cooperation between technical experts in the Technical Committee ISO 2007, experts and technical terms ISO organization workers. This version of specification will be made available in the form of a dictionary that includes all the definitions contained in the international specification series and will be issued in both English and French languages[15],[16].

History and Formation of Marble and Granite

Marble is one of materials used in Islamic art and religious in many areas, it is a rocky substance witch is formed by warming transition of limestone, it consists of calcium carbonate, which is evolving from rocks dominated by white red and black colors. Egypt did not know the use of marble until the end of the Al Ayobi times. In recent ages marble and ornamental stones in embellishing buildings whether outside or inside. Solid types of marble are chosen for these embellishment which have bright colors, can be burnished and polished, they give beautiful reflections of light. Marble is also used in the furniture industry in making boxes for electricity and in the establishment of memorial and upright tombstone and the clinics[17].

Granite is a ground fiery rock formed under high temperatures characterized by coarse fabric granules. It freezes slowly under earth surface, which allowed the growth of clear crystals There are other types of granite characterized in terms of fabric, which are characterized with the rest of fire rocks, this fabric indicates that the granite freezes in two stages. The First slowly and the other rapidly[18].

The ancient Egyptians knew granite especially the black and pink granite. They used it in temples and the unique pieces of arts, this industry has prospered a great prosperity in the times of the modern nation. Egyptian granite is internationally described as the strongest kind of high solidity, one of its advantages is that it does not absorb water. this gives it a high proportional advantage especially in the areas of high humidity such as beaches. The colors of Egyptian marble lie exclusively between beige and yellow with their degrees. There is a proportional advantage for the Egyptian marble, beside its desired color, its price is still an international competent, especially in the circumstances of low exchange rate of the Egyptian pound, compared with dollar[19].

Marble and Granite Industry and its Effects on the Environment

Granite is a ground firestone with coarse textile, rich with Quartz, Feldspar, Potash, Muscovite, poor of iron and magnesium minerals, so it is classified as acidic[20].

Formation of Marble and Granite in the Earth

The industry of building materials from natural stones is considered as one of the most important industries which helps in the civilization spread on the surface of the earth, Fig. 13.1 shows international market of marble

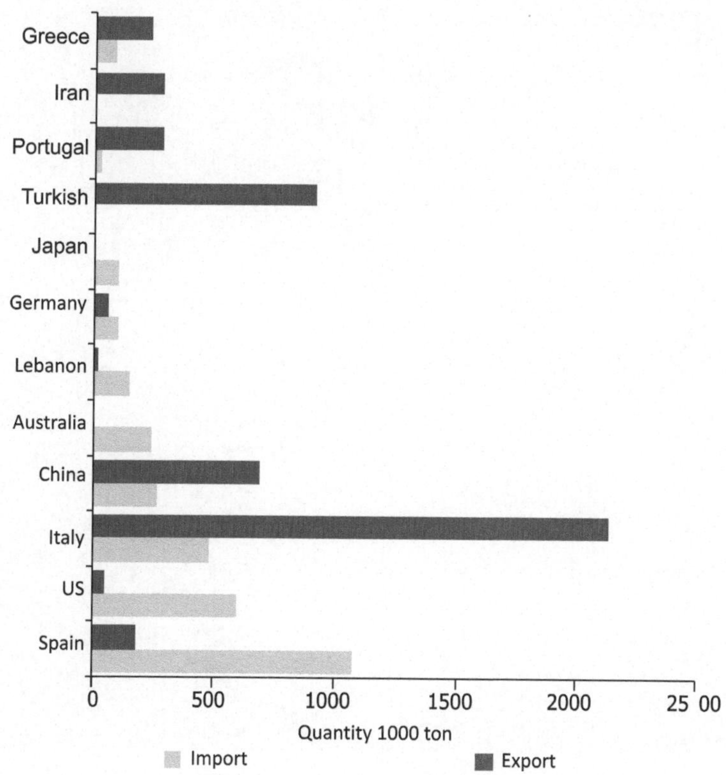

Fig. 13.1: International market of marble and granite

and granite, but the dust resulting from this industry has great damage on agriculture, human being and animal who are exposed to it. Despite of the non stopping calls to get rid of this dust and prevent it from coming out through the chimneys of these manufactures by using filters, but pollution of the environment is still going on[(21),(23)].

Production of Marble and Granite in Egypt

The mining of marble and granite are one of the most important mining industries, which are spread in different areas in Egypt Fig. 13.2 and fig. 13.3 show the mining areas of granite and marble in Egypt respectively.

The most important area for mining of marble and granite is Shak El Toaban, which lies on the road of the Autostrad, in the southern area, in Cairo. This area lies in the south of Maadi on the Autostrad road. It has many manufactures for marble, granite and other building materials, its total space is estimated at 1000 acre. This area is the most important area in the world for the production and manufacturing of raw marble which is exported to all countries in the world. It has been given this name for its natural conditions and its geographical form as well as its characterized history, it has gone through

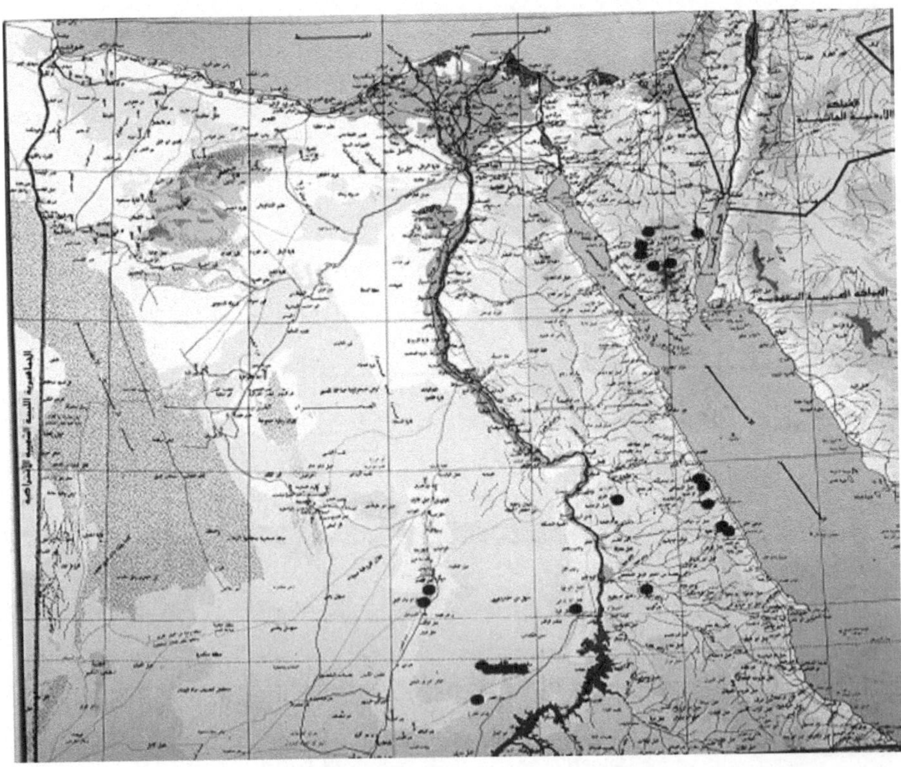

Fig. 13.2: Mining areas of granite in Egypt[(9)]

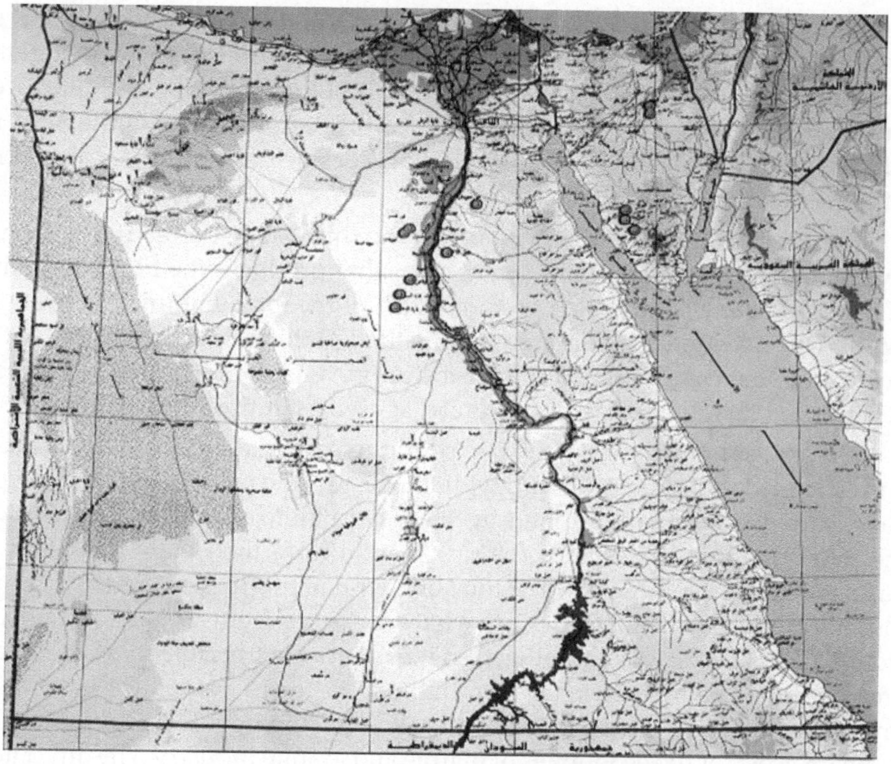

Fig. 13.3: Mining areas of marble in Egypt[9]

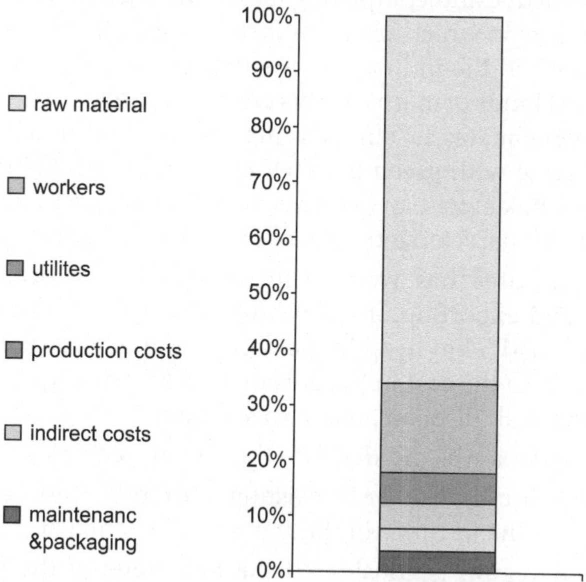

Fig. 13.4: Estimated cost for the economies of marble and granite industry

different periods till it reached what it is now, it is a mountain area far away from inhabitedness, it was specialized in lime Articles and stone pit materials, it did not produce marble in the beginning. It holds about 300 manufactures and more than two thousand workshop for the supplementary industries in which about 25 thousand are employed that is beside the indirect employment which is estimated at 30 thousand workers[(23),(24)].

The area of Shak El Thoban comes in the third stage on the international level in the list of the most important areas that produces the highest quality of marble in the world. It also produces 78% of the total amount of marble in Egypt. The investment in this area is more than 3 billion Egyptian pounds, it is expected to increase to 5 billion after the improvement of the area to provide 35 thousand direct working opportunity, as well as indirect opportunities[(25)].

The amount of exports are expected to increase in the near future. Today, it is estimated to be 225 million Egyptian pounds, the owners of the stone pit have started using the wild land in the area to build marble manufactories, the area has started to receive the raw marble from the Galala mountain in Suez, the Red sea and Aswan. The total of Egyptian production coming to Shak Elsoban area is reached 70% besides what are arrived from abroad for example from Turkey, Italy, India and others, so it has become a marble manufacturing area beside of being stone pit area, the manufactures procedure have been improved and have used the highest level of technology. Fig 13.4 shows the estimated cost for the economies of marble and granite industry. The direct and indirect work opportunities in the area are estimated at 75 thousand, it starts from lime, constructive and completing tasks. The total space of the industrial area reaches 400 acre in which 235 manufactories and 300 workshop are found most of them work in the industry of marble, granite and stone of all kinds. There are different kinds of marble in this area such as marble of Zafarana, pink, peige, yellow, perlatau, tersta, elmenya, alpechino, white and black marble, al galala, white marble with green lines, chrestina marble, alfelto and different kinds of granite. Shak el thoban becomes one of the biggest industrial area for granite, this area is characterized by people with experience and skills[(5),(9)].

Shak El soban area has won an international and local reputation in manufacturing and exporting of marble and granite. It is located in the east of the Autostrad road 5 km deep in the desert on the border of the sanctuary of the valley Degla in the east in the area of Tora Maadi. Fig. 13.5, fig 13.6 and fig. 13.7 show the shak Elsoban area from satellites[(8)].

Shak el Soban area was divided into three main regions:-

The First region is the area existing currently and has the marble manufactories, it is the territory of the status of the hands of.

The Second region is considered the first stage of the project to plan and specify the industrial area in Shak el Thoban and the space available for investment is 35 acre and the specified space is 30 acre and the spaces that have not been specified is 5 acre ,the number of projects is 39 projects ,working opportunities are 1980 opportunities, the amount of investment is 21.9 million Egyptian pounds.

Fig. 13.5: The location of shak elsoban and its borders from satellite(15)

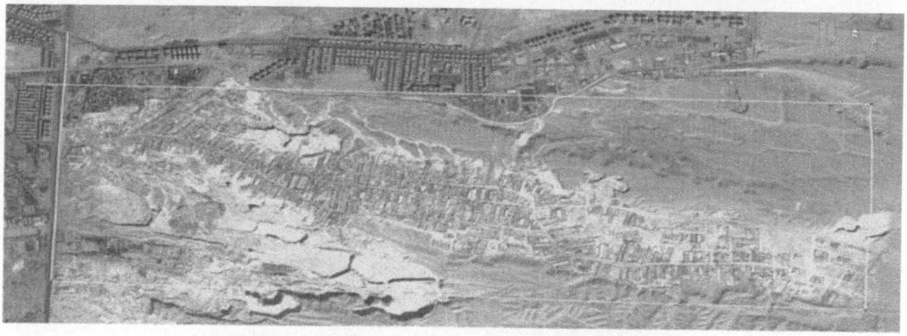

Fig. 13.6: Shak Elsoban from satellite(15)

Fig. 13.7: Stone pit area from satellite(15)

The Third region it is the second stage of the project to plan and specify the industrial area in Shak el Thoban and the space offered for investments 290 acre, the space specified is 104 acre and the spaces that have not been specified are 186 acre the number of project is 103 industrial projects. the opportunities of work are 5346 opportunities, the amount of investment is 308 million Egyptian pounds. the dominating characteristic in the market of marble and granite is the randomness of distribution this is why the locale product does not contribute to the marble and granite in big portion. **Fig. 13.8 shows the strategies of marble and granite wastes in Egypt and randomness in distribution, while fig. 13.9 shows volume of investment of marble in the Egyptian market and fig. 13.10 shows the marble imports and exports in tons[(13),(14)].**

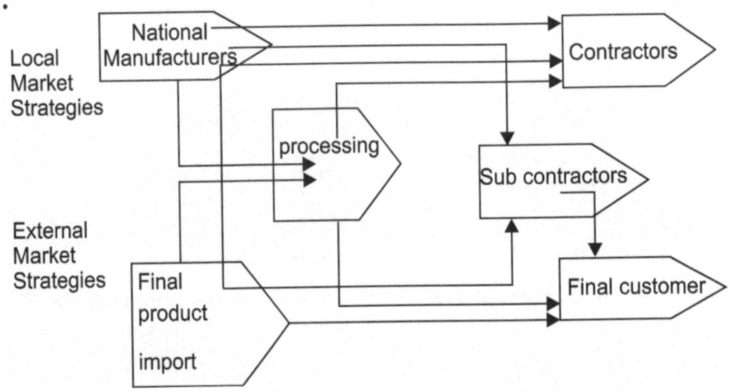

Fig. 13.8: The strategies of marble and granite wastes in Egypt[(16)]

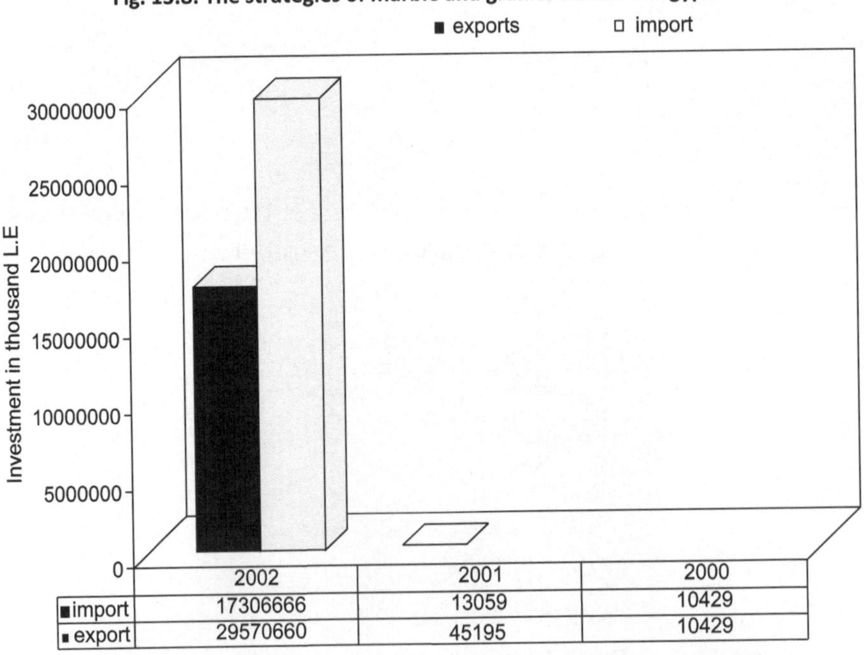

	2002	2001	2000
■ import	17306666	13059	10429
■ export	29570660	45195	10429

Fig. 13.9: Volume of investment of marble in the Egyptian market[(17)]

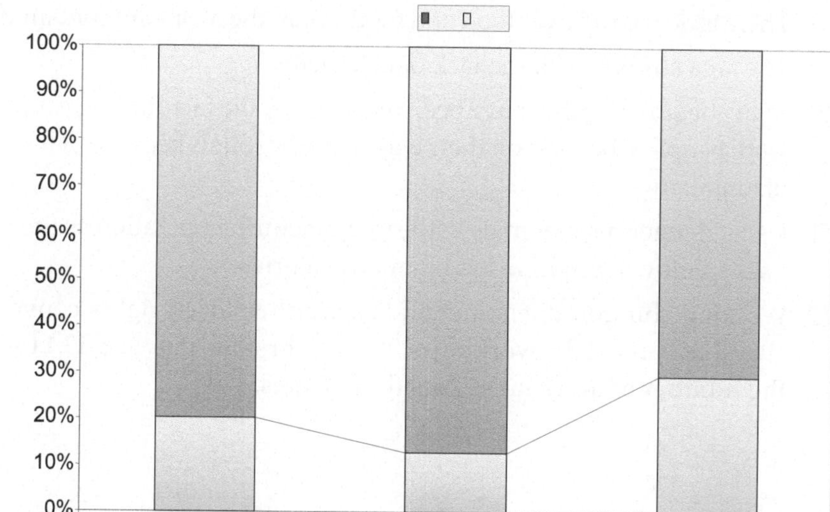

	2002 year	2001 year	2000year
■ Export	26471828.00	29330.8	6699.0
□ Import	6691538.0	4329.5	2788.4

Fig. 13.10: The marble imports and exports in tons(17)

Reasons of Problem Increase

1. One of the most important areas of marble industry in the world is Shak el Thoban is still suffering from randomness and lack of services and utilities
2. Most factories in shak el Thoban do not have the necessary licenses to carry out the business
3. The area does not have proper drinking water. The water is being sold in vehicle which is brought directly from the Nile covered with moss and bacteria and there is no sanitation to help taking away the remains
4. Accidents are repeatable because of low level of vision high temperature and humidity, large number of impurities and suspended objects in the surrounding environments, sand and dust resulting from the cutting and polishing operation of marble specially the humid remains which calls (alsohla)
5. The road is not surfaced, narrow and always crowded which lead to many accidents.
6. Hinders private cars are carry injured people to the hospital because the ambulance serves only the housing area and not the industrial area
7. The emergency unit is a new building that have no helpers, no doctors and no medical devices

8. There is no control over food and food stores, the meals are contaminated
9. The area suffers from the lack of electricity
10. Many death cases that have been recorded by the fact-finding committee were people who died on their way to the hospitals because of the delay of ambulance.
11. Using dangerous materials in the manufacturing operation as fire water used in glowing marble lead to many injuries
12. Working children phenomenon is against children rights convention 1989 that banned the working of children in stone pits. **Fig. 13.11 shows the number of accident as function of ages.**

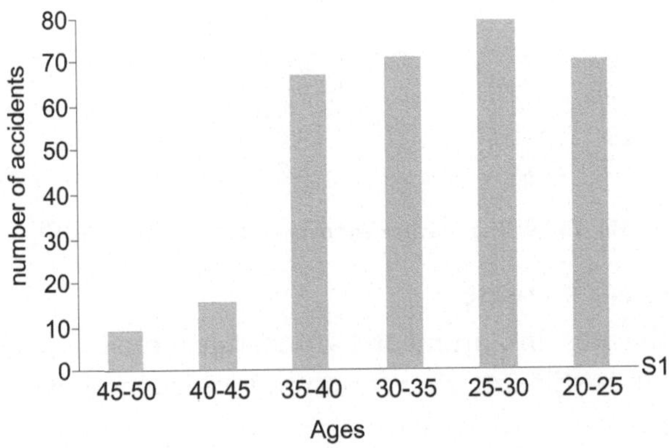

Fig. 13.11: The number of accident as function of ages[1]

The Negative Effects of the Marble and Granite Remains

The outbreak of chest and allergy disease between workers and residents due to dust and sand caused by sawing and cutting marble that can even be respiratory rigidity and cancer, they cause death specially with negligence of gloves and chest filters, chest disease are spread between workers because of drinking water and food contamination which in turn caused kidneys ache, diseases also caused by high temperature and lack of clean water, vomiting cases and intestinal ache between workers caused by eating contaminated food. Fig. 13.12 Rate and kind of accidents. Breaking bones injuries in feet and legs occur in front of the accidents then followed by head injuries while death cases are due to electric stun and falling of marble blocks on the victims.

The Economic Effects

The quantity of wastage lift up the price of the final product and affects the economies of the industry. Fig. 13.13 show the rate of cost increase with losses increase.

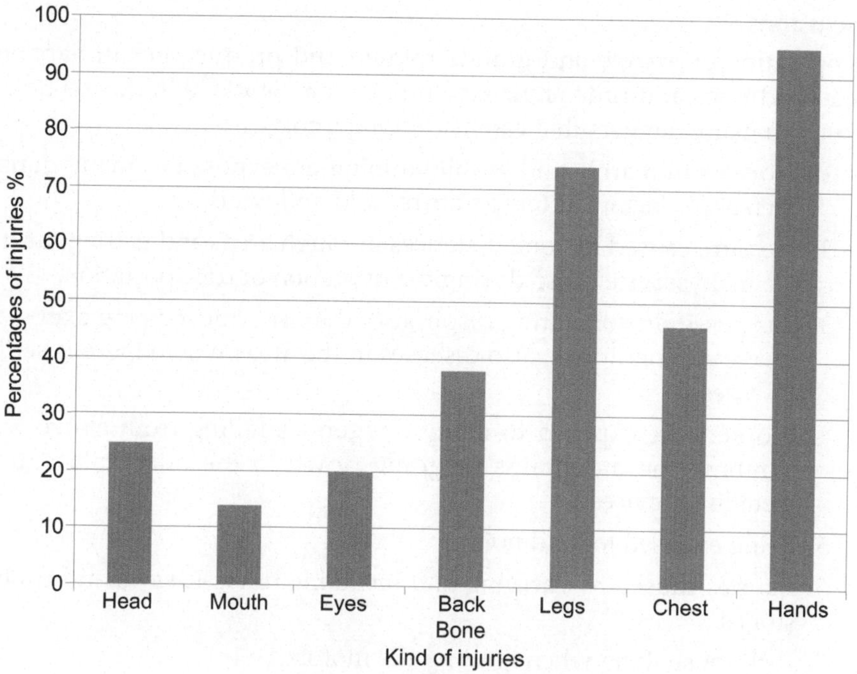

Fig. 13.12: Rate and kinds of accidents(1)

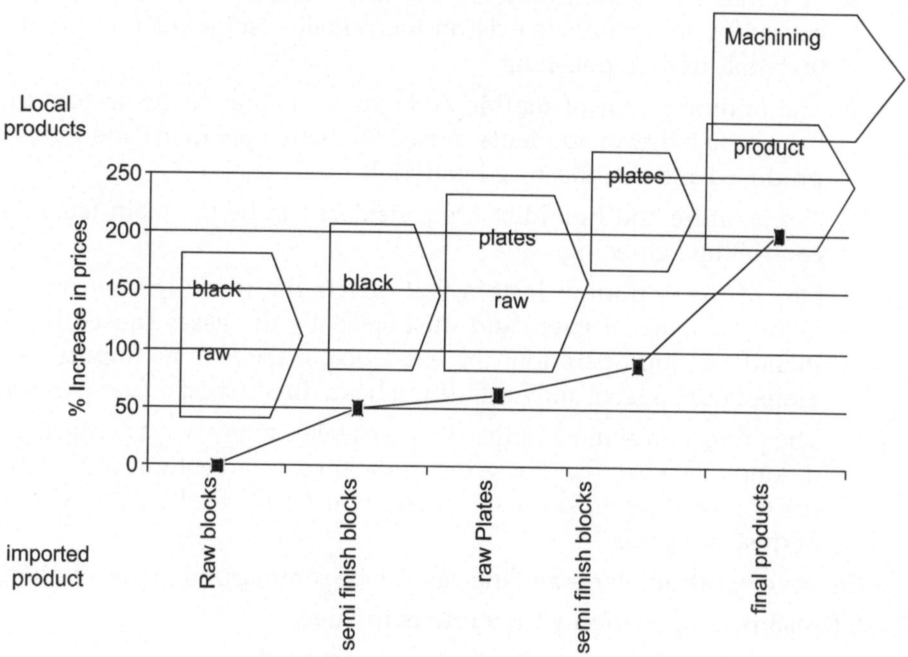

Fig. 13.13: Rate of cost increase with losses increase

Conclusions

The operation of marble and granite mining and production can happen in all air conditions and rude environmental factors, workers in this section are exposed to many dangers that can be divided into:

1. Workers in marble and granite mining are exposed to many dangers such as air factors as temperature, cold and wind.
2. Pressure caused by long distances in tough areas and getting far from the main service camp during the operation of transportation.
3. The possibility of getting respiratory diseases due to being exposed to severe air conditions, also diseases in the areas where there is settling diseases.
4. Workers are exposed to many dangers as falling from above when climbing the mountains or going down to the mines also during installing devices.
5. Being exposed to loud noise.
6. Injuries caused by carrying and installing devices, saws and rubbing stones.
7. Risks of shaking when igniting the motors.
8. Risks of slipping.
9. Skin infection caused by dust and contaminated water and diseases caused by the materials exist in the remains (sohla) or the chemical materials used in polishing.
10. The mining sector of marble and granite is one of the sectors that have probability of accidents caused by many operations and kinds of produced and manufactured materials.
11. Temperature and humidity are considered to be the main factors in controlling lightening.
12. One of the important factors that affects the working environment is the existence of gases and dust specially the gases caused by the manufacturing operation .the existence of gases is as important as temperature degree and humidity, it has a direct effect on temperature.
13. The protection against industrial gases takes many ways according to its kinds and effects and risks regarding poison and volume of granules, use of protective masks against gases which suite the kind and volume of dust and gases .

Causes of work accidents and injuries can be summarized in the following:

First: Reasons have relation with workers include:

1. not paying attention and concentrating at work.
2. lack of training and experience

3. the failure to follow rules and instructions of safety
4. lack of experience and training to use tools and devices
5. not wearing personal protective equipment

Second: reasons have relation with work environment:

1. chemical factors (vapor, gases ....)
2. physical factors (noise, temperature.......)
3. biological factors (bacteria...................)
4. lack of cleaning and tidiness of work place
5. mistakes at planning and execution periods
6. lack of safety tools
7. risks of materials and tools that have radioactivity which appear naturally

Conclusions concerning the case study

Through the study of work accidents and injuries in this important site Shak el Soban, it is clear that the main reason for work accidents and injuries were detected as follow:-

1. Workers do not stick to rules, instructions and guidelines of safety in carrying out the business
2. Summer months are the months in which work accidents and injuries happen because of high temperature degree
3. The first age group are more exposed to accidents and injuries, accidents decrease as one gets older and have the necessary experiences
4. The rate of absence days for each injury is in betterment from one year to the other
5. The main reason for most accidents was electric stun and negligence
6. The accident and injuries were distributed along all positions in the site.

Recommendations

1. a mechanism to deal with the remains weather, gases and harmful dust by recycling it or by safely getting rid of it must be mentioned.
2. providing rescue cars in the area that can provide protection and first aids to the probable injury.
3. changing the emergency point into a small hospital to be able to deal faster with injury cases.
4. controlling the use of dangerous tools and chemicals in the productive and industrial operation.
5. it is necessary to create sidewalk, surfacing, lighting in all roads, preplanning the area to provide clean water and industrial drainage with cooperation of governmental and public efforts

6. awakening workers in this section of following guidelines, and safety instructions in doing the jobs.
7. the use of gloves masks because the nature of work in this area is dangerous and requires precautions
8. choosing the right persons for each kind of job and excluding children employment
9. having commitment towards the conventions and international laws dealing with workers rights and children employment
10. develop new laws that guarantee workers and residents rights through clear environmental policies
11. training in all stages and all levels to reduce accidents and injuries of work
12. giving and arranging breaks in summer and winter to be fitting with temperature degree.
13. Legalization of working hours according to age categories and work type
14. having health insurance to all workers, periodic disclosure and providing healthy food to be suitable with the kind of effort, perform and awakening them to their rights in cases of disability death and injury.
15. planting the area with green spaces and making wall around it to prevent pollution from creeping to the housing area.
16. measurement devices that have to be used in the industrial environment to supervise the suitable conditions of work such as hygrometer to measure humidity, gases detectors, temperature sensor and antimatter which give an indicator of work state in work environment.

REFERENCES

1. The Fact-finding Comittee Reports (non governmental organizations) about Situation in Shak Elsoban, 2007.
2. Hose G, Hyne R, Lim RP, How important is the 'eco' in Ecotoxicology, Australian Marine Sciences Association Annual Conference, Australian Marine Sciences Association, 50, Sydney 2002.
3. Recommendation of 10th World Congress of the International Organization of Psychophysiology (IOP), Elsevier Science, 39, Sydney, 2000.
4. Industrial safety. (Google advanced search)
5. Martin Grayson, Encyclopedia of Composite Materials and Components, 1983, pp. 324-340.
6. www.britannica.com/bcom/eb/article/printable/2/0,5722,118752,00.html, 1999.
7. Doetze J. Sikkema (2002). "Manmade Fibers one Hundred Years: Polymers and Polymer Design". *J Appl Polym Sci, John Wiley & Sons, Inc.* (83): 484-488.
8. http://www.construction-institute.org

9. Atlas of mining wealth in Egypt, National projects, HBRC,2007.
10. http://www.hse.gov.uk/construction/designers/index.htm
11. http://www.designforconstructionsafety.org
12. http://www.workcover.nsw.gov.au/Publications/OHS/SafetyGuides/chairsafetyin designtool.html
13. Industrial Accident Prevention, the Dresden Institute for Industrial Safety and Protection, Technical fundamentals series, 2002.
14. Sarkar, P.B., *Sci. & Culture,* 1 (1935) 60, 3 (1937) 411, 485, 551.
15. www.googleearth.com
16. Report of Prime minister center, imports and exports annual report,2009.
17. Reports of
18. Gravitis, J. and P. Erins. *J. Appl. Polym. Sci.,* Appl. Polym Symp., 37 (1983) 421.
19. Staudinger, H., Ber 53B (1920) 1073.
20. Carothers, W. H. and J. W. Hill, *j Am. Chem. Soc.,* 54 (1932) 1559.
21. E.1. Dupont de Nemours and Company, US Patent 2,130,523, (1938).
22. Shlack, P., US Patent 2,241,321, (1941).
23. Whinfield, J. R. and J. T. Dickson, British Patent 578,079, (1941).
24. Proceedings of the American Association for Cancer Research 41, Cadmus Journal Services, 709, San Francisco, 2002.
25. I. Ghosh, *P., Polymer Science and Technology-Plastics, Rubbers, Blends and Composites,* 2nd ed., Tata McGraw-Hill, New Delhi, 2002.

14

Tribology of Laser Irradiated Nano and Micro Composite

ABSTRACT

In these work, new composite material is manufactured from poly methyl metha acrylate PMMA matrix reinforced by fiber glass Type E. The effect of volume fraction of fiber and length to diameter ratio are studied, The effect of reinforcement amount, size and distribution on the structure are discussed, friction and wear characteristics were determined at different volume fractions and fiber sizes. The hardness and the wear resistance of randomly distributed PMMA matrix composite were significantly enhanced, the maximum conditions for reinforcement of PMMA matrix composite to improve tribology characteristics were evaluated. The effect of laser irradiation on the mechanical properties were evaluated by irradiation of composite material after manufacturing with different kinds of lasers, CW argon ion laser and Pulsed Nd-YAG laser were used to irradiate composite material. Hardness, wear rate and coefficient of friction were evaluated at the same test condition of the un-irradiated composite. The significant improvement in the mechanical properties at certain irradiation conditions were evaluated.

Keywords: *Structure, Hardness, Wear, PMMA, randomly distributed.*

Introduction

Composite will not, split, delaminate or absorb moisture. Therefore, its life span will be many times more than traditional materials.Fibers are the most commonly used reinforcement in many types of composite. If the fiber density is known you also have a fiber diameter, otherwise it is simpler to measure diameters in micrometres[1]. Microfibers in technical fibers refer to ultrafine fibers (glass or meltblown thermoplastics) often used in filtration. Newer fiber designs include extruding fiber that splits into multiple finer fibers[2-5]. Most synthetic fibers are round in cross-section, but special designs can be hollow, oval, star-shaped or trilobal. The latter design provides more optically reflective properties. Synthetic textile fibers are often crimped to provide bulk in a woven, nonwoven or knitted structure. Fiber surfaces can also be dull or bright. Dull surfaces reflect more light while bright tends to transmit light and make the fiber more transparent. Very short and/or irregular fibers have been called fibrils. Natural cellulose, such as cotton or bleached kraft show smaller fibrils jutting out and away from the main fiber structure[5-7].

Polymer based Composites with randomly distributed filler are used in a wide range of applications in aerospace, marine, automotive, surface transport and sports equipment markets. Damage to composite components is not always visible to the naked eye and the extent of damage is best determined for structural components[8].

Polymers are used in tribological applications for many reasons. In many instances, polymers perform a dual function as both a structural and a tribological material. An example of dual functionality is self–lubricated polymers. Concerns such as weight, cost, and manufacturability are some of the same issues with the use of polymers and polymeric composites for sliding applications as in structural applications. Polymer failure in tribological applications is often catastrophic and occurs in a very short time scale, work was performed with curved short glass fibers and has found great applicability in the contact and subsequent friction of electrometric sliding. However, the glass is roughened, the real contact is reduced from the hertzian contact area[9].

Composite is also user-friendly in many applications. It is suitable for applications such as drop in floor panels for truck-bed; slate gate; decking; porch and stoop ceiling; siding and fencing; concrete forming panel; yacht interior or exterior decking and paneling. Many other applications where flexural strength and lightweight are important. Composite is pre-finished with colored surface[10-12].

II. EXPERIMENTAL WORK

Materials

Matrix (PMMA)

The matrix is polymethyl metha acrylate (PMMA). It is thermoplastic prepared from monomer (methyl methacrylate) by additional polymerization process; polymer was in the granule form[13-15].

Filler

Fiberglass (brand milled fibers) are glass filaments coated with a specific sizing to enhance resin compatibility and hammer milled to a specified bulk density. Fibers are hammered milled to an average fiber length. Average fiber length is determined by the input glass and process conditions. In the current work, milled fibers are made from "E" (electrical) glass which conforms to MIL-R- 60346C specification with average bulk density 0.55g/cm^3 in floccular and powder form with length to diameter ratio (L/d=50 and, L/d=1) respectively[16].

II. Preparation of Material

Grinding

A blinder with variable speeds is used to change the pieces of thermo-plastics into powder form, The blinder speed is about 15,500 rpm, work at 200 volt - 50 Hz, and the grinding time is about 90 sec. Switch off for cooling is lasted about 180 sec to prevent the agglomeration of the particles and achieve reasonable degree of quality in grinding. The retained granules after sieving will be returned to blinder[17].

Mixing

Automatic mixing for thermoplastic in the powder form with short fibers at different aspects ratio was done. The amount of material required was calculated by changing the volume fraction percent into weight percent (L/d=50 and, L/d=1) respectively[18].

The material prepared by grinding and mixing of thermoplastic in the powder form. The mixing of fiber with thermoplastics and other modifiers[19-21]. The process is done with certain volume fractions depend on the properties required in the final composite, the composite material find finally in the solid form and have different characteristics depends on the fiber percentages (volume fraction of fibers ≃ 20% to 17%) and fiber size (length to diameter ratio = 50).

Manufacturing process

Plastic powders and short fibers were mixed together in the solid state. The mixture is heated at the required temperature, according to its components. The heating rate depends on the type of the joining material, compression and cooling were done for heated mixture. Nano composite material is fabricated, the new composite material is distinguished with the light weight and the ability to endure scratch and damping capacity. It is also liable for the easy formation and is distinctive with different colors and shapes

Laser Irradiation

Samples used in this investigation were in a shape of disk of 25mm diameter and 7mm length. The irradiation is done on both sides of the samples in different positions to cover all the area of the sample and achieve homogeneous surface suitable for testing. The different lasers irradiated samples at different conditions were examined before and after laser irradiation and the effect of laser was determined.

CW Argon ion Laser Irradiation

(innova400) which have power of 25 watts multi-line wavelength from 514.5 nm to 465.5 nm, the power used in the experiment is 1 watt.

Pulsed Nd-YAG Laser Irradiation

The first harmonic lies in the IR region (wavelength = 1064nm) with power of about 60mw, duration time 6ns, repetition rate 10Hz and energy (360mj/pulse), the third harmonic generation (wavelength = 355nm) in the UV range, power 10mw, duration time 7ns, repetition rate 17Hz and energy per pulse (40mj/pulse).

Mechanical Test

Hardness

The hardness of the specimens were measured by using means of Barcol impression according to ASTM-D2583, the indentor cone with 26° and 0.157mm, the sample must have smooth and polished surface with specified thickness, the load ranges from 6.8kg to 4.5kg each hardness value is an average of 29 reading for every specimen (5) specimen at each condition were examined). The measurements are good up to ± 6%.

Friction and Were Testing

The test was carried out in normal atmosphere include weighing the test specimen before and after test for assessing the wear properties in such contacts, pin-on disc wear test machine are used in this work. The tested specimen was held in sliding contact with rotating hardened alloy steel (Mn-Cr) disc with hardness (HRC65). The test specimen is mounted to holder which was designed for easy change of pin (tested samples). The normal load range (0.2 - 3kg) is applied by dead weight at the end of level to cause the actual normal applied load on the test specimen to increase by a factor (liver ratio=2.75). At the end of loading beam there was a counter weight for oppose the beam weight, so the applied forces on the specimen come from the applied dead weight only cause a sliding speed ranges from (0.12:1.31) m/sec applied for 10min. The friction force between the vertical stationary specimen and rotation hardened steel disc was measured by strain gauges fixed on a cantilever attached to the tribo-testing machine from the signal, strain gauges was fed through an electric circuit F10MK11. Digital strain bridge reading are calibrated to read frictional force value by applying known dead weight later on the arm. The effect of Brinell hardness number of different specimen on properties are recorded.

Table 14.1: The Density of the Composite Material at different Volume Fraction of Fibers and different Length to Diameter Ratio

Specimen no	L/D	Fiber volume %	Density
1	0	0	1.12
2	1	17	1.191
3	1	35	1.224
4	1	50	1.246
5	1	65	1.247
6	50	17	1.342
7	50	35	1.327
8	50	50	1.584
9	50	60	1.729

The coefficient of friction is determined by :

$$U = \frac{F}{N} \tag{1}$$

F is the friction force.

N is the normal load.

U is the coefficient of friction

The wear volume is calculated from the relation

$$V = \frac{w}{\rho} \tag{2}$$

W is the wear weight the difference in weight of specimen before and after test.

ρ is the density of Composite in gm/cm^3. Table 14.1) shows the density of the composite material at different volume fraction of fibers and different length to diameter ratio.

The sliding distance calculated from the relation

$$L = 2\pi rn \tag{3}$$

r is the mean radius of the rotating disc.

L is determined to be 78.5m (sliding distance)

n is the number of revolution

The following relation is used to calculated wear coefficient:-

$$V = K\frac{LW}{3P} \tag{4}$$

V the volume removed by wear from the surface.

K The wear coefficient.

L Length of travel.

W The normal load.

P The Indentation hardness of the softer body.

Liver ratio = 2.75

Results and Discussions

Hardness

The mechanical properties of the samples were recorded, the barcoul hardness of composite is evaluated at different volume fraction of fiber at different length to diameter ratio. The effect of laser irradiation on the mechanical properties were evaluated by irradiation of composite material after manufacturing with different kinds of lasers, CW argon ion laser in the visible rage 510nm and Pulsed Nd-YAG laser (third harmonic generation 355nm), each value was the mean of five (29) readings. Hardness value is strong function of the amount of reinforcement presented due to manufacturing process. The maximum value was recorded for laser irradiated structures at 50% volume fraction fibers when the fiber size (length to diameter ration) L/D is 50 and the minimum one was recorded for un-reinforced plastics at fiber size L/D equal 1.

The correlation between the Barcoul hardness of the composite specimen and the amount of total fiber volume fraction at different laser irradiation condition is shown in figure 14.1. Figure 14.2 shows the same correlation at different fiber size (length to diameter ratio) L/D= 50. It is clear that hardness increases by increasing the amount of fibers which may be attributed by the accumulative strain hardening effect.

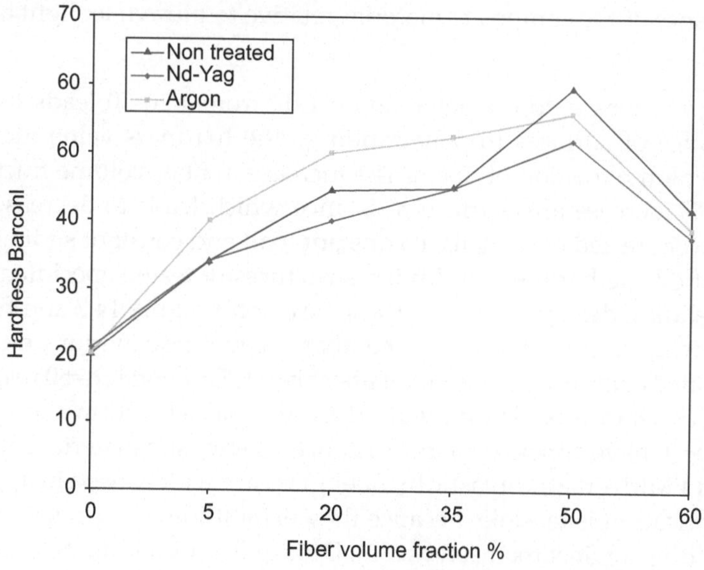

Fig. 14.1: The effect of fiber volume fraction on hardness at L/D=1

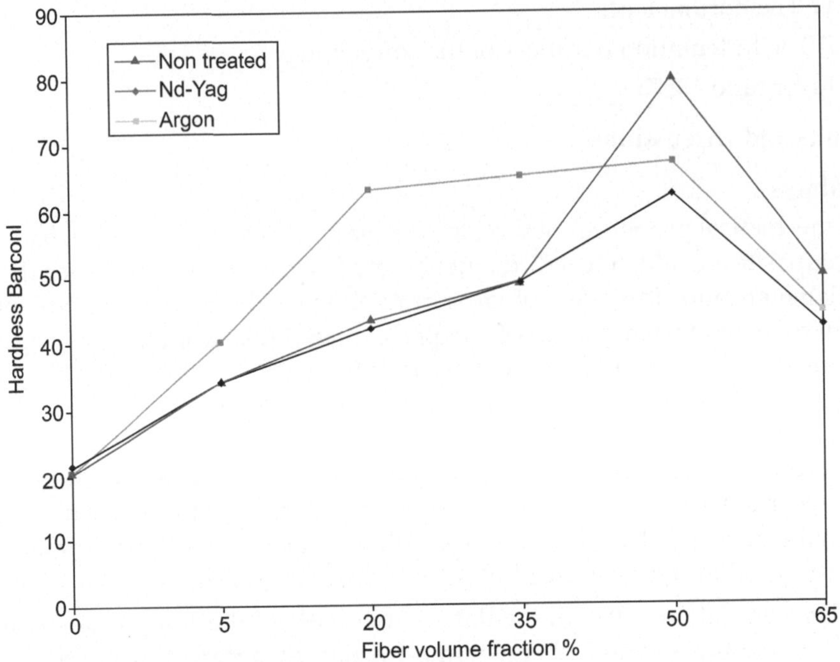

Fig. 14.2: The effect of fiber volume fraction on hardness at L/D=50

The laser irradiation conditions include the type of laser used and the amount of energy absorbed have significant effect on hardness, the CW laser at 510nm in the visible range have ability to improve the mechanical characteristics of the composite material relative to ultraviolet light at 355nm.

Wear

Increasing the length to diameter ration L/D from 1 to 50 leads to increase the resistance of surfaces to penetration so the hardness value increased at the same volume fraction of fibers. The increase in fiber volume fraction from 17% to 50% increase also surface resistance which leads to decrease in wear rate. The wear tested specimens at constant load and constant sliding speed is dependent on the hardness and microstructures of tested specimens, during wear test sliding deformation of surface may occur, figure 14.3 and figure 14.4 show the wear rate as function of the fiber volume fraction for un-irradiated and irradiated composite materials at fiber sizes L/D=1 and L/d=50 respectively. The wear resistance is also influenced by the particles form the cylindrical shape L/D=50 have superior wear resistance. Composite material prepared by reinforced PMMA thermoplastic by fiber glass are widely used in applications where lubrication is feasible, because they exhibit low wear rates and can be used as sliding against themselves (35). During the initial sliding of composite reinforced by fibers. The basal planes of composite shear appear and provide a continuous source of a solid lubricant due to the crystallographic structure,

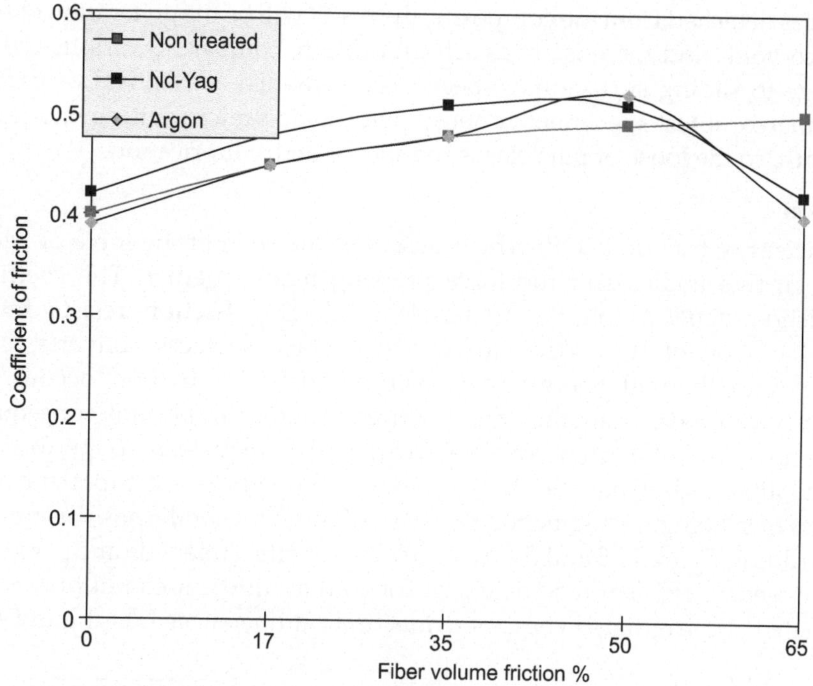

Fig. 14.3: The effect of fiber volume fraction on coefficient of friction at L/D=1

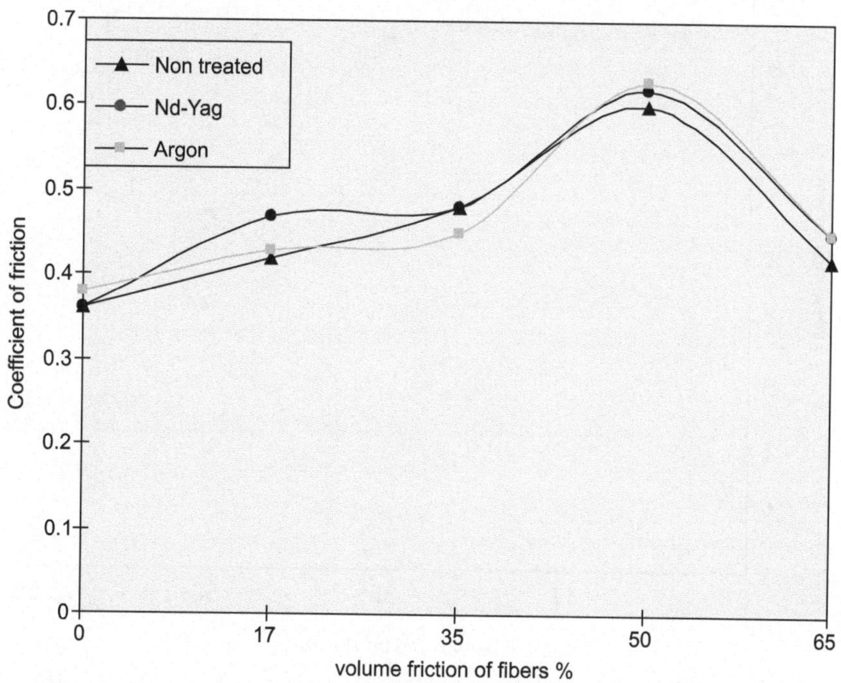

Fig. 14.4: The effect of fiber volume fraction on coefficient of friction at L/D=50

particles detached from the composite, the result will be the generation of series of mico-voids and there is act as self lubrication, comparing various types of damage to sliding surface have been observed such as removal of particles from matrix of test specimens reduced deformation micro cutting and tearing in depth, so the loose of particles is the source of dry lubrication.

Friction

Coefficient of friction (COF) which describes the ratio of the force of friction between two bodies and the force pressing them together. The coefficient of friction depends on the materials used. **Dry friction** resists relative lateral motion of two solid surfaces in contact, surfaces converts kinetic energy into thermal energy whenever motion with friction occurs. This property can have dramatic consequences. Another important consequence of many types of friction can be wear, which may lead to performance degradation and/or damage to components. Friction is a component of the science of tribology. The fraction behavior of different conditions was function on hardness, figure 14.5 and figure 14.6 show the effect fiber volume percentage on the wear coefficient (coefficient of friction) at different conditions, for un-irradiated and irradiated composite materials at fiber sizes L/D=1 and L/d=50

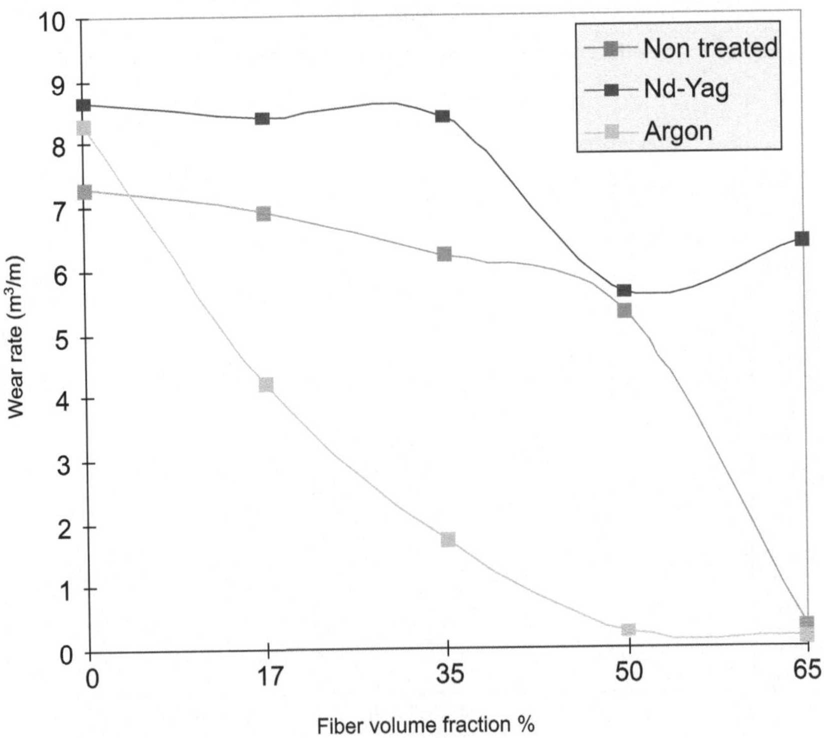

Fig. 14.5: The effect of fiber volume fraction on wear rate at L/D=1

respectively. Dry friction arises from a combination of inter-surface adhesion, surface roughness, surface deformation, and surface contamination. The force of friction is always exerted in a direction that opposes movement (for kinetic friction). The origin of kinetic friction at nanoscale can be explained by thermodynamics.Upon sliding, new surface forms at the back of a sliding true contact, and existing surface disappears at the front of it. Since all surfaces involve the thermodynamic surface energy.

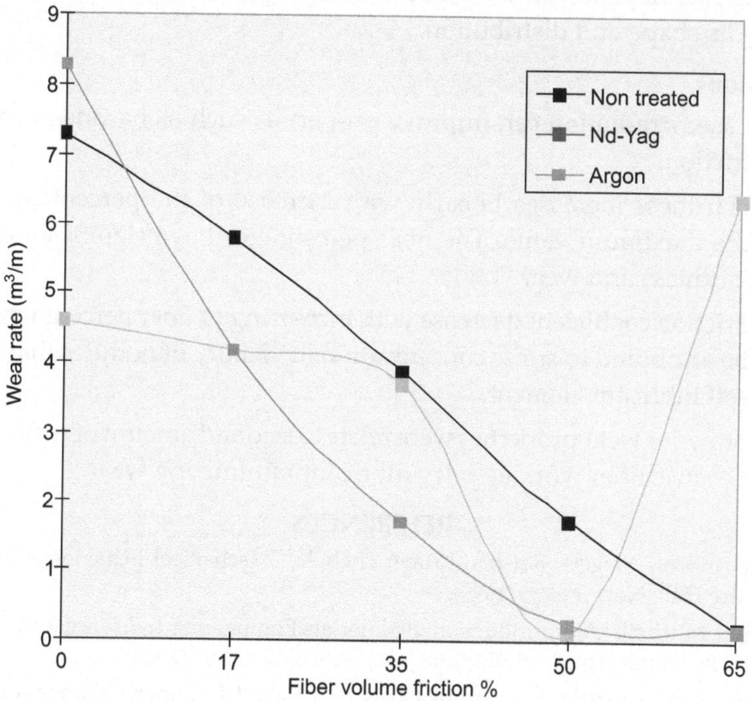

Fig. 14.6: The effect of fiber volume fraction on wear rate at L/D=50

Work must be spent in creating the new surface, and energy is released as heat in removing the surface. Thus, a force is required to move the back of the contact, and frictional heat is released at the front, however, do affect kinetic friction for micro- and nano-scale objects where surface area forces dominate inertial forces, to be primarily caused by chemical bonding between the surfaces, rather than interlocking.[21]

The improve in the resistance to surface penetration which leads to improve in hardness and wear resistance increase with fiber volume fraction till a certain limit, it reach maximum value at 50% fiber percentages, when increasing fiber volume fraction up to 65%, both hardness and wear rate decreased to lower level, the matrix will not be able to bind the additives at higher concentration. Each fiber concentration depends on the type of laser used which leads to change in the amount of energy absorbed. The amount of laser energy absorbed is function of the fiber size the spherical particles L/D=1 have smaller surface area for the same volume comparing with cylindrical one at L/D=50.

During laser irradiation, when the amount of laser energy go through the semi transparent material, the laser will not be coherent inside the composite specimen, laser is scatter when strike the particles inside the structure, the scattering rate depends on the amount of fiber particles inside the structure , specially its shape and distribution.

Conclusions

1. Laser irradiation can improve properties such as hardness, wear and friction.
2. Hardness increases linearly with increase of the percentage of fiber the maximum value. The fiber percentages have significant effect on hardness and wear
3. Friction coefficient decrease with increasing of fiber percent which may be attributed to stress concentration in vicinity of nodules that work as self lubricant element.
4. Superior wear properties were relate to size and amount of reinforcement because fiber work as a dry lubricant minimizing wear.

REFERENCES

1. Marc Andrew Megers, Krishan Kumar chalwla, "Mechanical Behavior of Materials", Prentice Hall, New Jersey, (1999).
2. Brain S. Mitchell, "An Introduction to Materials Engineering & Science for Chemical & Materials Engineering", 1th Edition, John Wily & Son, Inc, (2004).
3. "Resistance to Brittle Fracture of Glass Reinforced Polymer Composites Used in Composite (Nonceramic) Insulators", Lucas S. Kumosa, Maciej S. Kumosa, Daniel L. Armentrout, IEEE TRANSACTIONS ON POWER DELIVERY, Vol. 20, No. 4, October, (2005).
4. "Comparison of Tensile Strength of Different Carbon Fabric Reinforced Epoxy Composites", Jane Maria Maulstick, Journal of Materials Research, Vol. 9, No. 1, December,(2006), P.P. (83-89).
5. Askeland D.R. & phule P.P, " The Science & Engineering of Materials", 4th Edition Thomson Brook. Cole, (2003).
6. W. Iohnson & P.B Meller, "Engineering plasticity", John wiley & Sons, (1983).
7. Dod Coordination Draft, "Polymer matrix Composite materials Properties", Department of Defense,washing D. C. (1996).
8. Hull.O & T.W.Clyne, "An Introduction to Composites Materials", Cambridge University Press, (1996).
9. W.D.Callister, "Materials science & Engineering An Introduction", Jown Wiley & Sons, Inc, (2003).

10. "Mechanical Properties of Composites Based on Low Styrene Emission Polyester Resins for Marine Application", Christophe Baley, Y. Perrot, Peter Davies, Journal of Applied Composite Materials , Vol. 13, No. 1, January, (2006), P.P.(1-22).
12. R. F. Gibson ,"Principles of Composite Material Mechanics", Mc. Graw Hill, Inc, New York, (1994).
13. K. K. Chawla, "Composite Materials", Springer-verlag, NewYork, Inc, (1987).
14. R. A. Higgins, "Materials for Engineering and Technicas", Elsevier Ltd, (2006).
15. Henning Kaiser ,Vistasp M. Karbhari "Quality and Monitoring of Structural Rehabilitation Measures", UCSD, Version 1.2, November, (2001).
16. Derek Hull, "An Introduction to Composite Materials", Cambridge University Press, first Published, (1981).
17. www. SP System. com. "SP System Guide to Composite Engineering Materials", (2004),
18. "Encyclopedia of Polymer Science & Technology", Sons & John Wiley, Inc, (2002).
19. Ivor H. up degraff, "Hand – Book of Composite", Van No Strand Reinhold Inc, Edited by George Lubin, New York, (1982).
20. Hibbeler R.C, "Mechanics of Materials", 6th Ed, Pearson Prentice Hall, (2005).
21. S.V. Kulkarni, J. S. Rice & B. W. Rosen "Composites", Vol. 6, No.5, (1975), p.p.(217-225).

15 Structure and Performance of Thermoplastic Based Composite with Zeolite Filler

ABSTRACT

In these work, new nano and micro thermoplastic based composite is prepared with zeolite filler, The method involves using zeolite in powder form, the preparation of zeolite powder from ores by crushing it into small - sized granules. The characteristics of the zeolite powder are determined. The physical properties and chemical composition (XRD) are evaluated before impeding it into the thermoplastic. Thermoplastics powder are added to the zeolite powder as granules in different sizes, The particles sizes ranging from the size of a millimeter to nanometer. The manufacturing quality parameters are optimized at volume percentages of filler in the range 20 to 25%, composite material is formed into molds. New Composite material is characterized by easy deformation into different shapes beside machine ability. The characteristics of new composite such as SEM, EDX,FTIR in absorption and transmission mode are evaluated and compared with the standard characteristics of Zeolite ores. The performance and characteristics of the new composite are completely different. The new composite is hard, solid and does not absorb water. The work end with list of recommendation about the new field and expected application of Zeolite when using it as filler in thermoplastic based micro and nano composites.

Keywords: *Zeolite, thermoplastic, composite, filler, micro -nano, characteristics.*

Introduction

Advantages of Thermoplastics over Thermosets in Composites

Compared to Thermoset resins, there are two major advantages of thermoplastics in composites. The first is that many thermoplastic resins have an increased impact resistance compared to comparable thermoset materials[1]. In some instances, the difference is as high as 10 times the impact resistance. The other major advantage of thermoplastic composites is the ability to reform. When heat and pressure impregnate reinforcing fiber with a thermoplastic resin, physical rather than chemical change occurs. This allows the thermoplastic composites to be reformed and reshaped. Thus, the thermoplastic composite can be recycled at the end of its life. Polymer/filler interface plays an important role in determining the overall performance of thermoplastic composites[2],[3].

Demands of these materials in high temperature service environment is constantly evolving (use of new polymers, weight reduction in automotive and building applications[4],[5]. Maximize the performance/cost ratio of your thermoplastics formulations by getting structured knowledge on fillers and the impact of their particle size/shape, distribution on final performance[6],[7]. Figure 15.1 shows the characteristics of thermoplastic based composite[3].

Thermoplastic composite materials that were initially developed primarily for use in the aerospace industry are now attracting interest in new applications[8],[9]. Structural and performance advantages, continuous emergence of new and unique applications are some of the factors leading to an increased interest in nano and micro thermoplastic based composite materials[10],[11].

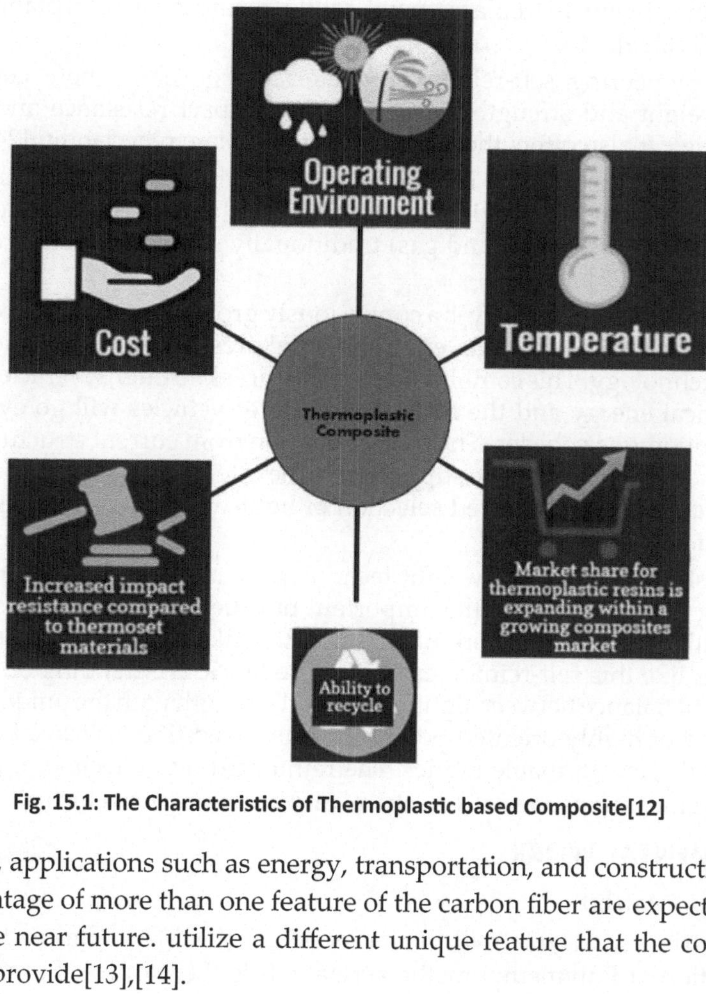

Fig. 15.1: The Characteristics of Thermoplastic based Composite[12]

Hence, applications such as energy, transportation, and construction, that take advantage of more than one feature of the carbon fiber are expected to be seen in the near future. utilize a different unique feature that the composite materials provide[13],[14].

The market share for thermoplastic resins is expanding within a growing composites market. For example, the automotive market is seeking new solutions for lighter vehicles and high volume production[15],[16]. Some applications of thermoplastic composites in the automotive industry include seat frames, battery trays, bumper beams, load floors, front ends, valve covers, rocker panels and under engine covers[17]. In many cases, thermoset resins, such as epoxies, are not satisfactory for these applications and, thus, there is an increased interest in the use of thermoplastic materials[18],[19].

The market of transportation components and parts is challenged by the growing requirement for high performance and lightweight elements, driven in large part by regulatory, sustainability pressure and fuel efficiency demands[20],[21].

However, the reduced weight should not come with a compromise on other properties like stiffness or processability. Today it exists a wide range of solutions likely to replace metal while insuring an acceptable level of strength[22],[23].

One pioneering self-reinforced material proposes a new combination of lightweight and strength, while insuring impact resistance and aesthetic possibilities. It also offers the advantage of complete recyclability[24].

High heat plastics have been among the fastest growing plastics products entering new and challenging applications (military/aerospace, automotive, electronics, down-hole oil and gas) traditionally served by metal, ceramics or thermoplastics[25].

The automotive industry is a continuously growing market with challenges coming from end-users needs, environmental pressure and innovations thanks to high technology. This combination leads to breakthroughs : vehicles powered by electrical energy and the next generation of vehicles will go even further with autonomous vehicles. The transformation from current structures to fully autonomous vehicles will be supported by new technologies to enhance driver support and also unrestricted selection of light-weight components for better fuel efficiency[26].

Investments in lighter-weight technologies and sustainability of material recycling have never been this important but the reduced weight should not come with a compromise on other properties like stiffness or processability. Solutions like this self-reinforced composite fabric are standing out thanks to an efficient balance between lightweight and strength with the unique structure composed of highly oriented polypropylene based fibers, weaved into a high strength thermo formable fabric. The reinforced fabric technology is able to support innovations towards electrical and autonomous vehicles.

EXPERIMENTAL WORK

Materials (Matrix)

The matrix is polymethyl metha acrylate (PMMA. Figure 15.4 shows preparation of Polymethyl metha acrylate. It is thermoplastic prepared from monomer (methyl methacrylate) by additional polymerization; polymer was in the granule form with 5mm diameter. The main properties of PMMA are explained in table 15.1.

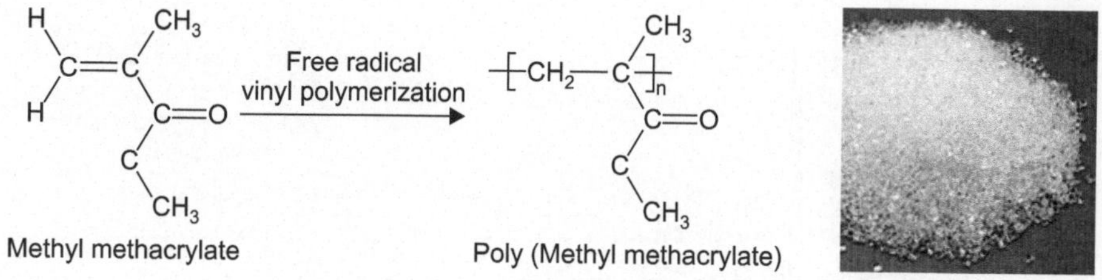

Fig. 15.2: Preparation of Polymethyl Metha Acrylate

Table 15.1: Physical properties of PMMA

Physical Properties	Value
Density	1.15-1.19 g/cm^3
Water Absorption	0.3–2%
Moisture Absorption at Equilibrium	0.3–0.33%
Linear Mould Shrinkage	0.003-0.0065 cm/cm
Melt Flow	0.9–27 g/10 min

Filler (Zeolite)

Hydrated aluminosilicate minerals that contain alkali and alkaline-earth metals. Figure 15.3 and 15.4 show the structure of zeolite powder used in this work while table 15.2 and 15.3 show its chemical composition and physical properties respectively

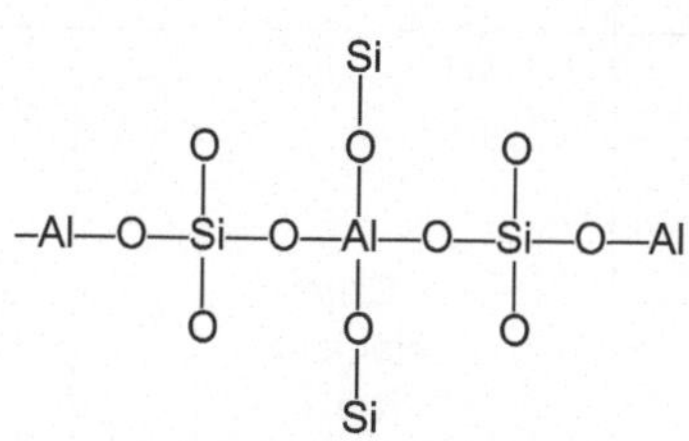

Basic Zeolite Structure

Fig. 15.3: Structure of natural zeolite

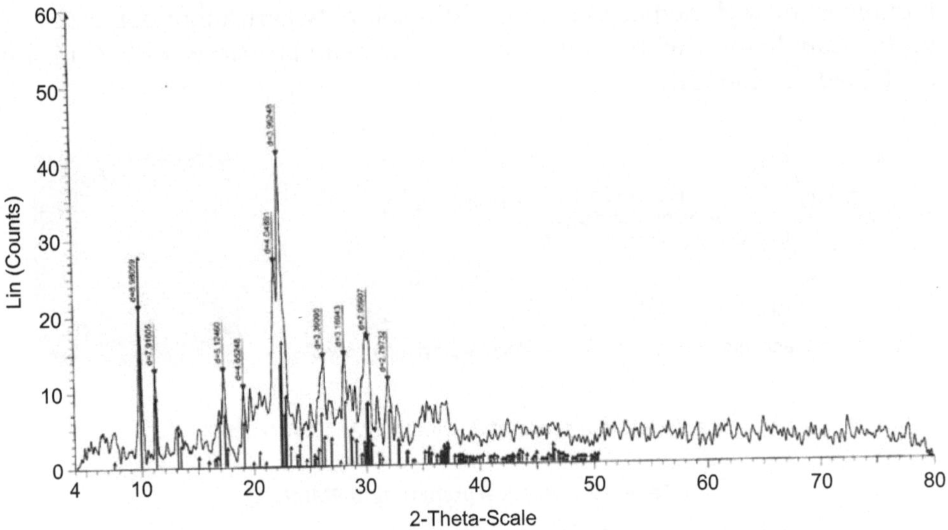

Fig. 15.4: X.ray analysis of the natural zeolite

Table 15.2: Chemical Compostion of Natural Zeolite

Compound	Type	Percents %
K_2O	Cations	3.266
CaO		3.583
Na_2O		0.780
SiO_2	Major Elements oxides)	62.22
Al_2O_3		11.096
Na_2O		0.78
MgO		0.599
CaO		3.583
Fe_2O_3		4.033
K_2O		3.266
TiO_2		0.339
ZrO_2		0.112
Cl	Other elements (trace)	0.025
BaO		0.085
P_2O_5		0.033
ZnO		0.025
SrO		0.047
PbO		0.002
MnO		0.120
SO_3		0.035

Table 15.3: Physical Properties of Natural Zeolite in Powder Form

Properties	Value	Unit
Bulk (Paticle) density	1.83	gm/cm^3
Apparent (skeletal) density	2.377	gm/cm^3
Over alls urface area	89.82	m^2/gm
Porosity	27.80	%
Total pore area	35.836	m^2/gm
Average pore diamter	0.0181	mm
Solubility	7.38	%
Swelling index	2.52	
PH	6.8	
Humidity	6.75	%
L.O.I.	13.6	%
Hardness	4	Moh scale
Grain size	6 mm <	
Non toxic		
Non combustible		
Loss on ignition		
Appearance color	Greyish-white	

A. Mixing and Sieving

The outcome of the two materials zeolite and PMMA after grinding are collected the automatic sieve. Automatic mixing for thermoplastic in the powder form with different aspects ratio was done. The amount of material required was calculated. The mixture moves to the final drying and mixing phase by laser irradiation. This is for guaranteeing the final drying of the two mixtures.

B. Manufacturing process

Plastic powders and natural zeolite were mixed together in the solid state. The mixture is heated at the required temperature, according to its components. Heating, compression and cooling were done for heated mixture. The heating rate depends on the type of the joining material, The heating rate depends on the type of the joining material.

Nano composite material is fabricated, the new composite material is distinguished with the light weight and the ability to endure scratch and damping capacity comparing with the natural zeolite It is also liable for the easy formation and distinctive with different colors and shapes. Figure 15.5 shows The manufacturing steps.

The Manufacturing Quality Parameters

The manufacturing parameters were adjusted and the effect of temperature, pressure and cooling rates were recorded. Design and test of the new system were evaluated. The nano- composite material consists of poly methyl metha acrylate as matrix reinforced with natural zeolite filler in powder form The manufacturing steps may be summarized in the following steps:-

1. Grinding of PMMA by electrical blinder-and control the grinding time to be less than 1.5 min to avoid temperature rise and agglomeration of particles after that use mesh < 300 μm diameter for sieving.
2. Zeolite have used in powder form.
3. Mixing of the two powders in multi speed mixture with continuous cooling to avoid agglomeration of particles.
4. Heating the empty mold which is lubricated by heavy oil.
5. The mixture added to the hot mold
6. Compress the mixture with (5:10 ton) hydraulic system with continuous heating and pressing.
7. Holding the compress and heating until the heat distributed uniformly
8. Cooling the mold with water JET.
9. Extract the final product by pressing.

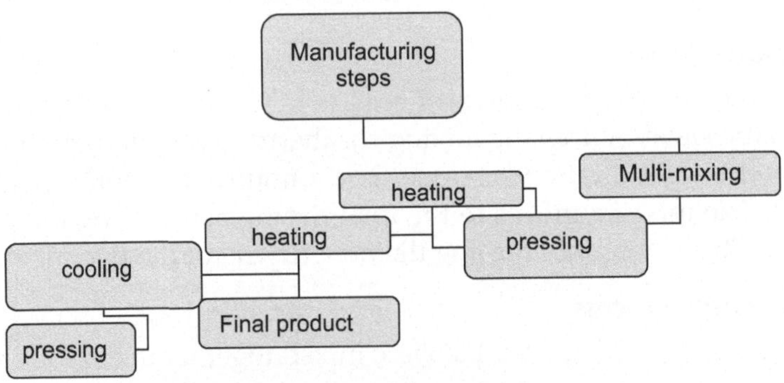

Fig. 15.5: The anufacturing steps

Scanning Electron Microscope (SEM)

The specimens were examined by scanning electron microscope (SEM) operating at a nominal accelerating voltage of 30kv. Specimen preparation is very simply accomplished by cutting a thin slice of the specimen containing the surface of interest, chemical and electro etching were done at standard conditions, the samples were inserting into the specimen chamber for direct examination of the structure.

Energy Dispersive X-ray " EDX"

The quantitative method of elemental analysis of the samples has been examined by SEM JSM-T200 at 25KV acceleration voltage, 20mm working distance, and magnification 200x, (1peak omitted 0.02 KeV). Each value is at least an average of 2 or3 readings at least.

FTIR spectroscopic Analysis

The Fourier Transform Infrared (FTIR) Analysis were carried out for samples Using FTIR Model Cary 630 FTIR spectrometer for both Qualitative and Quantitative for solid samples analysis produced by Agilent technologies Company, Samples were investigated in spectral range (wave number cm^{-1}) from 4000 cm^{-1} to 400 cm^{-1} Without any treatment

XRD

The XRD technique is used to determine the mineralogical phases of the investigated limestone and clay as well as the prepared clinker. The limestone samples were prepared by fine grounding to 20 μm using HERZOG (Herzog Co., Germany) grinder, to minimize the effect of absorption and extinction of the x-ray beam. Rectangular type sample holder was used to pack about 0.2 gm of the examined sample. The sample holder is then fed into the PAN-Analytical X' Pert Pro MPD PW 3050/60 X-ray diffractometer, provided with a proportional digital counter and Nickel-filtered Cu-kα radiation at 40 kV and 30 mA, and scanned over an interval of 5 - 50° 2θ at a scanning speed of 5°/min. The obtained XRD patterns were converted to a series of lattice spacing (Å) and identified by computer software "X'pert HighScore" using ASTM cards of International Center of Diffraction Data (ICDD 2006).

Results and Discussion

The new green composite material with natural zeolite filler has morphology and properties completely different from the natural zeolite. Table 15.4 show comparison between the properties of the new composite material and natural zeolite, While figure 15.6 shows the shape of the new composite material and its appearances difference from natural zeolite.

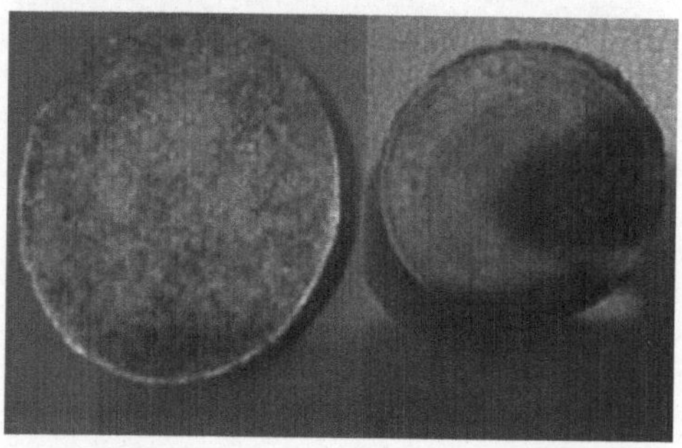

Fig. 15.6: The final products of new composite material

Table 15.4: Comparison between New Composite Material and Natural Zeolite

S.No.	Properties	Natural zeolite	Composite with zeolite filler
1.	Hardness	4 Mohs scale	65 barcoul
2.	Water absorption	High water absorption	No water absorption
3.	Porosity	High	Very low
4.	Water content	High moisture content	Free of water content
5.	Wear rate	Very low	High
6.	Dimension stabiliy	Irregular shape	Dimensional stable
7.	Resistance to compact (compression)	Low resistance	High resistance
8.	Reaction with water	High water retention	Does not interact with water
9.	Particles size	6 mm	150-300 mm

The structure and performance of the new composite material were analyzed by SEM, Figure 15.7 shows the structure of new composite. In

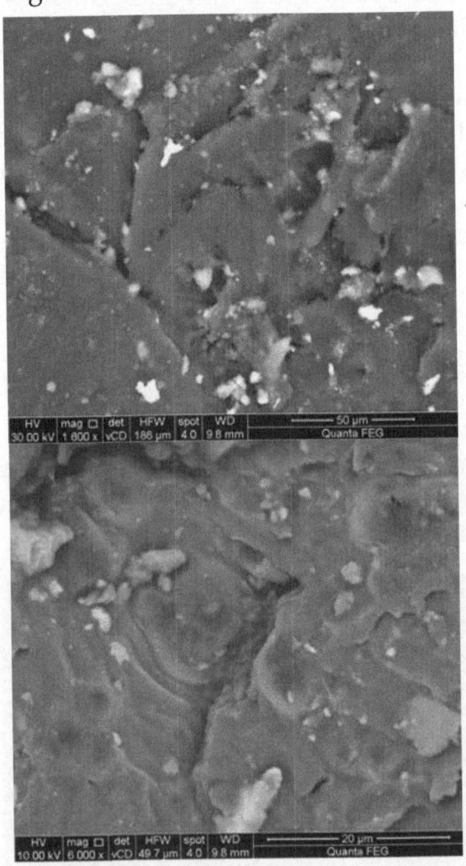

Fig. 15.7: SEM of the new composite material with zeolite filler

comparison with SEM images of natural zeolite powder in the literatures and references (appendix A). The random distribution of the zeolite particles in the PMMA matrix is clear, the very fine particles of zeolite powder are agglomerated as spots in the structure. This random distribution of the natural zeolite powder play the significant role in the elimination of the crack propagation. The matrix characteristics and manufacturing parameters eliminate micro voids and water content, the change in the properties of composite in comparison with natural zeolite due to the change in the structure of composite and distribution of particles inside the thermoplastic matrix.

Green composite with zeolite filler is analyzed by Scanning Electron Microscopy coupled with Energy Dispersive X-Ray apparatus. The surface morphology and mineral contents of the zeolites were obtained, respectively. Figure 15.8 and table 15.5 show the elemental analysis of the composite.

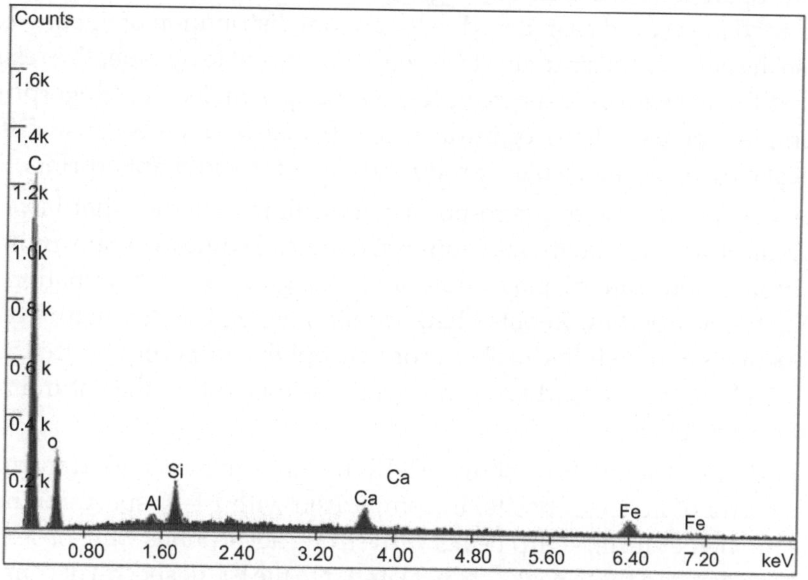

Fig. 15.8: EDX analysis of the new composite material with zeolite filler

Table 15.5: EDX Analysis of the New Composite Material with Zeolite Filler

Element	Wt %	At %	K-Ratio	Z	A	F
C K	66.00	74.12	0.3356	1.0086	0.5040	1.0003
O K	28.16	23.75	0.0416	0.9944	0.1484	1.0001
Alk	0.51	0.26	0.0029	0.9318	0.5995	1.0014
Sik	1.98	0.95	0.0141	0.9601	0.7411	1.0005
CaK	1.31	0.44	0.0128	0.9258	1.0525	1.0040
FeK	2.04	0.49	0.0183	0.8589	1.0447	1.0000
Total	100.00	100.00				

When comparing the weight percent of the composite material with the natural zeolite samples in the references (appendix A), the carbon percentages is dropped in the composite to 66% weight percentages, while the oxygen weight percentage increase to 28%, while the silicon weight percentage almost unchanged. The main reason of this difference related to the percentage of carbon and oxygen in the matrix (PMMA) as shown in the figure 15.2. The reactions during manufacturing at elevated temperature leads to the formation of gases such as Co, Co_2 and other hydrocarbon gases which leads to the change in weight percentages of Carbon and oxygen in the final product.

When IR radiation is passed through the composite material with zeolite filler, some radiation is absorbed by the sample and some passes through (transmitted) due to the properties of the PMMA matrix composite which is semi transparent material. In the origin the gloss grade of PMMA (polymethyl metha acrylate) is used as matrix due to random distribution of opaque zeolite filler. so the new composite material is semi translucent to opaque. The resulting signal at the detector is a spectrum representing a molecular 'fingerprint' of the sample. The usefulness of infrared spectroscopy arises because different chemical structures (molecules) produce different spectral fingerprints.

Zeolites are a class of micro-porous crystalline materials that have been widely used as adsorbents and ion-exchangers. Zeolites contain uniformly sized pores and can display molecular recognition, discrimination, and organization properties. Zeolite characteristics depend on the nature of their pore openings and their hydrophobic or hydrophilic properties figure 15.9 and figure 15.11 show the absorbance and transmission mode of the natural zeolite powder respectively.

Figure 15.10 and 15.12 show FT-IR the absorbance and transmission mode spectra of new composite. In comparison with FT-IR spectra of natural zeolite in powder form, sharp peaks with strong absorptions were observed at 1000^{cm-1} region and these peaks are not similar to the FT-IR spectra of composite with zeolite filler which have more absorption bands observed at 1700^{cm-1}, 1150^{cm-1} and 1400^{cm-1} these absorptions bands give indication about the change occur in the structure.

The micro void and porous structure of natural zeolite are changed to solid and confirmed the formation of strong bonds between the zeolite particles and matrix.

Broad band of zeolite also can be seen in both absorbance and transmission mode where the main bands associated with vibration transitions of PMMA matrix can be observed, However, it is possible to see some of them present attributed to C-C and C-H stretch vibrations of the matrix. Some peaks related to vibrations in bonds between matrix and filler were observed.

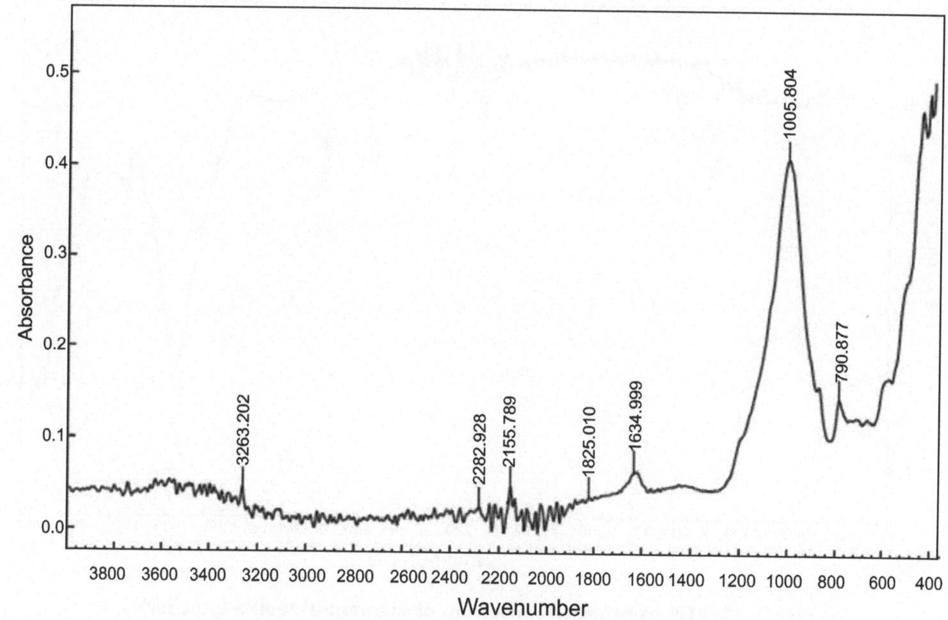

Fig. 15.9: FTIR absorption spectrum of the natural zeolite (powder)

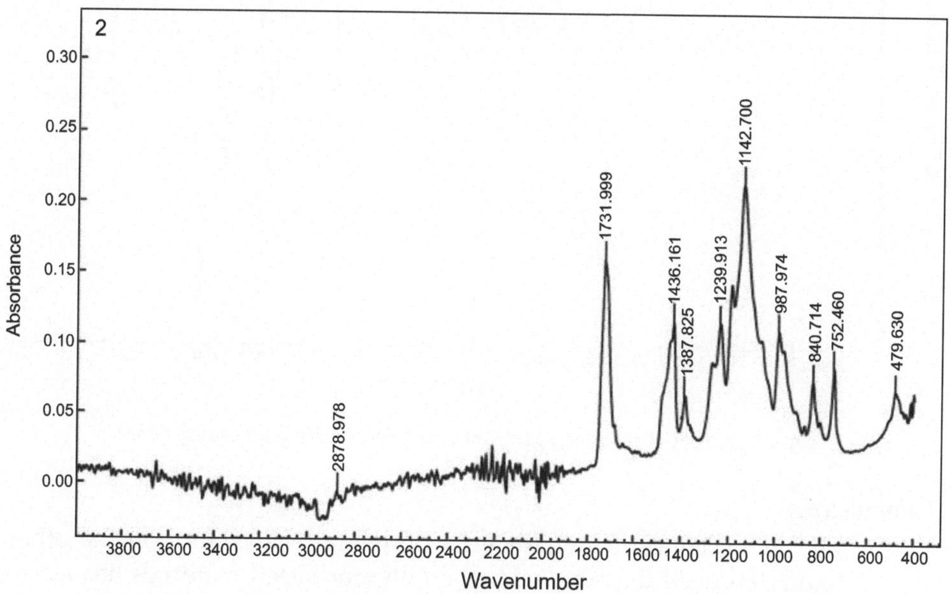

Fig. 15.10: FTIR absorption spectrum of the composite with zeolite filler

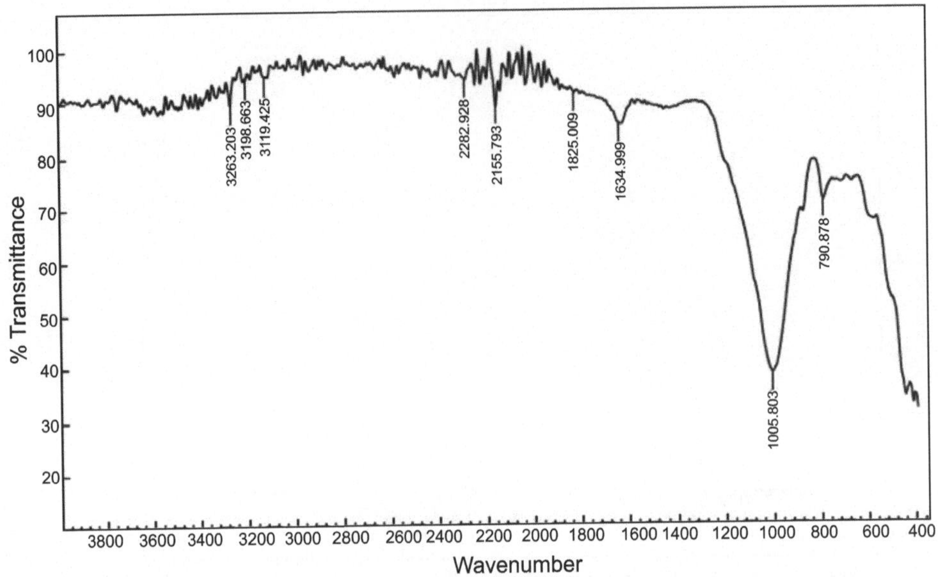

Fig. 15.11: FTIR transmission spectrum of the natural zeolite (powder)

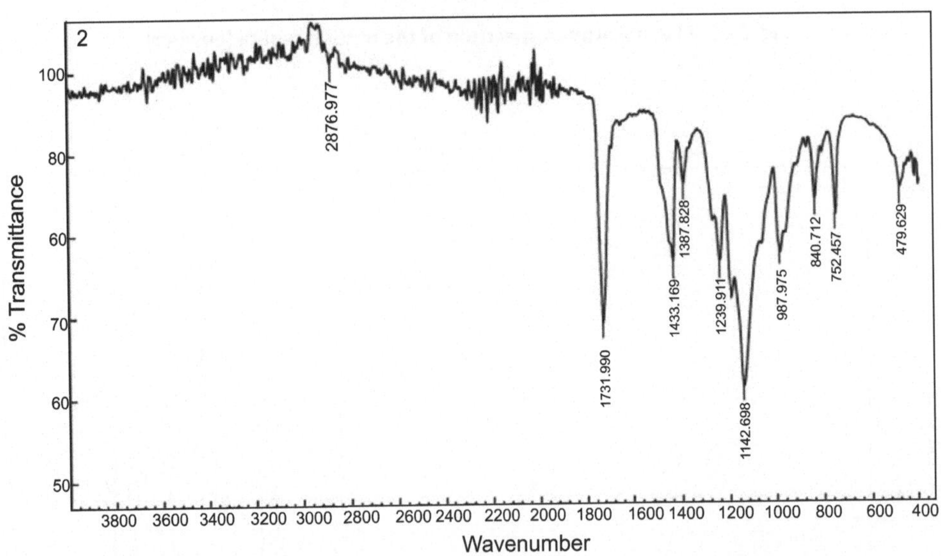

Fig. 15.12: FTIR absorption spectrum of the composite with zeolite filler

Conclusions

1. The rising concern towards environmental issues and, on the other hand, the need for more versatile polymer-based materials has led to increasing interest about polymer composites filled with natural-organic fillers.

2. The new composite material has properties completely different from natural zeolite, it does not interact or absorb water, compact, dimensionally stable with high resistance to wear and compression.
3. The manufacturing parameters such as temperature, pressure, heating and cooling rates play significant role in the new characteristics created in thermoplastic based composite reinforced with natural zeolite filler.
4. The new composite can be further environment-friendly when the polymer matrix is biodegradable and comes from renewable sources as well
5. There are several natural substances which are not degradable and renewable, such as zeolites, that are the right solution to environmental remediation.
6. Future prospects are wide ranging, especially in the field of functionalized nano green composite materials for environmental remediation using very economical systems.
7. The development of new economic manufacturing method for manufacturing of green composite material create new materials with superior characteristics.

Recommendation

The mechanical, chemical and electrical characteristics of the new composite material with zeolite filler should be studied to identify all possible applications of the new green composite.

REFERENCES

1. http://www.sciencedirect.com/science/article/pii/S1359836812004350
2. https://www.hindawi.com/journals/amse/si/347874/cfp/
3. http://www.cuttingdynamics.com/thermoplastic-composites/
4. https://tprc.nl/research-overview/new-thermoplastic-composites-materials
5. http://www.iza-structure.org/databases/ (accessed: March, 2017). Database of Zeolite, Structures,
6. https://books.google.com.eg/books?id=SSlDWXXa0xQC&pg=PA49&lpg=PA49& dq=thermoplastic+composite+references&source=bl&ots=5S9slZCnDJ&sig=QD-sYKI0ho2tbZmdmicWWbOpks4&hl=ar&sa=X&ved=0ahUKEwjw75_4tLTYAhXBshQKHahDCwoQ6AEIcjAJ#v=onepage&q=thermoplastic%20composite%20references&f=false
7. M. Moliner, C. Martínez, A. Corma, *Angew. Chem., Int. Ed.* 2015, **54**, 3560;
8. Angew. Chem. 2015, **127**, 5750.
9. J. Liu, L. Chen, H. Cui, J. Zhang, L. Zhang, C.-Y. Su, *Chem. Soc. Rev.* 2014, 43, 6011.
10. H. Chughtai, N. Ahmad, H. A. Younus, A. Laypkov, F. Verpoort, *Chem. Soc. Rev.* 2015, 44, 6804.
11. H. He, J. A. Perman, G. Zhu, S. Ma, *Small* 2016, **12**, 6309.
12. M. Rimoldi, A. J. Howarth, M. R. DeStefano, L. Lin, S. Goswami, P. Li, J. T. Hupp, O. K. Farha, *ACS Catal.* 2017, **7**, 997.

13. Y.-B. Huang, J. Liang, X.-S. Wang, R. Cao, *Chem. Soc. Rev.* 2017, **46**, 126.
15. T. Hupp, O. K. Farha, *Nat. Protoc.* 2016, **11**, 149.
16. X. Guo, Y. Feng, L. Ma, D. Gao, J. Jing, J. Yu, H. Sun, H. Gong, Y. Zhang, *Appl. Surf. Sci.* 2017, **402**, 53.
17. P. Falcaro, R. Ricco, A. Yazdi, I. Imaz, S. Furukawa, D. Maspoch, R. Ameloot, J. D. Evans, C. J. Doonan, *Coord. Chem. Rev.* 2016, **307**, 237.
18. Y.-Z. Chen, Z. U. Wang, H. Wang, J. Lu, S.-H. Yu, H.-L. Jiang, *J. Am. Chem. Soc.* 2017, **139**, 2035.
19. J. A. R. van Veen, in *Zeolites for Cleaner Technologies* (Eds: M. Guisnet, J.-P. Gilson), Imperial College Press, London, UK 2005, p. 131.
20. I. E. Maxwell, J. K. Minderhoud, W. H. J. Stork, J. A. R. van Veen, in *Handbook of Heterogeneous Catalysis*, Vol. **4**(Eds: G. Ertl, H. nözinger, J. Weitkamp), Wiley-VCH, Weinheim, Germany 1997, p. 2017.
21. http://www.iza-structure.org/databases/
22. http://www.sciencedirect.com/science/book/9780444530646.
23. https://en.wikipedia.org/wiki/Zeolite
24. *Ferraz, E.; et al.* "Synthetic Zeolite Pellets Incorporated to Air lime–metakaolin Mortars: Mechanical Properties". *Construction & Building Materials*, 2014. **69**: 243–252.
25. Handbook of Zeolite Science and Technology, Scott M. Auerbach, Kathleen A. Carrado, Prabir K. Dutta, eds. CRC Press, 2003, p. 16.
26. First, E. L.; Gounaris, C. E.; Wei, J.; Floudas, C. A. "Computational Characterization of Zeolite Porous Networks: An Automated Approach". Physical Chemistry Chemical Physics. **13** (38): 17339–17358. 2011.
27. H. van Koningsveld, Compendium of Zeolite Framework Types. Building Schemes and Type Characteristics, Elsevier, Amsterdam, 2007.

APPENDIX–A

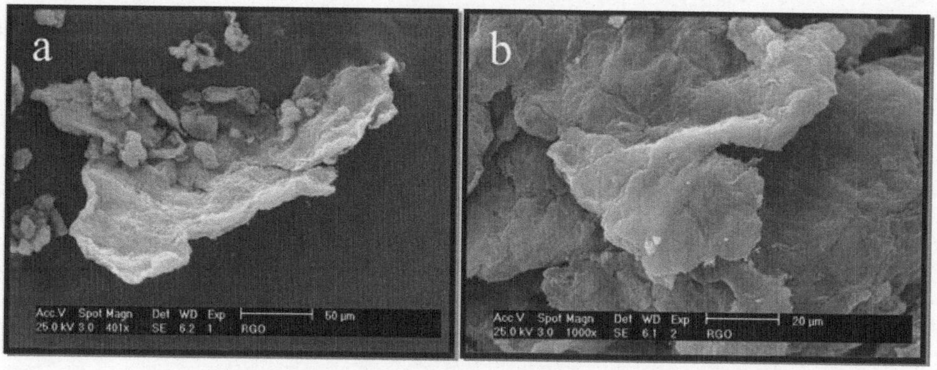

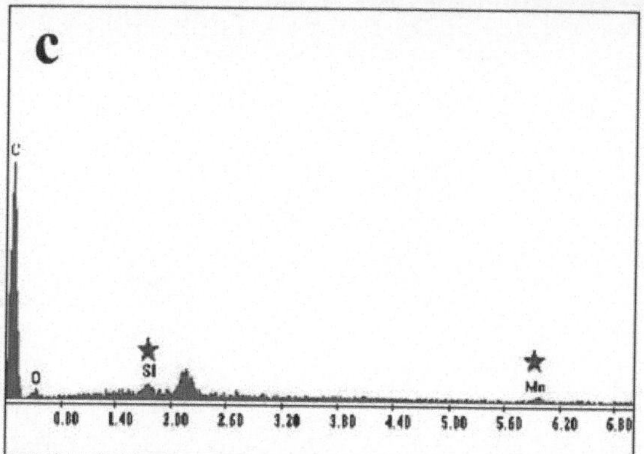

Elem	Wt %	At %	K-Ratio	Z	A	F
C K	91.73	94.36	0.7079	1.0025	0.7697	1.0000
O K	6.47	5.00	0.0078	0.9874	0.1222	1.0000
SiK	1.09	0.48	0.0092	0.9507	0.8861	1.0001
MnK	0.71	0.16	0.0062	0.8276	1.0481	1.0000
Total	100.00	100.00				

Index

Z